RACING POST
100 Favourite Racehorses

RACING POST
100 Favourite Racehorses

edited by
Nicholas Godfrey

Raceform

Photographs: Gerry Cranham Racing Library, Edward Whitaker, Martin Lynch, Alec Russell, Caroline Norris, Ed Byrne, Jon Winter, Dan Abraham, Bill Selwyn, George Selwyn, Alan Johnson, Racing Post, Sporting Life, Daily Mirror, Press Association, Reuters, Getty Images, Central Press Photos Ltd, Sporting Pictures, Alpha, Empics, Sport and General, Topham Picturepoint

Special thanks for their invaluable assistance to Robin Gibson, John Randall, Lee Mottershead, Steve Dennis, Victor Jones, Nigel Jones, Tracey Scarlett, Gerry Cranham, Bryan Pugh, Martin Smethurst and Rodney Masters

Published in 2005 by Raceform Ltd
Compton, Newbury, Berkshire, RG20 6NL
Raceform Ltd is a wholly owned subsidiary of Trinity-Mirror plc

A CIP catalogue record for this book is available from the British Library.

ISBN 1-904137-81-2

Designed by Robin Gibson and Tracey Scarlett
Picture research by Victor Jones and Nigel Jones
Printed in Great Britain by William Clowes Ltd, Beccles, Suffolk

RACING POST

100 Favourite Racehorses

contents

foreword
Brough Scott

HERE was the proof, as if it were needed, that the horse is still at the heart of it all. Set up a vote for 'Your Favourite Racehorse' and the floodgates of nostalgia and subjective advocacy open. The arguments begin.

Choosing a horse gets even more passionate than picking a player, for the important ones have imprinted not just images in the memory but weight (and often holes) in the wallet. They become phantom figures on to which we ascribe every superlative in the lexicon. In my case, it is both thrilling, and maybe slightly nerdishly sad, to find that the list goes back not just five decades but six.

Not many of you will remember Sir Ken, Champion Hurdle winner in 1952, '53 and '54, but the image of him and Tim Molony jumping the last and putting their heads down to face the Cheltenham Hill will never fade – even if it was on the most flickering of early TVs. Add Tulyar, the little Derby winner on whom crafty old Charlie Smirke beat a 16-year-old Lester Piggott (on Gay Time) at Epsom before adding the Eclipse and King George treble.

The 1960s were a special time. For me, not just with Arkle, the nonpareil, and Sir Ivor, the most exciting of all Lester Piggott's Derby winners.

The '60s were when I was going round too, so otherwise unsung horses suddenly gallop out of the scrapbook – Arcticeelagh, the blinkered 'thinker' who produced my first win on both the Flat and over hurdles, although self-congratulation at the latter was tempered by the runner-up's jockey being warned off for not trying.

There was the trail-blazing Wirswall Major who held his head so low he would cut his lip on his knee. And, bravest of all, three-times Champion Hurdle winner Persian War, only a morning ride for me, but as gentle as he was big-hearted.

The '70s were the hurdlers' golden age – Bula, Comedy Of Errors, Lanzarote, Night Nurse, Monksfield and Sea Pigeon. But 1970 and 1971 also gave us three of the greatest Flat horses ever to look through a bridle in Nijinsky, Mill Reef and Brigadier Gerard, whilst come 1973 we had started the five-year epic that was Red Rum at Aintree. Riding him flat out up Southport sands one misty morning in '75 remains just about my best and most alarming moment in the saddle – next stop looked like being Blackpool.

The '80s had Dancing Brave: will there ever be a Flat-race finish as fantastic as his Arc victory at Longchamp? The '80s also had Desert Orchid, whose cause as leader of the pack I have advocated later in these pages. The '90s had Lochsong at the beginning of the decade, Istabraq at the end. This latest span has already given us Best Mate and High Chaparral.

Looking back overbrims the memory but it also highlights a truth best stated back at Ascot on April 7, 1993. Peter Scudamore had just ridden Sweet Duke to be the 1,678th and final winner of his mould-breaking career.

As the cameras and the hoopla began, Peter said straight to camera: "I want first to thank all the horses who have done so much for me down the years."

Reliving these pages, so should we.

Arkle: all-time favourite

introduction
Nicholas Godfrey

WE WEREN'T asking a lot. We were only looking to compile the definitive list of the 100 most popular racehorses of all time in Britain and Ireland.

That's how, in December 2003 and then for a period of two months, I found myself knee-deep in letters and emails after an astonishing response from *Racing Post* readers who had answered the paper's call for them to identify their favourites. And that's how, using the list we compiled from them as the basis, we had the idea to put it all together into the book you are now holding in your hands.

No doubt we would get a slightly different result if we held the poll when this book was published, a year after the event, but this is how it was then: *Racing Post* readers' 100 favourite racehorses, as voted for between late December 2003 and February 2004.

It was quite a poll. Over 2,000 readers answered the initial challenge; even more took part when the telephone lines were opened to determine the final order of the top ten.

While the concept was simple, that is not to say there weren't rules. Every horse selected had to have raced under Rules in Britain or Ireland, and every reader was allowed just one vote each, naming their 1-2-3 in order, after which we totted up the votes, with first choices earning more points than second, a second choice more than a third.

Remember, we were not interested in who readers considered to be the greatest racehorse – we decided to leave that to the handicappers and slide-rule merchants. What we were after were personal favourites: it could be the equine superstar who took your breath away every time he raced, or the dodgy old handicapper who kickstarted a lifelong affair with racing all those years ago, when he got up on the line to win you what seemed a small fortune at the time.

We asked readers not to select a horse such as Persian Punch or Red Rum simply because they believed such a superstar was likely to be voted the public number one. If Quixall Crossett was your favourite, we said, despite his extraordinarily hopeless career, then you should vote for him. Or, if you had fallen in love with a once-raced two-year-old maiden, then vote for him instead.

Readers were also invited to write letters in support of their first choice – and those who did earned a small bonus in the points for their selection.

You clearly relished the task. There were a lot of letters, although some were not slow to tell us just how difficult a job it was. "Thank you for asking the hardest question a racing fan will ever have to answer," said Mark Franklin, of Saul, Gloucestershire, neatly summing up the thoughts of many. He voted for Cavalero, by the way.

"Start the competition again!" demanded Paul Tweddle of Edinburgh (Arazi). "Pick your ten favourite racehorses of all time. That's what you need to ask us!"

Maybe so, but we didn't, and our concept seemed to strike a chord with racing fans across the globe: we had responses from Sydney to Kentucky, from Rio to, well, Lambourn. Fortunately, most people managed to whittle it down to just their top threes –

and, despite the restriction, a total of 967 different horses eventually received at least one third-place vote. They were all there, from the undisputed champions to the horse who was unplaced in three runs in Ireland before earning himself a reputation in Central Europe, to the little-known Irish-based gelding who has a few friends in the lofty realms of academe in the Galway area. We kid you not.

They couldn't all make the top 100, of course, but all of them have managed to claim a place in at least one person's heart.

The final countdown of the 100 favourite racehorses of all time in Britain and Ireland was originally published in the *Racing Post* in January 2004 following the initial six-week voting period, during which several apparent attempts to rig the ballot were noted and outlawed, as is detailed elsewhere in this volume.

Although we listed numbers 11-100 in finishing order, the ten horses with the most points according to our voting system were listed alphabetically. Then, with their scores back to zero, telephone lines were opened alongside email and internet voting to find the number one.

What a list of champions it was: Arkle, Brigadier Gerard, Dancing Brave, Desert Orchid, Istabraq, Nijinsky, One Man, Persian Punch, Red Rum and Sea Pigeon. In order to help voters make up their minds, a team of the *Racing Post*'s best writers penned profiles of these luminaries, essays that have been updated for inclusion here by the likes of Brough Scott, former sportswriter of the year, and Tony Morris, the world's foremost bloodstock expert.

As well as these essays, we have added extended pieces about the horses who comprised the bottom half of the top 20 – a list only a little less exalted than the top ten, including some of the very biggest names, among them triple Gold Cup winner Best Mate, that history-making mare Dawn Run and true Classic greats such as Mill Reef and Shergar. Writers featured in this section include the sport's greatest historian John Randall, whose expertise and dedication throughout this project has been invaluable. (While we are on the subject of expertise and invaluable assistance, I must also mention the *Racing Post* design editor Robin Gibson, without whom this project would never have seen the light of day.)

However, as choosing a favourite is a subjective exercise, other top *Post* writers and regular contributors have explained their own selections, among them two of the biggest names in racing journalism in Alastair Down and Paul Haigh. We also have Richard Birch, who explains exactly why one Reg Akehurst-trained handicapper is synonymous with garage doors to him, and Peter Gomm, whose affection for one Henry Cecil-trained star has lasted his entire adult life and is so great he once had the horse's name stencilled into his hair.

That may sound strange, but who am I to talk? I once threatened to have Alderbrook and Master Oats (right) tattooed on the left and right cheek of my bottom respectively after a particularly memorable Cheltenham. Why is it that you can never find a good tattoo parlour when you need one?

Everyone else has had a go, so now seems as good a time as any to reveal my own top three. At number one was the aforementioned would-be tattoo-inspirer Master Oats, who endeared himself to me with his clumsy but effective way of getting from start to finish that seldom seemed to stop him. At least, it didn't stop him landing one of my all-too-rare winning ante-post bets, after which it was nearly impossible for anyone to stop me doing an impression of this wonderful horse – known to me simply as 'The Master' – every time a session in the pub neared closing time. (You had to be there. Then again, you could be forgiven if you'd have preferred to give it a miss.)

My second choice was that wonderful filly Indian Skimmer. She may have lit up the racecourse, but I remember her primarily for lighting up my 21st-birthday celebrations when she turned up – in decorative icing form, Steve Cauthen up in Sheikh Mohammed's maroon-and-white silks – on top of a cake sent special delivery to my then-seat of learning by my Auntie Sally.

And third was Tingle Creek. If you need to ask why, then you never saw him. (What? No Mill Reef? Reference Point? Power Bender? Rock Hopper? Dubai Millennium? Monksfield? Remittance Man? See More Business? Rooster Booster? Harbour Pilot? Perhaps that Arazi fan Mr Tweddle was right after all.)

Several racing personalities have also given us their top three choices, which are featured in this volume – but as the list was compiled from the choices of the racing public, we have also reprinted what we judged the five best letters from more than 600 written in support of some beloved favourites.

The final ballot involving just the top ten lasted a fortnight. Initially four horses seemed to be battling it out, then three, then just two who, in the end, after thousands of votes, took more than 40 per cent of the ballot between them.

In the end, it made no difference that we had asked people to nominate their favourite, not simply the best.

The winner *was* simply the best. I hope you enjoy reading about him – and the 99 horses who, like so many others before them, were beaten by Arkle.

about the contributors

100 Favourite Racehorses features work from the *Racing Post*'s top writers, both journalists employed on the staff at the paper and occasional columnists alike.

The book's editor Nicholas Godfrey is the paper's deputy editor, while the list of contributors reads like a who's who of racing's best-known writers.

The essays on the top ten were also written by *Post* regulars, including a handful of former racing journalists of the year who are among the biggest names in the business, namely David Ashforth, George Ennor, Rodney Masters, Tony Morris, Tom O'Ryan and Brough Scott. Others to feature in this section are Tony O'Hehir, the voice of Irish racing, and his colleague Michael Clower, as well as two of the new stars of racing journalism, Peter Thomas and James Willoughby. The sport's No.1 historian, John Randall, played a major role in the project and is responsible for nearly half the remaining essays, many of which were also penned by the highly respected Lee Mottershead.

Much-decorated members of the *Racing Post* team feature elsewhere, including leading columnists Alastair Down, Paul Haigh, Sir Clement Freud and Howard Wright, senior reporter Jon Lees, chief race analyst Graham Dench, bloodstock aficionado Rachel Pagones, 'dark horse' expert Marten Julian, sports betting editor Bruce Millington and Emily Weber, head of the revered Spotlight team.

In *Racing Post* terms, John Oaksey is of an older vintage. His articles from the pages of *Horse and Hound* that followed the career of Arkle are regarded as classics in the field of racing journalism. One of them is reproduced in these pages – while Oaksey also reveals the reasoning behind his choosing a steeplechaser other than Arkle as his own personal favourite.

Other contributors include *Post* staffers Richard Birch and Peter Gomm, and Ian Balding and Bill O'Gorman, who boast around 70 years of training experience between them, as well as submitting the occasional column to the paper.

Although the work of a host of excellent photographers across the decades graces these pages, the vast majority are from the libraries of three of the best in the business, namely Edward Whitaker, Gerry Cranham and Martin Lynch.

RACING POST
100 Favourite
Racehorses

Notes on the text: All statistics are correct until December 31, 2004 // Trainers and jockeys named in brackets, while not chiefly associated with the horse, played a significant role in their career // All writers are credited in full on numbers 1-20; where initials are used on 21-100, the writers are John Randall (JR), George Ennor (GE), Nicholas Godfrey (NG) and Lee Mottershead (LM)

Arkle's race-by-race record

1961/62

Date	Course	Race	Weight	Jockey	Result
Dec 9	Mullingar	Lough Ennel Maiden (NH Flat)	11-4	Mr M Hely-Hutchinson	3rd
Dec 26	Leopardstown	Greystones Maiden (NH Flat)	10-11	Mr M Hely-Hutchinson	4th
Jan 20	Navan	Bective Novice Hurdle	11-5	L McLoughlin	WON
Mar 10	Naas	Rathconnel Handicap Hurdle	11-2	P Taaffe	WON
Apr 14	Baldoyle	Balbriggan Handicap Hurdle	10-1	L McLoughlin	unpl
Apr 24	Fairyhouse	New Handicap Hurdle	10-5	L McLoughlin	4th

1962/63

Date	Course	Race	Weight	Jockey	Result
Oct 17	Dundalk	Wee County Handicap Hurdle	11-13	P Taaffe	WON
Oct 24	Gowran Park	President's Handicap Hurdle	10-5	P Woods	WON
Nov 17	Cheltenham	Honeybourne Chase	11-11	P Taaffe	WON
Feb 23	Leopardstown	Milltown Chase	12-11	P Taaffe	WON
Mar 12	Cheltenham	Broadway Novices' Chase	12-4	P Taaffe	WON
Apr 15	Fairyhouse	Power Gold Cup	12-5	P Taaffe	WON
May 1	Punchestown	John Jameson Gold Cup	12-4	P Taaffe	WON

1963/64

Date	Course	Race	Weight	Jockey	Result
Oct 9	Navan	Donoughmore Maiden (Flat)	9-6	T P Burns	WON
Oct 24	Gowran Park	Carey's Cottage Handicap Chase	11-13	P Taaffe	WON
Nov 30	Newbury	Hennessy Gold Cup	11-9	P Taaffe	3rd
Dec 26	Leopardstown	Christmas Handicap Chase	12-0	P Taaffe	WON
Jan 30	Gowran Park	Thyestes Handicap Chase	12-0	P Taaffe	WON
Feb 15	Leopardstown	Leopardstown Handicap Chase	12-0	P Taaffe	WON
Mar 7	Cheltenham	Cheltenham Gold Cup	12-0	P Taaffe	WON
Mar 30	Fairyhouse	Irish Grand National	12-0	P Taaffe	WON

1964/65

Date	Course	Race	Weight	Jockey	Result
Oct 29	Gowran Park	Carey's Cottage Handicap Chase	12-0	P Taaffe	WON
Dec 5	Newbury	Hennessy Gold Cup	12-7	P Taaffe	WON
Dec 12	Cheltenham	Massey-Ferguson Gold Cup	12-10	P Taaffe	3rd
Feb 27	Leopardstown	Leopardstown Handicap Chase	12-7	P Taaffe	WON
Mar 11	Cheltenham	Cheltenham Gold Cup	12-0	P Taaffe	WON
Apr 24	Sandown	Whitbread Gold Cup	12-7	P Taaffe	WON

1965/66

Date	Course	Race	Weight	Jockey	Result
Nov 6	Sandown	Gallaher Gold Cup	12-7	P Taaffe	WON
Nov 27	Newbury	Hennessy Gold Cup	12-7	P Taaffe	WON
Dec 27	Kempton	King George VI Chase	12-0	P Taaffe	WON
Mar 1	Leopardstown	Leopardstown Handicap Chase	12-7	P Taaffe	WON
Mar 17	Cheltenham	Cheltenham Gold Cup	12-0	P Taaffe	WON

1966/67

Date	Course	Race	Weight	Jockey	Result
Nov 26	Newbury	Hennessy Gold Cup	12-7	P Taaffe	2nd
Dec 14	Ascot	SGB Handicap Chase	12-7	P Taaffe	WON
Dec 27	Kempton	King George VI Chase	12-0	P Taaffe	2nd

Won 27 from 35 starts (22 out of 26 over fences)

**A legend is born: Arkle (Pat Taaffe) fights his way
through the crowd after his first Gold Cup victory in 1964**

1
Arkle

Bay gelding foaled 1957
Archive - Bright Cherry

Owner Anne Duchess of Westminster
Trainer Tom Dreaper **Jockey** Pat Taaffe
Record (jumps) 26 wins from 34 starts
(including 2 bumpers)

Career highlights Won 1963 Broadway
Novices' Chase, Power Gold Cup, John
Jameson Gold Cup, 1964 Thyestes Chase,
Leopardstown Chase, Cheltenham Gold Cup,
Irish Grand National, Hennessy Gold Cup,
1965 Leopardstown Chase, Cheltenham Gold
Cup, Whitbread Gold Cup, Gallaher Gold
Cup, Hennessy Gold Cup, King George VI
Chase, 1966 Leopardstown Chase,
Cheltenham Gold Cup, SGB Chase

Arkle jumps the last on the way to his third Cheltenham Gold Cup success in 1966

Arkle
by tony
o'hehir

Since the horse who became known simply as

'Himself' was officially retired 36 years ago countless young steeplechasers, especially those trained in Ireland, have been cursed with the tag of being the 'new Arkle' or the 'best since Arkle'. Understandable as it has been for newspaper sub-editors to leap on that particular bandwagon, they have inadvertently burdened good horses with expectations that have proved beyond them. To state that Arkle was a hard act to follow takes understatement to a new level.

The undisputed champion chaser of the 1960s achieved fame and immortality by completely dominating the sport in what was a relatively short racing career between 1961 and 1966. His early clashes with Mill House brought to racing like never before the type of Ireland-versus-England fervour usually associated with other sports – and while Mill House, the Cheltenham Gold Cup winner of 1963, won their first duel in the Hennessy Gold Cup at Newbury later that year, he was never again able to match his great rival.

Arkle won 26 of his 34 starts under National Hunt Rules. He was beaten only four times over fences and he also won over a mile and three-quarters on the Flat. Before Best Mate matched the feat, he was remembered by many as the last triple Cheltenham Gold Cup winner (1964-1966), but what made him outstanding were his achievements, in victory and defeat, under big weights in handicaps.

Arkle was so superior that there was one set of weights for when he was declared, and another for when he was absent

He was so superior to his fellow Irish steeplechasers that the authorities introduced a system of two handicaps for races he was entered for: one set of weights for races for which he was declared, and another for when he was absent.

Arkle came into the world at Ballymacoll Stud in County Meath on April 19, 1957. Bred by Mary Baker, he was bought at Goffs August Sales in 1960 by Anne, Duchess of Westminster, whose yellow-and-black colours he was to carry with such distinction. Tom Dreaper, who had made his name as the trainer of Prince Regent, the 1946 Gold Cup winner, and his stable jockey Pat Taaffe were to be associated with Arkle throughout a career which began with a third in a bumper at Mullingar in December 1961. He was ridden on that occasion, and on his only other bumper start, by amateur rider Mark Hely-Hutchinson, who afterwards was to claim, entirely accurately, that he was the only person who rode Arkle and never won on him!

Four wins over hurdles with Taaffe and two other Dreaper jockeys, Liam McLoughlin and Paddy Woods, gave some indication that more was to follow when Arkle – whom Taaffe once described as having hindlegs so far apart that "you could drive a wheelbarrow between them" – went chasing. From his 20-length debut win over fences in the Honeybourne Chase at Cheltenham in November 1962 until he fractured a pedal bone when losing out narrowly to Dormant in the 1966 King George VI Chase (his final race), Arkle amassed a portfolio of top races. Besides his three

Enter the dragon: Arkle seems to breathe fire after winning his first Gold Cup

Cheltenham Gold Cups, he won two Hennessys, a King George, a Whitbread, a Gallaher Gold Cup, an SGB Chase, three Leopardstown Chases, an Irish Grand National, a Thyestes Chase, a Broadway Novices' Chase (now the Royal & SunAlliance Chase), a Power Gold Cup and a John Jameson Gold Cup.

The Anglo-Irish build-up to his first Cheltenham Gold Cup in 1964 had much to do with the arguments that raged after Mill House had beaten Arkle into third place in the Hennessy three months earlier. Ireland claimed Arkle would have won at Newbury but for slipping on landing at the final open ditch; England tut-tutted at such heresy. Arkle got his revenge, though, beating Mill House by five lengths – and Ireland had a new hero. The nation agreed with Peter O'Sullevan – this was the best we had seen for a long time.

Back at Cheltenham a year later, the gap back to Mill House was 20 lengths, and his great adversary's spirit had been crushed. Colour television had not arrived and racing coverage on TV was less frequent and less attractive than it is today. Nevertheless, Arkle's big-race outings were televised in both Ireland and Britain. He frequently made the nightly news bulletins on a then-infant RTE and was a regular feature on the front pages of Ireland's newspapers – and, in the end, he had as many, if not more, admirers in Britain and abroad as he had at home.

Cards and letters, many of them addressed simply to 'Arkle, Ireland', arrived regularly at the Dreaper stables in Kilsallaghan, County Dublin. Sunday afternoon

Cards and letters, many addressed simply to 'Arkle, Ireland', arrived regularly at the Dreaper stables

drives often produced a procession of cars jamming up the roads around the Dreaper yard, a song was written about the horse, and pubs were named after him.

Arkle's ability to give lumps of weight away to horses who in their own right were very smart chasers was the true mark of his greatness. By comparison, the modern-day big-name chasers have a relatively easy life. He carried 12st 10lb when Flying Wild and Buona notte beat him by a head and a length in the Massey-Ferguson at Cheltenham. Those two classy chasers were carrying only 10st 6lb and 10st 12lb respectively. And when Stalbridge Colonist, another chaser who most definitely did not belong in the 'slow boat' category, beat him by half a length in the 1966 Hennessy, Arkle was conceding 35lb. Arkle's only other defeat in a chase came on his final start when, despite the pain of his foot injury, he almost lasted home.

Arkle had to be put down because of advancing arthritis in May 1970. His outstanding trainer and the tall man on his back who shared in his big-race successes have also long since left this world. Then in 2003, Arkle's owner, who named him after a mountain peak in Scotland, died.

But if the Arkle team belong to another era, Himself set the standard by which all chasers are still measured. It was no surprise whatsoever that the steeplechaser universally regarded as the greatest-ever also proved to be the best-loved.

We have not seen his like since – and nor are we ever likely to.

arkle what they said

He was a great, great friend and a great racehorse. He was very special, an amazing character. I rode him a lot at home. I was a little worried about him in his races. Pat Taaffe and Mr Dreaper wanted to run him in the National, but I wouldn't allow it. His Gold Cups were the highlights, especially as there were so many good horses, like Mill House, around. It was a very sad day when he died. Like all great athletes, after he'd been inactive for a while he became very stiff and found it hard to get up. His original injury, the pedal bone, healed and he was sound again on that, but he had lumbago or sciatica.
Anne, Duchess of Westminster, owner
(Anne, Duchess of Westminster died in 2003; her words are taken from the Racing Post)

The memory can play tricks and when people ask me about Arkle, I find it hard to separate what I remember about him from what I was told about him. My first real memory was all the hype and build-up to his first Gold Cup in 1964. I was at Headfort school near Kells at the time and one of the teachers, Jack Sweetman, used to keep me up to date with all the news. Arthur Moore was at school with me and I remember the school caretaker used to head off to the bookies in Kells with our half-crowns when Arkle was running.
Jim Dreaper, son of trainer Tom Dreaper

His first Gold Cup is the one I remember best. The British reckoned Mill House, who had won it the previous year, was unbeatable and he was long odds-on. Arkle was 7-4 and won by five lengths. How we felt the pride. I wish I'd appreciated at the time how lucky I was to look after such a star. No-one who has ever worked in a stable could have been more fortunate because my other horse was Flyingbolt, whose three wins at the Cheltenham Festival included the Champion Chase. Perhaps if I'd been a bit older I would have appreciated it. But I was a kid.
Johnny Lumley, Arkle's groom

One morning I schooled him alongside Pat Taaffe, who was on Flyingbolt. To say it was exhilarating would be an understatement. They just kept going, getting quicker and quicker. They were the two best horses of their generation. It was such a thrill to be involved. He loved life and he loved people. Compared to Flyingbolt, Arkle was a gentleman. Flyingbolt would try to bite you or kick you, and on the gallops he was always ducking or diving. He was a mule. At home and on the track Arkle was a saint. I never pass the yard without looking across to box number seven, where he was stabled. I think of him every day. I think back to the mornings when he'd jig-jog back from exercise on his own.
Paddy Woods, regular work-rider

I'm delighted Arkle has won. A remarkable horse, ridden by a supreme horseman in Pat Taaffe: Arkle was the best I've seen, though my father would have said the same about Golden Miller. I rode Mill House against Arkle in the Gallaher Chase at Sandown. I thought we'd burned him off, but he came sweeping by as if we were standing still and went on to win by 20 lengths and set a course record. He was giving Mill House 16lb. Earlier, I'd ridden Border Flight against Arkle in the Broadway Chase at Cheltenham. We'd been upsides at the last fence, but I got the sack for not giving my horse a ride!
David Nicholson, who rode against Arkle on several occasions

All of us who lived in the Arkle era must count ourselves as privileged, but I probably saw rather too much of him! To this day, I cannot quite believe what he did to Mill House in the 1964 Gold Cup. That day Peter O'Sullevan described him as "the best we've seen for a long, long time". Nobody could argue with that, and we've seen nothing to touch him since. Arkle was the most magnificent athlete, superbly balanced. A major talent. His achievements did a lot to promote jump racing at the time and it became a golden period for the sport – he introduced countless new people to jumping. Some say we'll see another Arkle one day. I doubt that. I'm thrilled he won the vote.
Willie Robinson, regular partner of Arkle's great rival Mill House

The story in Ireland was that Arkle's heart was twice the size of normal. I don't know if that was true, but he was a class apart. A horse without a flaw.
Tommy 'TP' Burns, who won a 14-furlong maiden on the Flat on Arkle at Navan

Some experts consider Arkle was 25lb clear of any chaser to have raced since, and I wouldn't argue with that. In many respects he was unlucky not to go unbeaten in Britain. It was a tactical race when Stalbridge Colonist won the Hennessy – a case of sink the Tirpitz. I stalked him, then pulled wide approaching the final fence and went for home. It was all a blur because we were travelling so quick. I didn't beat Arkle that day – he was cantering and I cheated him! My horse had that one bit of speed and we just caught Arkle by surprise. Arkle was in such a league of his own the handicapper would publish two sets of weights for races in which he was entered, because if he wasn't declared at the overnight stage it would make a nonsense of the handicap. I remember, at the time, I said he should run in just three races – the King George, the Gold Cup and the French Grand National. I'm delighted he came out top in the poll. A magical horse.
Stan Mellor, who rode in two of Arkle's three Gold Cups and beat him on Stalbridge Colonist in the 1966 Hennessy at Newbury

Generally, I'm not convinced the public have much sense, but they've shown a considerable degree of sense on this occasion by voting for Arkle. When the Duchess of Westminster was asked by the organisers of the Horse of the Year Show if they could play a song in Arkle's honour while he paraded in the arena, she suggested *There'll Never Be Another You*. How true that was. For me, his best performance came in defeat, when third to Flying Wild in the 1964 Massey-Ferguson Gold Cup. Arkle had won the Hennessy the previous weekend and a 3lb penalty topped up his weight to 12st 10lb. He was beaten little more than a length, giving 32lb to the winner and 26lb to the second, Buona Notte. And still he was coming back at them at the finish. Can you imagine Henrietta Knight running Best Mate under 12st 10lb?
John Oaksey, award-winning journalist

It was the result I expected. Arkle was a seriously incomparable talent and his dominance required the rules of racing to be rewritten. Many of his finest performances came in handicaps. I don't know if we'll ever see another Arkle. I'll certainly not.
Sir Peter O'Sullevan, broadcasting legend

john oaksey charted Arkle's racing career in a series of brilliant articles in Horse and Hound. Here, we reproduce the piece he produced following the death, in May 1970, of 'Himself', the hero of two nations and the horse voted for by Racing Post readers in their thousands

A proud warrior who fought to the bitter end

FOR A moment last week the election, the Derby, the World Cup and all the other preoccupations of an English June seemed unimportant. A single four-word news announcement put them abruptly in perspective – and sent a stab of almost personal bereavement through who knows how many million hearts.

"The end of Arkle," the radio said, and, as the voice droned on, laconic, uninvolved, the rest of its sad message was drowned in a flood of memories.

With them, at first, came bitterness – anger at the cruel fate which has cut short the happy retirement Arkle so richly deserved. For he was only 13 years old and might fairly have looked forward to another decade of sweet grass, warm beds and careless ease. He was far too intelligent to be one of those horses who pine when their active life is over and, after all, if from time to time he wanted to hear the roar of the crowd again, what racecourse or showground in the world would not have been proud to receive him?

So it *is* cruel – to Arkle himself and perhaps even more to those who loved him best. Almost everyone who owns a domestic animal has to face, sooner or later, the dreadful decision Anne, Duchess of Westminster, faced last week. Once it was clear that the pain in Arkle's feet could not be cured and would get worse, there could only be the one decision. But only one person could take it and this great horse, unlike so many others, was lucky enough to have an owner who both deserved and appreciated the gift from the gods that he was.

But set against his sad, untimely ending, Arkle was lucky in other ways as well. Throughout his life, in a world it takes all sorts to make, his selection of human beings was as unerring as his jumping.

An owner who wanted to bet, a trainer who specialised in hurdlers or a jockey with clumsy hands – any one of them could have sent his life careering off down false, dark-ending trails. But the Duchess was prepared to wait, Tom Dreaper saw the big, ungraceful youngster's full potential, Johnny Lumley, Paddy Woods and all the others at Greenogue worked long and hard to develop it – and in the end, in Pat Taaffe's gentle, steely fingers, it flowered to the thing of magic that was Arkle.

So he was lucky in his friends – and even luckier perhaps never to know the downward sag to mediocrity and failure which is, inevitably, the lot of so many.

That tragic Boxing Day at Kempton, Arkle's supremacy was as great as it had ever been. Not for him the agonising battle with advancing years, the steady, too slow progress down the handicap, the defeats by younger horses, the excuses, the knowing nods and patronising words – "I told you so – he's gone." No-one ever said that about Arkle.

To the very end there was no hint of deterioration and now there never will be. Our memories of him may fade with time, but they can never be tarnished by failure – and of all the great chasers since the war I can think of only one, Mandarin, who went out on anything like so high a note.

But if, in these ways, Arkle was lucky, how much luckier were we who lived to watch and enjoy his greatness. And how lucky – though not all racecourse managers might agree – that television came in time to convey that greatness to millions for whom, without it, Arkle would only have been a name.

Of all those millions each will have his memories. My own are so many and vivid that it is difficult to choose, but, oddly enough, a defeat, one of the only four he ever suffered over fences, stands clearest in my mind.

Only a week before, Arkle had turned the Hennessy Gold Cup into a hollow procession beating poor Mill House by 100 yards and looking, quite literally, invincible.

Even with 12st 10lb on his back, even over two miles and five furlongs, a distance patently short of his best, he was still made a red-hot favourite for the Massey-Ferguson Gold Cup. And it was only between the last two fences at Cheltenham as Flying Wild and Buona notte went past him, that we realised he wasn't invincible after all.

But the moment I remember came *after* the last fence that day. Buona notte, who had blundered horribly, was fighting back in a vain attempt to catch Flying Wild and the two of them, the elegant, grey mare and the massive, powerful bay, would in any case have made a thrilling sight.

But look back behind them and you will see something far more memorable. Head low, dog-tired, giving 32lb to one rival and 26lb to the other, Arkle *gained ground* up the Cheltenham hill.

With everything against him, he never for one moment thought of giving up and even now, shutting my eyes, I can see the angle of his out-thrust neck with every nerve and sinew strained to the limit and beyond.

It wasn't, thank heaven, how we usually saw him. Far more often, of course, it was the others who struggled in vain and he who toyed with them.

But a lot has been written of Arkle's alleged "conceit" – a ridiculous and inaccurate word in any case to describe the natural elegance and gaiety which were his outward trademarks. And even if he had an air of pride, conceit is still the wrong description. For conceit is a balloon that can all too easily be pricked.

In all his four defeats – that fatal, misleading slip at Newbury, against Flying Wild and Buona notte, trying to give Stalbridge Colonist 35lb and, finally, on three legs in the King George VI Chase – Arkle's courage never once deserted him.

So used to victory, he might so easily have sulked when things got tough – but the tougher they got, the harder he tried. Effortless supremacy is one thing – dogged persistence in pursuit of the impossible quite another.

It is very hard to shift, as Arkle did, from the first to the second without losing either his own or anyone else's respect. So call him proud if you like, for proud he was. But not, I beg of you, "conceited" – for braggarts seldom fight, as he did, to the bitter end. The facts and figures of Arkle's record are too well known to bear repeating in detail. Only six horses ever beat him over fences. Mill House and Happy Spring did so in the 1963 Hennessy Gold Cup, after one of the only two mistakes which ever affected Arkle's career.

The second, at the last open ditch in the 1966 King George VI Chase, was the one which smashed his pedal bone, brought about his defeat by Dormant and drove him into premature retirement.

Between those two disasters I can only remember seeing Arkle hit two fences hard. One was the second in the Railway straight at Sandown (he took off a full stride too soon) and the other was the last fence first time round in his third and final Cheltenham Gold Cup.

He had the shamrock in his bridle for St Patrick that day and, looking at the crowd instead of where he was going, he simply galloped straight on. But so great was his strength, so perfect his balance, that the shamrock never even nodded and Pat Taaffe never moved. In public I suppose he must have jumped well over 500 steeplechase fences and, even if you add a few mistakes unnoticed from the stands, his record – unblemished by a single racing fall – can never have been excelled by any chaser, let alone one who was so often asked to concede huge weights in top-class handicaps.

I have no wish to revive the sterile argument comparing him with Golden Miller, but to suggest that the Aintree fences would have been too much for Arkle has always seemed to me insulting nonsense.

From the moment when, as a headstrong yearling, he came off second best in an argument with a strand of barbed wire, only one obstacle ever did prove too much for him. That was a schooling hurdle and the crashing fall he took over it taught him a lesson he never forgot.

Perhaps that, in the end, was the underlying secret of his greatness. For while there may well have been horses with hearts, lungs, muscles and bones as efficient as Arkle's – horses who could gallop as far and as fast – there has never been one who combined with those physical qualities the intelligence, co-ordination and timing to jump 500 fences at racing pace and misjudge only five or six.

Had Arkle ever gone to Aintree, I for one have not the slightest doubt that, barring sheer bad luck, he would have carried any weight up to 12st and won any of the Grand Nationals run during his lifetime.

But there is no need for such speculation. The facts alone are quite enough. They are, simply, that no other horse in steeplechasing history ever dominated his contemporaries half as completely as Arkle did. No other horse in the whole history of thoroughbred racing was ever so much loved and admired by so many people, and to no other horse does the sport and all who follow it owe so huge and unpayable a debt.

It is a slightly sobering thought that, in under three minutes this week, a three-year-old colt will, by galloping 12 furlongs on the Flat, have earned nearly as much (£60,000) as the total (£75,000) Arkle won by galloping almost 100 miles and jumping 500 fences and hurdles.

Such are the topsy-turvy values of modern racing – but it wasn't for money that Arkle ran his heart out. He did it because he had been bred for the job and taught to do it well by kindly men whose kindness and skill he was glad to repay.

He did it because he loved his own speed and strength and agility – and perhaps because he loved the cheers they brought him. He was, more certainly than any other Thoroughbred I can think of, a *happy* horse who enjoyed every minute of his life.

In that sense perhaps the human race did repay some small part of the debt it owed him and at least when his life ceased being a pleasure it was quickly and humanely ended.

But mostly the debt remains unpaid. We can only try to pay it by remembering Arkle as he was – brave in defeat, magnificent in victory, kind and gentle in repose.

Now he is gone and we must search for others to warm our blood on winter afternoons, to fill the stands and set the crowds on fire. No doubt we shall find them – but they will be pale shadows of the real thing. For those who saw Arkle will never forget the sight and, until they see another like him, will never believe that two such miracles can happen in a lifetime.

June 5, 1970

Reproduced by permission

Arkle and Pat Taaffe

He was the warrior we took to our hearts. Desert

Desert Orchid

by brough scott

Orchid was not just good but brave, not just brave but front-running bold, not just bold but fearless and sometimes flawed. He was the grey attacker who put his neck on the line, and the world loved him for it.

It was utterly typical of him that he should go out on his shield. That he began and ended his 71-race, 34-victory, ten-season jumps career with a sickening somersault at Kempton. That the final crash came in his sixth consecutive King George and, when he got up and galloped riderless past the stands, the whole crowd stood and cheered him just as they had roared home his record four victories in the race.

With Desert Orchid you knew exactly what you were going to get. The tapes would go up and 'Dessie' would charge off to the first as if Prince Rupert had recruited him to his cavalry. In an increasingly evasive and spin-doctoring world there was something wonderfully rewarding in this increasingly white horse who threw caution to the winds and, unlike Prince Rupert's one-charge wonders, kept returning to the fray.

Our relationship with him was all the stronger for its taking time to grow. Sure, he won six in a row and ended up running in the Champion Hurdle in his first full season.

Trainer David Elsworth seemed game to run him in everything, as did the splendidly batty Burridge family. Solicitor Jimmy Burridge had bred Dessie from his headstrong hunter mare Flower Child; his son Richard was a tall scriptwriter who had won a hurdling blue at Cambridge. They were not quite the Distressed Gentlefolks'

The grey attacker put his neck on the line – and the world loved him for it

Association but they had to borrow a horsebox to take Dessie to Elsworth's and it took them two days – and much kicking – to get him there. They had never expected anything and were having the time of their lives – Richard used to sneak off and jump the fences himself.

After four seasons we thought they had a good horse but not a great one.

Time for comparisons. In March 2004, when the nine-year-old Best Mate emulated, wonderfully, the third Cheltenham Gold Cup that Arkle achieved at the same age, his record stood at 13 wins and six seconds from 19 starts. As a nine-year-old, Desert Orchid was second to Pearlyman in the Queen Mother Champion Chase – but at this stage, he had already won 19 races from 45 starts, had won and been beaten in the King George, had earlier been good enough to run in two Champion Hurdles, had also fallen in three other hurdle races, had been pulled up twice, and had once been ignominiously and unsuccessfully tried in blinkers. Best Mate is the blueblood, Desert Orchid the hustler.

It was on that foundation that the fairytale took flight. That year, Desert Orchid may have got beaten again in the Champion Chase at Cheltenham – many people still thought him best as a two-miler – but then he won over three miles at Aintree, followed by a sensational, all-the-way, ears-pricked victory in the Whitbread over three miles five. The next season he won everything. The Tingle

2

Desert Orchid

Grey gelding foaled 1979
Grey Mirage - Flower Child
Owner Richard Burridge **Trainer** David Elsworth

Jockeys Colin Brown, Simon Sherwood, Richard Dunwoody **Record (jumps)** 34 wins from 71 starts

Career highlights Won 1984 Tolworth Hurdle, Kingwell Hurdle, 1985 Hurst Park Novices' Chase, 1986 King George VI Chase, 1987 Gainsborough Chase, 1988 Chivas Regal Cup, Whitbread Gold Cup, Tingle Creek Chase, King George VI Chase, 1989 Victor Chandler Chase, Gainsborough Chase, Cheltenham Gold Cup, King George VI Chase, 1990 Racing Post Chase, Irish Grand National, King George VI Chase, 1991 Agfa Diamond Chase

Desert Orchid (Richard Dunwoody) en route to winning his third King George

Creek and the Victor Chandler over two miles, the King George and the Gainsborough over three miles, and then – wonder of wonders – the Gold Cup itself over three and a quarter miles in conditions so rough that all faint-hearts advised withdrawal.

But he always gravitated to the eye of the storm. After becoming front-page news at Cheltenham, he practically brought the nation to a halt by then having his first ever steeplechasing fall at Aintree in April 1989 in the Martell Cup.

By now, Dessiemania was a full-scale epidemic and it had a good two seasons to run. He won seven more races, two more King Georges, got beat in two Gold Cups and it wasn't just his colour that was easy to recognise. Everyone had an inkling of why this was a phenomenon on the hoof. They could see that Dessie did not just like to lead, he loved to rumble. This was a horse who would race you until you quit.

The memories blur together but two clear images remain: the punch-in-the-stomach certainty of Dessie's jumping as he destroyed his rivals round Kempton in the 1990 Racing Post Chase, and the absolute I-will-not-be-denied set of his head and neck as he saw off Nick The Brief and a 15lb weight disadvantage in what was to be his last ever victory a year later at Sandown.

The legend had invaded the ether and was distorting into the land of the cuddly toy. One day at Kempton a 'coochie-coo' infant in a pram was stationed next to the paddock. As assorted bay and brown brutes filed past, the child gurgled "horsey,

He was the horse who led the charge under the banner 'Fear and Be Slain'

horsey". When a grey finally arrived, the burble changed to "Dessie, Dessie". Up close the real thing was never so sweet.

Before that closing King George in 1991, David Elsworth had us all down to Whitsbury. With the extraordinary intuitive, untutored eloquence that is the trademark of a man who managed to train not one, but two, of the top ten favourite racehorses of all time, Elsworth talked to us about how the strain of getting the now 12-year-old to racing peak was beginning to get to both him and the horse, of how Dessie "had to take his coat off at Sandown", of how the end was near.

Dessie himself put up with the hacks and camera crews with plenty of his old swagger until exercise was finally over and his groom Janice Coyle put his food in the manger.

An eager lensman moved forward to get the cosy picture of 'Dessie's breakfast'. The old fighter's patience snapped. The white face came up, the ears laid back and the guy was sent panicking through the door. In six decades with thoroughbreds I have never seen a horse so clearly express the sentiment "eff off".

In the search for wider interest, we are apt to drag up all sorts of soft and inappropriate analogies for famous quadrupeds. With Desert Orchid there is no such difficulty. He was the warrior who would not weaken, the horse who led the charge under the banner 'Fear and Be Slain'. That's why we loved and admired him. That's why I thought he would win.

desert orchid what they said

Without doubt the best horse I rode. He was the ultimate in courage. Just when I feared he was beaten, he would dig deep and find fresh reserves. In his second Gold Cup, I thought he would drop out at the top of the hill, but then he picked up and ran all the way to the line to finish third. He was an outstanding competitor and it was a privilege to have been associated with him.

Richard Dunwoody, regular rider for the last two seasons of Desert Orchid's career

Desert Orchid was the first racehorse I bought. I had been broke for years, had just sold my first screenplay and, instead of buying a car or a carpet or something remotely sensible, I decided, out of compulsion, to buy a horse – it's been downhill ever since. From the moment I saw him twitch his head and take off across a field, I was lost. It never occurred to me that he'd eventually rival Arkle; in fact, throughout his career, I was in a state of shock. Desert Orchid has meant so much to so many; he has touched so many lives and left so many memories. I thought he might win the vote, but it is impossible to be disappointed to be second to a legend. Jump racing has lived in Arkle's shadow for as long as I can remember, and he came from a more sporting age.

Richard Burridge, owner

Desert Orchid gave us so many great days that it is impossible to pick out one as the highlight. He was a wonderful piece of machinery; he was a phenomenon. As for the attention he got – if I hadn't trained him, I'd have got sick of hearing about him! We started Dessie off in obscurity and we grew with him. I was on the inside looking out and it became like watching your boy at the school sports. We were possessive and got offended if anyone said something derogatory about him. Finishing runner-up to Arkle is a huge honour, be it in a race or in a poll such as this.

David Elsworth, trainer

The highlight of my career was riding Desert Orchid. He's a brilliant horse – I love him. Every time I rode him, it was exhilarating. I never won a King George on him but I rode 17 of his 34 wins and in the early days he was a real tearaway and not the easiest of rides. He was pretty good and I just used to sit still on him and let him do his own thing.

Colin Brown, Desert Orchid's rider 1982-88

He was simply the most complete racehorse I ever sat on. His greatest attributes were his courage and jumping, his incredible soundness and his trainer. When you got on Desert Orchid, you knew you were on a racehorse who was 100 per cent fit and just as honest. He enabled me to fulfil so many ambitions. His two greatest performances for me were his victory in the Whitbread and his defeat of Pegwell Bay in the Gainsborough Chase.

Simon Sherwood, who partnered Desert Orchid to his Gold Cup victory in 1989, as well as his first two King Georges

Red Rum reached hearts never touched by

Red Rum

by david ashforth

horseracing before, or since. To this day, he stands on a pedestal, in fitting tribute to his spirit, courage and resilience, and to the lasting memories he created.

Admiring crowds willed him to win with a fierce passion and when, in 1977, Red Rum won the Grand National for the third time, an emotional eruption carried him to a special place in racing history.

Red Rum was a Cinderella horse who arrived with nothing, boasted no qualifications, raised no expectations – yet achieved the impossible. He brought neither fine breeding nor an imposing physique; he wasn't fast, he didn't jump spectacularly. Red Rum had other, deeper qualities.

Mared, on the other hand, was mad, the winner of a maiden race at Galway, and Red Rum's mother. His father was Quorum, chosen because he was owned by friends of the mare's owner.

This unpromising union produced an unpromising foal, bought without competition for 400gns by Tim Molony, a former champion jump jockey. Molony was acting for Maurice Kingsley, a gambling owner who had the Grand National meeting in mind for Red Rum – the five-furlong Thursby Selling Plate for two-year-olds.

On April 7, 1967, the day before Foinavon attracted huge attention, Red Rum attracted none when dead-heating for a share of £266. Molony bought him in for 300gns. Almost a year later, when Red Rum won another selling race, at Warwick, he was forced up to 1,400gns. Kingsley doubted that he was worth it.

He stands on a pedestal, in fitting tribute to his spirit, courage and resilience

In 1968, it was the turn of veteran trainer Bobby Renton and owner Lurline Brotherton to place their optimism in Red Rum. By the summer of 1972, they decided it had been misplaced. The horse had graduated into an occasional winning chaser but, hard-raced and often hard-ridden, he seemed to be deteriorating. When foot problems surfaced – the potentially fatal pedalostitis was diagnosed – Red Rum was sent to the Doncaster Sales.

There was another unpromising visitor to the sales – Donald 'Ginger' McCain. Part taxi driver, part used-car salesman, part trainer, McCain had finally persuaded one of his regular fares, Noel Le Mare, to buy a horse. Le Mare, 84, had once worked as a trawlerman for fourpence an hour. Now a Liverpool millionaire, it was his ambition to win the National; it was McCain's ambition to show that he was the man to do it.

Le Mare's limit was 7,000gns; McCain bought Red Rum for 6,000gns, four times more than he had ever paid for a horse before.

Feisty and opinionated, McCain trained from an eccentric little yard near Southport, working his small string on the beach. On his first day there, Red Rum was lame. McCain walked him in the sea, and the lameness walked away.

The partnership flourished, with Red Rum winning his next five races. When the eight-year-old lined up for the 1973 National, he was 9-1 joint-favourite with Crisp.

3

Red Rum

Bay gelding foaled 1965
Quorum - Mared
Owners Noel Le Mare (Lurline Brotherton)
Trainers Ginger McCain (Bobby Renton, Tony
Gillam) **Jockeys** Brian Fletcher, Tommy Stack
(Paddy Broderick) **Record (jumps)** 24 wins from
100 starts

Career highlights Won 1973 Grand National,
1974 Grand National, Scottish Grand National,
1975 Haydock Park National Trial, 1977 Grand
National; 2nd 1973 Haydock Park National Trial,
Hennessy Cognac Gold Cup, 1975 Grand National,
1976 Grand National

The crowd goes wild as Red Rum (Tommy Stack) wins his third Grand National in 1977

Red Rum played the villain to Crisp's tragic hero in one of the greatest of Grand National dramas. Crisp, magnificent, way out in front, one majestic leap after another, 12st on his back. His rival, off 10st 5lb, closing remorselessly and finally catching Crisp, to smother a story seemingly even better than Red Rum's fairytale. The time was 18 seconds faster than Golden Miller's 1934 record, and would stand until 1990.

It was the following year, 1974, that Red Rum became a horse apart, a National hero. This time it was Red Rum's turn to carry 12st, making him 24lb worse off with dual Gold Cup winner L'Escargot, third the previous year. Red Rum was not a big horse, but he and Brian Fletcher won by an easy seven lengths, the first horse since Reynoldstown in 1936 to have won the great race twice.

The National fences were more formidable in the 1970s than they are today and, granted good ground, Red Rum was wonderfully well equipped to jump them. Beautifully balanced, nimble, carefully accurate and economical, his jumping didn't bring gasps of amazement but it gave Fletcher and then Tommy Stack well-founded confidence. Red Rum also had stamina, galloping on with grit and relish. Three weeks after that second win, he won the Scottish Grand National, carrying 15lb more than any of his 16 rivals.

Red Rum was to be Aintree's salvation, for the course was in crisis. After the 1973 National, Mirabel Topham sold it to property developer Bill Davies. He raised the admission charges so much that in 1975 the smallest crowd on record – just 9,000 – watched Red Rum, a heart-over-head 7-2 favourite, finish a gallant runner-up, again under 12st, to L'Escargot, now receiving 11lb.

Red Rum had stamina, grit and relish – and he was to be Aintree's salvation

Time was ticking on. When Red Rum battled bravely to get to grips with Rag Trade in 1976, and failed by only two lengths, again under top weight, cold reason declared that the marvellous tale had reached its end. It was a great National record, two wins and two seconds, the last with Ladbrokes in charge of the race, before a revived crowd of 42,000.

By 1977, Red Rum was a 12-year-old and there were calls for his retirement. He arrived at Aintree having finished last in three of his latest four races, yet was still burdened with top weight, set to give 9lb to Davy Lad, the recent Gold Cup winner. You know the rest, because the occasion, and Peter O'Sullevan's rousing finale, are seared in racing's collective memory.

Left in the lead at Becher's, coming home 25 lengths clear for an improbable third National. The record will never be broken – three wins and two seconds in five successive runnings. "Bloody marvellous," said Ginger McCain. "Just bloody marvellous!"

McCain, remarkably, won another Grand National after a 27-year gap in April 2004 with Amberleigh House, a victory over which the shadow of Red Rum loomed large.

The Grand National legend himself enjoyed an active, adulation-filled retirement and, ever the survivor, had lived to be 30 when he died in October 1995. Fittingly, he is buried near the winning post at Aintree. There will never be another.

red rum what they said

The old lad had a wonderful life and was a marvellous friend. He was a tremendous old competitor but much more than that – he switched on the Blackpool lights and was Chieftain of Honour at the Highland Games. He was a very remarkable old horse, seriously magical.

He was the most lovely-looking horse with a character to match, not a brilliant horse but a true professional who never accepted he'd been beaten. He loved the public and they loved him too.

He just loved it at Aintree, of course. Horses like him, highly intelligent, can get bored on those park courses but at Aintree they have to use their brains – and he was very, very intelligent.

I thought Red Rum would finish second to Arkle in the poll, not third. When Red Rum died he was on the front page of every national newspaper, apart from the *Financial Times*.

Ginger McCain, trainer

To my mind, he was the true steeplechaser – a great jumper, a great stayer, with a big heart and the ability to avoid trouble. He was almost cat-like with his jumping. He was a real character – and there was something special about him in the sense that when you got on his back he immediately lit up and became aware of where he was and what he was doing.

Brian Fletcher, who won two Grand Nationals and finished second in another on Red Rum

Red Rum was one of the best advertisements racing has ever had and he got a lot of people interested in the sport.

I had some wonderful days with him and obviously winning the 1977 National on him was something very special. I had been associated with him earlier in his career and he was already a big hero when I got back on him.

One thing will always stick in my mind about that win. That night Red Rum was led up the steps into the Southport hotel where everybody was celebrating. They took him through the reception area and down into the ballroom where he took the applause like a film star. He hardly turned a hair.

Tommy Stack, Red Rum's rider in the 1977 Grand National

A Cheltenham Festival winner is something

to be. To be a triple Champion Hurdle winner is something else – but even that does not do full justice to the aura of invincibility that the mighty Istabraq earned on jumping's greatest stage.

Few notable racing careers pass by without an 'if only' – if only he hadn't fallen, if only he hadn't gone lame, if only he'd had his ground – and Istabraq, already one of the greatest hurdlers of all time, would surely have had the strongest of claims to be regarded as the best of the lot if only the 2001 Cheltenham Festival had survived the foot-and-mouth outbreak. 'If only' indeed . . .

His fast, accurate jumping, coupled with high cruising speed and devastating acceleration, made Istabraq a jockey's dream and a nation's hero. At four consecutive Festivals he came storming up the final hill to a crescendo of cheering that seemed to echo all round the Cotswolds. But could it have been five?

Despite being beaten on his hurdling debut, Istabraq, trained by Aidan O'Brien and owned by the legendary JP McManus, quickly established himself as the leading Irish novice and endeared himself to his public in the best possible way – by landing a massive gamble – in the 1997 Royal & SunAlliance Novices' Hurdle, despite working himself into a bag of nerves.

Many expected him to be trained for the Stayers' Hurdle the following season – it was the logical route for a SunAlliance winner – but O'Brien was convinced he had enough speed to go for the Champion Hurdle, even though no horse had ever completed the SunAlliance-Champion Hurdle double.

At four consecutive Festivals he stormed up the hill to a crescendo of cheering

Istabraq, the young prince of Cheltenham, duly brought it off. Indeed, he didn't just win, he scored imperiously by 12 lengths over his stable companion Theatreworld, the biggest winning margin in the Champion Hurdle for 66 years.

Such was the level of public esteem Istabraq commanded that he started at 4-9 for the following year's Champion and duly notched a straightforward success. Although Theatreworld cut the deficit to just three and a half lengths, Istabraq still won with total authority after injecting a smart turn of foot at the second-last.

His progress towards a third successive victory – to match the record of Hatton's Grace, Sir Ken, Persian War and See You Then – wasn't all plain sailing. The stage was set for the star to deliver the result that his adoring public wanted – demanded – but it was a case of 'noises off' when, on the eve of the 2000 Champion, a trickle of blood was found to be coming from a nostril shortly after his arrival in the racecourse stables.

O'Brien agonised about running him and decided to do so only because he did not want to thwart the horse's chance of joining the immortals. Istabraq settled all the doubts by sweeping home majestically in record time, and bloody noses were strictly for his rivals.

A fourth successive Irish Champion Hurdle in the foot-and-mouth campaign – albeit one achieved following a fall at the Leopardstown Christmas meeting – served

4

Istabraq

Bay gelding foaled 1992 Sadler's Wells - Betty's Secret Owner JP McManus **Trainer** Aidan O'Brien **Jockey** Charlie Swan **Record (jumps)** 23 wins from 29 starts

Career highlights Won 1997 Royal & SunAlliance Novices' Hurdle, Punchestown Champion Novices' Hurdle, Hatton's Grace Hurdle, December Festival Hurdle, 1998 Irish Champion Hurdle, Champion Hurdle, Hatton's Grace Hurdle, 1999 Irish Champion Hurdle, Champion Hurdle, Aintree Hurdle, Punchestown Champion Hurdle, 2000 Irish Champion Hurdle, Champion Hurdle, 2001 Irish Champion Hurdle, December Festival Hurdle

Charlie Swan salutes the crowd as Istabraq wins his second Champion Hurdle in 1999

as a tasty *hors d'oeuvre* for the fourth Cheltenham Champion success that would have given him a unique place as a hurdling legend. But the main course was never served as plumes of smoke and the stench of burning carcasses spoke of greater tragedy.

Twelve months on, the build-up to the 2002 Champion Hurdle was marred by another Leopardstown fall and, by Cheltenham, the rumour mill was grinding remorselessly with the suggestion that Istabraq was not the horse he had been. The aura of invincibility was finally dispelled on his fifth visit to the Festival as he was pulled up after the third flight with tendon damage. Never has such an abject effort been greeted with such warm, heartfelt applause. Jumping folk have long memories, and the tribute to a fallen gladiator borne away on his shield from the arena he had made his own was an emotional one, shorn of venal concern for the losing betting ticket.

Istabraq was retired with the remarkable record of having finished behind only three horses in his entire jumping career when he managed to complete the race – and he completed 26 of them. His glory days were a far cry from his early career, however, which can only be classed as a disappointment, certainly to his owner-breeder Hamdan Al Maktoum, who gave the horse his name – old Arabic for 'lightning', as in lightning-fast – in the hope he would justify an illustrious pedigree.

Born at the Derrinstown Stud in County Kildare, Istabraq was sent to John Gosden with high hopes for a Flat career. However, he managed only one undistinguished

Istabraq, the old warrior and one of the greatest hurdlers of them all

run as a two-year-old and, while he won twice at three, there was still little sign of the speed suggested by his name.

Istabraq also had his share of problems – a dodgy hoof, a bone chip and, for good measure, flat feet. The chip came off the front of a fetlock joint and was not thought to be serious enough to be removed, but the quarter-crack had to be patched and at one stage, for three weeks, he was confined to walking and trotting. He was to develop a similar problem in the run-up to his third Champion Hurdle victory – but the flat feet stayed with him for the rest of his career.

Gosden's assistant during the horse's Flat career was an enthusiastic amateur rider called John Durkan, and thereby hangs another, sadder chapter in the Istabraq legend. In 1996, Durkan was planning a training career and was convinced that the then four-year-old would make a top hurdler. McManus agreed to buy him, but Durkan was never to fulfil his dream. He was diagnosed with leukaemia before he was able to take out a licence, but he recommended that Istabraq should join O'Brien while he concentrated on his treatment. Durkan never recovered, dying before the first of Istabraq's Champion Hurdle victories.

O'Brien thus became keeper of the flame, and the man who has since enjoyed so many wonderful Flat triumphs tended it faithfully, seeing home Istabraq, the old warrior and one of the greatest hurdlers of them all, to a safe and honourable retirement at his owner's Martinstown Stud.

istabraq what they said

It was a privilege for me and everybody at Ballydoyle to have a horse like him. I don't think we will ever see such a good hurdler again and I know I will never have another like him.

I am indebted to the late John Durkan for recommending that the horse should come to Ballydoyle and I will never forget that it was John who first recognised his talent. He told me before Istabraq had even run over hurdles that he would win the SunAlliance, and that was a big statement to make.

Istabraq was a natural athlete and a very clear-winded horse who had brilliance, but he tended to live on the edge – there was always a very fine line involved.

He gave us wonderful memories to cherish and all who were associated with him feel especially privileged. We will cherish those memories forever.

Aidan O'Brien, trainer

He was a great horse – not just to me but to a lot of other people and it's great he finished up there so high in the list. There are great horses ahead of him and below him and I'm proud to be able to say I rode a horse so famous and so good.

Istabraq meant everything to me. You only come across a horse as good as him once in a lifetime and he was an unbelievable racehorse. He had everything – speed, stamina,

jumping ability, you name it. He was an all-round brilliant horse.

He loved racing and winning. You could settle him and he would go at whatever speed you wanted, on any ground and over any trip, and it made no difference whether the course was right-handed or left-handed.

His greatest asset was his jumping; he always landed running. His hind legs were down almost before the front ones, enabling him to get away from his hurdles so quickly.

It's hard to say what were the best moments, but I suppose winning the third Champion Hurdle was the icing on the cake.

The biggest disappointment was when the Festival was called off in 2001. I am convinced he would have made it four on the trot, as he was in great form at the time.

Charlie Swan, who rode Istabraq in every one of his 29 starts over jumps

He's a horse who gave everyone so much pleasure and I'm thankful particularly to Aidan and his team at Ballydoyle for all they achieved with Istabraq. Istabraq had a great innings at Cheltenham and he finished his career safe and well.

JP McManus, owner

In spirit he belonged to England, to all who

stood in admiration around him, to the thousands who followed his career and had never seen him, even to those ignorant of his name.

"In him every Englishman justly could take an equal part, for he was part of our heritage, evolved from 300 years of thought and endeavour by those dedicated to perfecting the breed of the racehorse."

Brigadier Gerard was England's horse. His owner John Hislop could not have composed a more fitting tribute than the one reproduced above. To this horse, every runner with pretensions to greatness must stand comparison.

Rocking horses were more my concern when Brigadier Gerard was doing his thing. The early 1970s are precious, however, because the dark period between birth and first memory holds a particular fascination.

While my parents were listening to the likes of Jimi Hendrix and Jim Morrison – who both died during this period – the US was at war with a technologically inferior nation, a duplicitous president was in the White House and the world was in turmoil. The Vietnam War and Watergate are fading into history, but some things never change.

On May 1, 1971, Brigadier Gerard lined up for the 2,000 Guineas at Newmarket with a point to prove. His unbeaten two-year-old season had culminated with success in the Middle Park Stakes at Newmarket, but even that had failed to convince everyone that he was right out of the top drawer.

Brigadier Gerard

by **james willoughby**

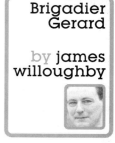

Brigadier Gerard was unflinchingly determined, impervious to circumstance

Correspondingly, the public preferred Mill Reef and My Swallow in the betting, both brilliant juveniles who themselves had a score to settle from the Prix Robert Papin, in which the former was thought to have been unlucky to go down by a short head.

Brigadier Gerard duly triumphed by three lengths and, while the result proved him a better horse than Mill Reef over a mile, the winning margin seemed not to be a true reflection of their relative merits. The latter was softened up in a duel with My Swallow while the winner waited in behind.

The modern-day racing fan owes it to himself not to accept the testimony of his elders on every matter of history. There is a wealth of video and literary material to help you make your own mind up about the worth of great horses of the past.

How dare they compare Hawk Wing with the mighty Brigadier, for example? Both won in the highest class at two, three and four years and had the Lockinge on their CV, but there the similarity ends. Brigadier Gerard was unflinchingly determined, impervious to circumstance and won 17 of his 18 starts. Enough said. Some of his most thrilling victories came on bottomless ground which was palpably not to his advantage. Time and again, he found a way to win, even if not running within a stone of his best form.

In the St James's Palace Stakes at Royal Ascot, for instance, the colt faced a situation the desperation of which could have been penned for the Conan Doyle

5

Brigadier Gerard

Bay colt foaled 1968
Queen's Hussar - La Paiva
Owner-breeders John and Jean
Hislop **Trainer** Dick Hern **Jockey**
Joe Mercer **Record (Flat)** 17 wins
from 18 starts

Career highlights Won 1970
Middle Park Stakes, 1971 2,000
Guineas, St James's Palace Stakes,
Sussex Stakes, Goodwood Mile,
Queen Elizabeth II Stakes,
Champion Stakes, 1972 Lockinge
Stakes, Westbury Stakes, Prince of
Wales's Stakes, Eclipse Stakes, King
George VI and Queen Elizabeth
Stakes, Queen Elizabeth II Stakes,
Champion Stakes

Brigadier Gerard and Joe Mercer after winning the Eclipse Stakes in 1972

character after whom he was named. Turning for home, he lost his action in deep mud and allowed the superb miler Sparkler an advantage of several lengths. Not content to lie down, however, he clawed back the deficit and won by a head.

When conditions were in his favour, Brigadier Gerard's natural ability did not require the bolster of his courage. He set Ascot track records at both a mile and a mile and a quarter. To anyone who can access the 1972 form book and knows how to calculate speed figures, assimilating the merit of his six-length victory in the Queen Elizabeth II Stakes is well worth the effort. Not bad considering he missed the break!

That race also marked the first time a horse eclipsed the 1min 40sec barrier for the Old Mile. Lesser horses regularly achieve the same feat nowadays, but only because of the combined development of the thoroughbred and the surface on which it competes. (A new mark of 1min 38.51sec was set by Russian Rhythm in the Coronation Stakes of 2003.)

One of the sport's most famous conundrums concerns Brigadier Gerard's defeat by Roberto in the 1972 Benson and Hedges Gold Cup at York.

Roberto had the advantage of far more natural early pace and was able to take a clear lead after a couple of furlongs. Brigadier Gerard's running style put him at a severe disadvantage because they just don't come back at York. Early in the straight, he looked to be travelling well, but he was more likely running with the choke out and was beaten before the furlong pole.

That he should suffer only one defeat is testament to his greatness

Hislop, initially as confused as anybody, eventually rationalised The Brigadier's three-length defeat by accepting that a hard-fought success in the King George at Ascot had caught up with him. According to this theory, the stress of running over a mile and a half for the only time, coupled with only 24 days to recover, had left its mark on The Brigadier, though there were no outward signs in the colt's demeanour.

An alternative explanation is provided by the evidence of the clock. Not only was Roberto's winning time a track record, but it was sensational when compared with others on the day. Moreover, the average speed at which Brigadier Gerard travelled (12.1sec per furlong) was by far the fastest of his career. It is therefore highly likely that his turn of foot was blunted by having to run hard from a long way out.

That Brigadier Gerard should suffer only one defeat given the aggressive manner in which he was campaigned is testament to his greatness. Hislop believed that honourable defeat carried more merit than an unbeaten record preserved by avoiding the issue. Brigadier Gerard combined the brilliance of the champion Flat horse with the courage of the jumper. He permeated the public awareness, even without being grey or winning the Grand National.

England expects, and sometimes England is not disappointed.

brigadier gerard what they said

I felt very proud of Brigadier Gerard. He was the sort of horse every trainer dreams of having because he seemed to be head and shoulders above his contemporaries.

Brigadier Gerard was a great racehorse, being beaten only once in 18 starts and putting up a very brilliant performance when he beat Mill Reef in the 2,000 Guineas. When I trained him I can never remember not being able to do with him what I wanted. Day to day, at exercise, he was never sick or sorry, he was very sound. He was great to train – after a while, I could never see him getting beaten as long as we kept him well.
Dick Hern, trainer (Dick Hern died in 2002; his words are taken from the Racing Post)

It is absolutely wonderful and a great feather in the old boy's cap that he was voted the most popular Flat horse. He gave a lot of people a lot of pleasure – he achieved an awful lot in his career and there were some very good horses around in his era. I reckon that if he was around today he would've won about three million quid! It was like losing one of the family when he died. He was a

great character and a lovely horse to be associated with. He was a freak horse with tremendous enthusiasm and speed and the class to win beyond his distance. He was a horse you never thought about getting beat on.
Joe Mercer, jockey

Like the star of wonder, his brilliance shone again and again during three magnificent seasons and his achievements will surely never be equalled. Answering the call to arms on ground he loved and on ground he hated, over all distances, racing from the front and from behind, in sickness and in health, never once did he desert the battlefield or flinch in the face of adversity. At a time when hyperbole and superlatives are too freely used, he is the one British Flat racehorse who can genuinely and unequivocally claim the mantle of greatness.
Laurie Williamson, Brigadier Gerard's groom

Brigadier Gerard defied the maxim that horses are not machines. For three seasons his brilliant performances made him consistently superior to the usual run of champions and, in winning 17 of his 18 races, he proved almost the perfect equine athlete, the culmination of 300 years of genetic engineering.

Even when conditions favoured his rivals – his supreme class and raw courage saw him through. He won 15 races before suffering his only defeat, when second to Roberto in the Benson and Hedges Gold Cup at York in 1972 – the most baffling result in racing history.

His tally of 13 Pattern victories remains a record, and his talent, courage and amazing consistency made him a champion among champions – a worthy Horse of the Century.
John Randall and Tony Morris (From the Racing Post series A Century of Racing, published in 1999, in which Brigadier Gerard was rated No.1 Flat horse)

There was something Churchillian about One

One Man

by **rodney masters**

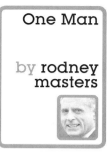

Man's career. His chronicle of achievement across half a dozen years in the 1990s was peppered with depressing lows that led to publicity regularly focusing on his shortcomings. The disparity between the extremes of his performance was wider than that of any other of the elite who made the top ten in this poll.

To his credit, no defeat was to dilute the grey's indomitable spirit. Setbacks that were due to a lack of stamina failed to diminish his popularity – in a way they enhanced it.

That resolute spirit was why we adored him and why we'll never forget him. He embraced the romance, heartbreak and unpredictable thrill of jump racing at its best.

It should be remembered that three times the impossible was asked of him at the Cheltenham Festival, where he was sent out for inappropriate combat – a Sun Alliance Chase and two Gold Cups.

On each occasion he ran himself to a wobbly standstill as his lungs deflated as rapidly as a pricked balloon. He was thrashed 49 lengths, 34 lengths and 35 lengths in those three races.

Ask One Man to leap over Cheltenham Town Hall and he'd be sure to give it a go, but beyond three miles that final push up the hill to the winning line at Prestbury was too far at championship level without the aid of a grappling iron.

One Man's finest hour came at the age of ten, and, although we didn't know it at the time, horribly close to his final hours. On his penultimate appearance,

Ask One Man to leap over Cheltenham Town Hall and he'd be sure to give it a go

fittingly at Cheltenham, a stunning mix of class and power carried him to a richly deserved and widely appreciated success in the 1998 Queen Mother Champion Chase, beating Or Royal by four lengths. This time he was on the right side of the wall.

Remarkably, it was only his second race over two miles. The first had been on his racecourse debut in a novices' hurdle at Hexham – six years, and 33 races, earlier when trained by Arthur Stephenson and ridden by Chris Grant.

Of course, it begged the question what might he have achieved at the Festival had he been campaigned over a more suitable distance there earlier in his career. After all, the two previous runnings of the Champion Chase had been won by Klairon Davis (1996) and Martha's Son (1997), neither one blessed with his ability.

As a spectacular jumper of the same hue and class, the general public had looked to him to fill the vacuum left by Desert Orchid. Scanning his record, one cannot make a case that he let them down: victories included the King George VI Chase (twice), the Hennessy, and that Queen Mother Champion Chase.

Gordon Richards had an unswerving belief that he was a horse in a million. He would refer to One Man as his rubber ball, an appropriate analogy considering the manner in which the horse bounced rhythmically over his fences. Another definition might be the way he bounced back from those three humiliating defeats at the

6
One Man

Grey gelding foaled 1988
Remainder Man - Steal On
Owner John Hales **Trainer** Gordon Richards **Jockeys**
Tony Dobbin, Richard Dunwoody, Brian Harding **Record**
(jumps) 20 wins from 35 starts

Career highlights Won 1994 Reynoldstown Novices'
Chase, Hennessy Cognac Gold Cup, 1995 Tommy Whittle
Chase, 1996 King George VI Chase (Sandown, postponed
from December 1995), Charlie Hall Chase, King George VI
Chase, 1997 Pillar Property Investments Chase, Charlie Hall
Chase, Peterborough Chase, 1998 Comet And Sony Chase,
Queen Mother Champion Chase

One Man (Richard Dunwoody) winning a rescheduled King George in 1996 at Sandown

Festival. Yet in no respect can connections be censured for their belief he was a Gold Cup horse.

There was tantalising evidence that suggested he would last home. For instance, as a six-year-old he'd won a Hennessy at Newbury over the Gold Cup distance, though admittedly off 10st.

The first of his King George wins in 1996 had come in the rearranged running over a stretched three miles at Sandown, and he had come up the hill there to swamp the Sun Alliance winner Monsieur Le Cure by 14 lengths. In the second, later the same year and back at Kempton, he broke the course record as he came home 12 lengths clear of Rough Quest.

Detractors will point to the fact that One Man made the final ten in the poll while a host of Gold Cup winners, including Best Mate and Dawn Run, failed to do so. However, several respected historians are of the opinion the King George represents a more authentic measure of a champion. Looking at the results of both races down the years, it's difficult to mount an argument to that school of thinking.

One Man had started life on the point-to-point circuit in Ireland, and after coming to Britain had won a third of his nine appearances over hurdles for Stephenson, the former winningmost trainer of all time in Britain. The latter was a man of few words, but nine of them to his friend and rival Richards sparked interest in this young

"After three races my wife said, 'I think we've bought a good one'."

grey. "Wait until you see him over the black ones," he said. The "black ones" in question were steeplechase fences; Richards, it seems, took careful note.

At Stephenson's dispersal sale in 1993, businessman John Hales, whose interest in racing had been motivated by Desert Orchid, the greatest grey of them all, was looking for a horse. Hales, who was later to make his fortune as the maker of toy Teletubbies for children, had a budget of 30,000gns. One Man was his for 68,000gns.

"Afterwards I thought it was the most stupid thing I'd ever done," he remembers. "When we got him home my wife looked at his huge feet and said, 'You paid what for this?' After three races she said, 'I think we've bought a good one'."

The canny Stephenson's assessment proved accurate. In his novice season over fences after being sent to Richards, One Man was beaten just once in half-a-dozen races – at the Cheltenham Festival, in the Sun Alliance Chase.

His first fall over fences came in the 1995 Racing Post Chase at Kempton. It was of the X-rated variety and connections feared they'd lost him.

His second fall, his fatal fall, came at Liverpool, 16 days after he was crowned two-mile champion chaser. As the horse was being saddled, a BBC television boom microphone eavesdropped the visibly distraught owner's whisper to One Man.

"Just come home safely," Hales said. "There's a summer at grass awaiting you at home."

Tragically, One Man would not live to see it.

one man what they said

There will never be another like him. We all thought the world of him.

[When he was killed at Aintree] we had many, many hundreds of cards, letters and faxes – far too many to mention. They came from people from all walks of life, grannies, children and grown men who just wanted to say how sorry they were about the loss of a great horse. We all loved One Man. He was one of the family and I'm proud to have had him. I pushed Mr Hales to buy him and the horse proved me right. He knew my voice – we loved one another.

Gordon Richards, trainer (Gordon Richards died in 1998, less than six months after the death of his greatest chaser; his words are taken from the Racing Post)

I always maintained that he was the best two-and-a-half-mile chaser that I have ridden. He had a lovely way about him. In the Gold Cup, when I was trying to hold him up, he couldn't use his jumping prowess properly, but he showed at Cheltenham in the Queen Mother just how brilliant he could be.

Richard Dunwoody, who partnered One Man to many big-race wins, including a pair of King Georges

Not a day goes by when I don't think about One Man. He was a truly great horse and when I watch others run they seem mortals by comparison, but the tears have stopped and at least I can watch his races on video.

He was not just a horse but a gentleman and a friend. He was never sad or lame, and always gave

the best he knew. He was the horse of a lifetime: a true champion.

John Hales, owner

One Man was a great horse and one with all the attributes to make him a public favourite. He was one of those rare animals who inspired love, affection and admiration right across the spectrum – from seasoned professionals all the way to the denizens of the high-street betting shop.

Perhaps one of the reasons he struck such a deep chord was that he mixed pure class with vulnerability. We could rejoice in his King George wins but we also saw him suffer during those grinding but unavailing efforts to get up that Gold Cup hill.

That we had seen him both rampantly triumphant and desperately humiliated somehow brought him closer – there was nothing we didn't know about him.

That he was a grey obviously set him apart, but there was a flamboyance about him that drew the eye – the way he bounced over the turf in the manner of the truly gifted.

Alastair Down (From the Sporting Life tribute to One Man after his death at Aintree in 1998)

It all ended in tears. Not just the tears of his

connections – owner Jeff Smith, trainer David Elsworth, groom Dick Brown and regular jockey Martin Dwyer – but the tears of so many ordinary racing fans, who love a born battler above all others.

Persian
Punch

by george
ennor

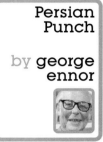

How could it not do so? Not when Persian Punch, newly voted the seventh-most popular horse in the *Racing Post* poll of 100 all-time favourite horses, collapsed and died in front of his adoring public in the Sagaro Stakes at Ascot in April 2004.

Not when a horse who had given so much over so many years had the most well-earned of retirements – whenever it might finally have arrived – so cruelly snatched away.

For Persian Punch, in sad contrast to that other Elsworth legend, there were to be no gallops past cheering stands at big meetings, no open days at which to be feted. But there will always be the memories.

Tributes to the gallant stayer poured in after his death, but there can be no better illustration of how the public loved him than a reception he was given when he was still alive, namely the reaction to what turned out to be Persian Punch's final victory, the Jockey Club Cup of 2003.

When judge Nick Haynes called "first, number two" as the result of the photo-finish, the Rowley Mile erupted. This number two was Persian Punch, who had once again come from what appeared to be an irretrievable position to win against all the odds.

A hundred yards from the line he had been fourth, but he had got up on the post to beat Millenary by a short head. Poor Millenary and his team might as well have been at the North Pole in the post-race excitement.

Persian Punch was the people's horse . . . the most popular horse in training

Persian Punch was the people's horse, far and away the most popular horse in training on the Flat. He was aged ten when he won that Jockey Club Cup – thereby equalling Brigadier Gerard's record of 13 Pattern-race victories – and ought to have been at the pipe-and-slippers stage, but such was his enthusiasm that nothing could have kept him from the racecourse.

For many at Newmarket that day, for all the excellence of Rakti's Champion Stakes success, the romance of 33-1 Milk It Mick in the Dewhurst and a first Cesarewitch at the last attempt for Pat Eddery, the memory they went home with was of Persian Punch and another last-gasp success.

Yet there is no doubt that much of his amazing popularity was due to the fact that, for all his wonderful courage and determination, Persian Punch was not an outstanding racehorse. He could and did run disappointingly sometimes, sometimes so badly, indeed, that people suggested he should be retired.

This was a big part of his appeal. He was a mere mortal; he was not invincible and he often had to grind out his wins by sheer resolution and will to succeed. His record of 63 runs and 20 wins makes it quite clear that it was never easy for him. Having to battle against the odds was truly a hallmark of his popularity.

At the end of 1999, when Persian Punch was six, Timeform observed – quite rightly

Persian Punch and Martin Dwyer after winning the Jockey Club Cup in 2003 at Newmarket

7
Persian Punch

Chestnut gelding foaled 1993
Persian Heights - Rum Cay
Owner Jeff Smith **Trainer** David Elsworth **Jockeys** Martin

Dwyer, Richard Quinn, Richard Hughes **Record (Flat)** 20 wins from 63 starts

Career highlights Won 1997 Henry II Stakes, 1998 Sagaro Stakes, Henry II Stakes, Lonsdale Stakes, 2000 Henry II Stakes, Prix Kergorlay, Jockey Club Cup, 2001 Goodwood Cup, Lonsdale Stakes, 2002 Jockey Club Cup, 2003 Goodwood Cup, Doncaster Cup. Jockey Club Cup; 2nd 1997 Irish St Leger, 2001 Ascot Gold Cup, 2003 Ascot Gold Cup; 3rd 1997 Prix du Cadran, 1998 Melbourne Cup, 2001 Melbourne Cup

on the basis of one win from six starts and a serious injury – that he was not as good as he had been. A year later, Timeform's opening sentence referred to how "Persian Punch defied the old sports writers' adage 'they never come back'".

Come back he most certainly did. He may or may not have been better than ever, but he was certainly as brave and determined. And even more popular.

Indeed, BHB marketing director Chris John remarked that if you wanted to increase racecourse attendances, Persian Punch should run every day.

It didn't really begin like that, though, and Persian Punch was hardly the most popular boy in the class when he made a winning debut in a mile-and-a-quarter maiden race at Windsor in May 1996. Ridden by Anthony Procter and starting at 25-1, he ran on too strongly for odds-on King Of Sparta. Someone, maybe Elsworth, for whose training of the horse no praise can be too high, knew something, as the 40-1 chalked up on a few boards was soon snapped up.

Persian Punch won twice more that year and was third in the Goodwood and Jockey Club Cups, races that became regular stopping-off points for him. But there was no adoration. Not yet.

During the next couple of years, Persian Punch won races such as the Sagaro and Henry II Stakes and put up a superb display in the Melbourne Cup of 1998, beaten a neck and half a length when trying to give almost a stone to the two who beat him.

It is not easy to define quite when he started to achieve hero status but, ironically, it may have been for a race in which he was beaten – the 2001 Gold Cup, when

What a horse, what a hero – no wonder the entire racing world loved him

he was eight and running in the contest for the fifth time. In a titanic struggle, he went down by a head to Royal Rebel, fighting back all the way to the line, having been headed a furlong and a half from home. He just refused to submit.

One national racing correspondent was tempted to write about "75,000 people all cheering for the runner-up", and Persian Punch returned to a reception that couldn't have been greater if he had won. He put Royal Rebel in his place in their two subsequent meetings that year. His popularity grew to such an extent that Luca Cumani apologised "for spoiling the party" after Boreas beat Persian Punch into second place in the 2002 Doncaster Cup, but the nation's favourite took revenge, as he usually did, in the Jockey Club Cup five weeks later.

Make no mistake: despite the tragic end to the story, there was never a sign of waning enthusiasm. Persian Punch loved the whole thing and his admirers adored him more and more as the years went by, which was hardly surprising when you consider the nature of his two highest-profile wins, as a ten-year-old in the 2003 Goodwood Cup and the aforementioned Jockey Club Cup. In both races he looked beaten, but he just would not have it. Down went his head, out stretched his neck, and he just galloped on.

What a horse, what a hero. No wonder the entire racing world loved him – the game could have no better ambassador.

persian punch what they said

He was a one-off, and to sum up what I feel about him is difficult. I know horses aren't that intelligent but he knew people and he could identify with us. He was so easy to work with and a privilege to be around – most people wanted to ride 'Punch' and most people had a go at some point, and he looked after everybody.

We knew him for so many years and he played a significant part in all our lives. We sent him to so many good races and he even took us to the other side of the world.

What hurts is that we were going to get so many more years of pleasure from him, but we've been robbed. I suppose you could say he went the way he would have wanted to go, in harness, and he didn't suffer, but I can't describe how much enjoyment we would have got from spoiling him, like we have with the old grey horse. Among the things I will miss most are those lovely summer days when I would throw a headcollar and lead rein on him, take him up the road and let him have a pick of grass and a roll in the paddock. It became a ritual.
David Elsworth, trainer

Ron Sheather, my racing manager, summed it up for me perfectly. He said that he knew I'd always wanted to win the Derby but that with Persian Punch I'd gone one better. Of course that's not true in terms of prize-money, stallion values and that

sort of thing, but in terms of the racing experience, it was a salient remark. To own a champion like a Nijinsky must be marvellous but, for me, Persian Punch, and all he did, was as good as it gets.
Jeff Smith, owner

In the end, he was a gladiator who died in the arena. Looking back on all the great days we had together, there are so many memories, but to me he was at his best in the Goodwood Cup. It was a big day and he showed tremendous battling qualities. It was a privilege to be associated with such a great horse. We had a lot of fun and I'll always remember him.
Martin Dwyer, regular rider of Persian Punch in the latter stages of his career

He was such a trier and he always gave 100 per cent – he was a true fighter. He wouldn't do a thing to hurt you; he loved the company and he always said hello. It's like Martin Dwyer says – he wasn't just a mate, he was a best friend.
Dick Brown, Persian Punch's groom

Dancing
Brave

by **peter
thomas**

Three-mile chasers are great, aren't they? You find them in all the old familiar places, winter after winter, giving you the same warm glow as a favourite cardigan on your golden wedding anniversary.

Warm glows and long-term relationships are nice, of course, but the ones you really remember are the ones who give you a thrill like you've never had before, and then leave you yearning for just one more summer.

Dancing Brave was a thriller. He smouldered for a season, he returned to seduce us and leave us gasping, then he was gone, out of the bedroom window, down the drainpipe and into the night.

There were many facets to the brilliance of this 1986 champion, but when all's said and done he was about speed, a streamlined gem, set in pure pace and finished with a shimmering patina of greased lightning.

To see him in the two strides between stalking and swooping was to taste the distilled essence of horseracing – a truly great middle-distance animal with a finishing kick like Armageddon.

Sadly for the great-lover analogy, Dancing Brave was not much of a looker – more Cyrano than Valentino, in fact. He had a parrot mouth and a wonky, off-centre streak on his snout that was damp squib rather than blaze. But handsome was as handsome did, and he looked a picture in a blur of green, pink and white.

I can't claim to have seen the attraction very early. Even when he hit the ground running as a three-year-old with a perfectly decent success in the Craven, I

Dancing Brave was a thriller – he left us gasping and was gone

was still not a convert, to the extent that I unwisely opposed him in the 2,000 Guineas.

In fairness, Mr Magoo could have spotted the star quality in this performance, as Dancing Brave put the likes of Green Desert through the shredder. And that's where the story really begins.

I was working as a cub reporter on the *East Grinstead Courier* at the time – the kind of job your employer describes as giving you "a good grounding". The kind of job you describe as giving you no wages. Money wasn't so much scarce as extinct, and a punting jaunt to the races wasn't something to be undertaken lightly.

Armed with Dancing Brave, however, I felt unassailable as I stood in the Epsom grandstand. I left the racecourse even more certain of the horse's superstar status, but sadly even less certain of how I was going to eat until payday.

This was the defeat that would etch him into folklore as the unluckiest Derby loser of the age, thereby handing him the one weapon most likely to penetrate the consciousness of any racefan looking for a legend – the potential for righteous revenge.

The fact that Dancing Brave was set a bigger task at Epsom than all of Hercules's put together didn't pass many witnesses by, but there were still some who claimed he was beaten because he had been ridden as a non-stayer and failed to overhaul the worthy Shahrastani.

Dancing Brave (Pat Eddery) swamps his rivals for an unforgettable Arc success

8

Dancing Brave

Bay colt foaled 1983
Lyphard - Navajo Princess
Owner Khalid Abdullah **Trainer** Guy Harwood **Jockeys** Greville
Starkey, Pat Eddery **Record (Flat)** 8 wins from 10 starts

Career highlights Won 1986 Craven Stakes, 2,000 Guineas,
Eclipse Stakes, King George VI and Queen Elizabeth Diamond
Stakes, Select Stakes, Prix de l'Arc de Triomphe; 2nd 1986 Derby

A scintillating 4-9 Eclipse success from the top-class mare Triptych quickly proved his superiority over his elders at ten furlongs, but for some he was still vulnerable at the longer trip.

So, on the trail to Ascot, Dancing Brave was the one in the white hat. His army of fans had him marked down as the good guy with a score to settle. I was chuffed that he was backable at sensible odds against, despite his glaring Derby superiority.

In the event, Shahrastani never got in a blow, as the avenger once again unholstered his glinting turn of foot to see off Shardari and Triptych.

For any normal horse, this result would have been the pinnacle of a memorable career, but the great thing about a beast like Dancing Brave – possessed of such potent and matchless velocity – is that the possibilities are limitless. The style of his successes precluded any accurate measure of his superiority, thereby elevating him, in the fevered imagination at least, to the infinite realms of the equine stratosphere.

For once, the final reckoning was not to be denied us. For our hero, there was to be no easy opt-out. Eleven Group 1 winners of all generations and nationalities would provide his stiffest test and the opportunity for his finest hour.

I recall snapping up a ludicrously generous 3-1 for the Arc soon after the King George. I didn't have my full stake on, though, reckoning that he might be a bit

He mowed down the greatest Arc line-up of the era like so many daisies in a field

bigger on-course, which seemed also to be the reasoning of every other Brit in Paris that weekend. He was sent off at 11-10 by a legion of invaders.

The French, however, were far from reticent about their own Derby winner, Bering, who challenged late and so apparently decisively that the home cameraman became fixated. Off camera, and out of view of this frantic loon, Dancing Brave was about to be unleashed.

The last I had seen of him was in the false straight, where Pat had taken a nerveless tug, to be certain he would not play his ace until all the others were on the table. Then he disappeared, deep, deep on the track, behind a French woman with a big hat. He was missing, presumed beaten, for a split second, before a flash of pink appeared. I bellowed manically, the lady in the hat had a coronary, and Dancing Brave mowed down the greatest Arc line-up of the era like so many daisies in a field.

Even defeat in the Breeders' Cup Turf (for which many unnecessary excuses were put forward) couldn't dim the glaring light of that glorious afternoon.

The gods had plotted to provide the perfect set of circumstances for a truly magical horse to sear his mark on the hearts of the racing public; they offered a glittering entrance, glorious defeat, sweet revenge and incontrovertible greatness in one unforgettable season.

And Dancing Brave soared, plucked the gifts from the clouds and presented them to us on a big silver plate.

dancing brave what they said

A great horse – I was lucky enough to get on him twice to win a King George and an Arc.

The Longchamp field was wonderful and he killed them; he was just brilliant that day. He came from a long way behind because in the King George he hit the front too soon.

I sat on the tail of Bering and then we zoomed past – he went past eight Group 1 winners in a furlong – and he didn't just beat them, he annihilated them. He was a lovely horse to ride.

The way he picked up was unbelievable. He was brilliant, a wonderful horse, so relaxed, so well-balanced and, like Grundy and El Gran Senor, so easy. They're special horses, horses that make you look good.

He was an outstanding horse, probably the best we'd seen for a long time.
Pat Eddery, who rode Dancing Brave in the King George and the Arc

He was an outstanding racehorse. Of course he should have won at Epsom – there can't be any doubt about it.

Greville [Starkey] let Shirley Heights have everything when he won the Derby in 1978, but he thought so highly of Dancing Brave that he got too far back and could never quite peg back Shahrastani.

Greville decided to sit in on the horse, but between the seventh and eighth furlongs they threw in a 17-second furlong – when the average is 13 – and that had a concertina effect which made it very difficult to make up ground.

He flew at the finish and was an unfortunate loser, as he was clearly a better horse than Shahrastani and the rest of the field, but it was just one of those things.

Two furlongs out [in the Arc], with plenty of horses to pass, I wondered what Pat Eddery was trying to do to me. But once he asked Dancing Brave to quicken, he showed the sort of devastating change of gear which differentiates the great horses. That was the pinnacle of a fantastic year for the yard.
Guy Harwood, trainer

He is deservedly the highest-rated horse since the International Classifications started in 1977. While it was obviously very sad to see him beaten in the Derby, I was certainly fortunate to be present when he won his Arc, which was one of the most remarkable performances I have ever seen.

You would have to put him in the same category as Mill Reef and Nijinsky, who I also rated as a handicapper, even if he didn't match their performances at two. 'Great' is a word used far too often, but each of those three horses could be described as great.
Geoffrey Gibbs, former senior handicapper (Gibbs was speaking in 1999, but Dancing Brave's official rating of 141 has not been matched since.)

Just the mere mention of his name does it for

many people. It puts a smile on faces, a glow in the heart, a vision in the memory of a special horse with a special talent. And style. Yes, that's the word. Think of Sea Pigeon and you think of style.

There's something tinglingly exciting about hold-up horses possessing cruise control, horses with the sheer class to sprint past toiling rivals on a tight rein, horses with enough character and intelligence to know when the job is done. Sea Pigeon was all of these, and a bit more besides. What made him so outstanding was his durability and versatility.

Here was a horse who started life – owned by Jock Whitney and trained by Jeremy Tree – as a Classic hope, winning his first and only race as a two-year-old at Ascot; who finished seventh in Morston's Derby at three; and yet who was nine years old when he won the Ebor Handicap, ten when he won his first Champion Hurdle, and 11 when he won his second. Any wonder that he had such a loyal legion of fans? Hardly.

He won 37 races in all, 21 over hurdles and 16 on the Flat. His range of gears was his forte, blistering finishing speed his trademark. His only fault, mainly early in his life, was his reluctance to settle. It was largely a combination of maturity, plus a vital input by Mark Birch, Peter Easterby's stable jockey on the Flat, which helped Sea Pigeon hone his considerable talents to the finest edge.

Sea Pigeon

by **tom o'ryan**

His range of gears was his forte, blistering finishing speed his trademark

Having been a member of the Easterby outfit in those glory years, I can well remember the day he arrived, along with about a dozen others, in a dramatic transfer by owner Pat Muldoon following a fall-out with Gordon Richards, his previous trainer.

Richards had been in the process of elevating Sea Pigeon to a high-ranking position as a hurdler. It was very much his loss and Easterby's gain when the horse was switched from Cumbria to Yorkshire in the autumn of 1976.

Birch's long-rein style suited the hard-pulling Sea Pigeon and, from riding him out regularly at home, he gradually won him over, getting him to drop his head, spit out the bit and lob along at the back of the string.

Birch got his reward. At the end of Sea Pigeon's first season hurdling with Easterby, during which he defied huge weights in three handicaps, finished fourth to his new stablemate Night Nurse in the Champion Hurdle and won the Scottish equivalent, he returned to Flat racing for the first time in three years.

The race was the Chester Cup, and so confident was Birch that he declared to anyone within earshot that if Sea Pigeon were beaten, he would bare his backside in front of Malton Town Hall. Thankfully, for all concerned, Sea Pigeon gained a handsome victory. And, just for good measure, they followed up in the same race the following year.

Sea Pigeon (Jonjo O'Neill) takes the last flight in the 1977 Scottish Champion Hurdle

9

Sea Pigeon

Bay gelding foaled 1970
Sea-Bird - Around The Roses
Owners Pat Muldoon (Jock Whitney)
Trainers Peter Easterby, Gordon Richards
(Jeremy Tree) **Jockeys** Jonjo O'Neill, John

Francome, Mark Birch, Ian Watkinson, Ron
Barry (Alan Brown, Lester Piggott) **Record
(Flat)** 16 wins from 47 starts **(jumps)** 21
wins from 40 starts

Career highlights Won 1975 Cheltenham
Trial Hurdle, 1977 Scottish Champion Hurdle,
Chester Cup, 1978 Scottish Champion Hurdle,
Chester Cup, Fighting Fifth Hurdle, 1979 Ebor,
1980 Champion Hurdle, Welsh Champion
Hurdle, Doonside Cup, Fighting Fifth Hurdle,
1981 Champion Hurdle; 2nd 1978 Champion
Hurdle, 1979 Champion Hurdle

The seeds, by then, had been sown for the shaping of one of the most remarkable dual-purpose careers in racing history. Winner of the Ebor, the Doonside Cup, the Tennent Trophy and three Vaux Gold Tankards, he was also a match for anything during a golden period of two-mile hurdlers.

To ride him in a piece of work at home, which I was privileged to do occasionally, was a treat in itself. It was like sitting in a Rolls-Royce. No matter what he was galloping with, he'd cruise effortlessly in its slipstream, pick up in the blink of an eye and then, once in front, would prick his ears and down tools.

Timing was crucial to him, as Jonjo O'Neill found out to his cost in the 1979 Champion Hurdle. Easterby has always maintained that what caused Jonjo to come too soon was Muldoon's insistence to the jockey not to leave it too late. The upshot was a three-quarter-length defeat by Monksfield, who had beaten him two lengths into an identical second place 12 months earlier.

Revenge was sweet. The following year, Sea Pigeon doled out a seven-length drubbing to his mighty arch-rival after O'Neill had counted to ten after the final flight before unleashing his mount's famous turn of foot. It was much the same scenario, though even more dramatic, the following year. John Francome, standing in for the sidelined O'Neill, rode the most cocksure of races and had the temerity to take a pull on Sea Pigeon after the last before cutting down Pollardstown and Daring Run in a matter of strides 100 yards from the line.

O'Neill and Francome have said that Sea Pigeon was the best horse they ever rode

The reception he got after winning his second Champion was fit for the king he'd become, and was matched only by the never-to-be-forgotten scenes among his local crowd at York following his short-head defeat of Donegal Prince in the 1979 Ebor under 10st, when O'Neill heart-stoppingly dropped his hands a stride or two from the line.

That both O'Neill and Francome have said that Sea Pigeon was the best horse they ever rode, and that Easterby describes him as "a horse of a lifetime", rightly places him on a sky-high pedestal.

For my part, as a fringe player at Habton Grange, he will forever be the source of the fondest of memories. And, in the unlikely event that I should ever forget him, I need only to admire four of the trophies he won – two Fighting Fifth Hurdles and two Scottish Champion Hurdles – which have adorned my dining-room sideboard since I managed to buy them in an auction several years back.

Other than that, I could, of course, pay my occasional respects. Less than two miles from my front door, the old soldier, who lived to be 30, is buried in a railed-off resting place at the Easterby yard. Alongside is his great rival and former stablemate Night Nurse, another dual champion hurdler, and between the pair, and beneath a beech tree, is the inscription "Legends in their lifetimes". Enough said.

sea pigeon what they said

Sea Pigeon was the best I ever rode, a fantastic horse with a blinding turn of speed. I wish I had a few like him to train!

He had lots of speed, plenty of toe. He could make you look fantastic or he could make you look stupid, because if you went too quick on him he'd turn it in. He loved jumping, and the longer you sat on him the easier you won.

Winning the Ebor on him was fantastic because I was a jump jockey winning a Flat race. I dropped my hands on him and everyone thought he'd got beat. It was a bit closer than I thought it was!

He had a lot of character, like all good horses are characters. He was a beggar to ride out at home – he'd pull your arms out all day if you let him.

Jonjo O'Neill, who partnered Sea Pigeon to many big-race wins over jumps including his first Champion Hurdle – plus the Ebor on the Flat

He had ability, it was as simple as that, and he's one of the best we've ever had. The most exciting part about him for the public was that they love a horse to come from behind, thinking 'will he or won't he get there?' That's more exciting than a front-runner.

When John Francome rode him in his second Champion Hurdle, that was a masterpiece. And when Jonjo won the Ebor, only Jonjo knew he'd won. He gave us heart failure and only won by a short head. We had some great days and bad heads because of him – I think the champagne was flowing down the stands one day at York.

Peter Easterby, trainer

My fondest memory from riding days is getting on Sea Pigeon and never having a moment's worry as he flew round to win the 1981 Champion Hurdle. I remember that I had seen him beaten by being in front too soon, so I was determined to leave it to the last moment before asking him to win the race.

But horses who travel as well as he did at Cheltenham are few and far between.

He was a great horse – my granny could have won on him.

He was a horse in a million. I don't think I ever rode one who could quicken like he could at the end of a top-class race.

John Francome, who rode Sea Pigeon to his second Champion Hurdle success

There will never be another Sea Pigeon, in racing ability or as a character. He was an absolute individual. He had strength of mind and lots of brains – there was something very special about him. He made a terrific impact on the racing world and people in general. It was a long time ago when he performed, but he was very popular and had a very strong band of followers.

Polly Perkins, owner of the Etchingham Stud in Malton, where Sea Pigeon spent his retirement

Nobody need apologise for naming Nijinsky

Nijinsky

by tony
morris

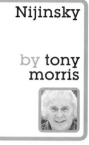

as his or her all-time favourite. Those who saw him run may feel that no justification of, or explanation for, their choice is necessary.

The trouble is, Nijinsky is history. Many of today's racegoers did not see him on the racecourse, perhaps have never even seen him on video, certainly cannot begin to imagine what he meant to those of us who were privileged to follow his career and witness his unparalleled achievements at first hand.

What can younger generations, who acquire their belief system about racing merit from form analysts, understand and appreciate about a horse whose rating proclaims him inferior to Brigadier Gerard, Mill Reef, Shergar, Dancing Brave, Dubai Millennium and others who came after him? Blind acceptance of those judgements means he can find a place in their pantheon only as one of the lesser gods.

We who knew him and experienced him in the context of his time can but respond with a wry smile and treasure the memories.

For me it was love at first sight, in the paddock before the Dewhurst. It was not just that he dominated his modest rivals in appearance; he was a commanding figure, all power and majesty, who would have taken the eye in any company. This was a two-year-old whose like I had never seen before. After 35 years, I can add 'or since'.

The race, of course, was a formality. Nijinsky treated his opposition with disdain, sauntering home in a style that allowed no doubts as to his championship status. He clearly ranked head and shoulders above the rest of his generation.

He clearly ranked head and shoulders above the rest of his generation

At home in Ireland, Nijinsky extended his unbeaten sequence to six before he returned to Newmarket for the 2,000 Guineas. Although he had 13 rivals this time, including proper racehorses, capable of top form in international company, he started at 4-7. And he brushed them aside, stringing them out like so many selling platers.

Nijinsky was odds against for the first and only time in his career on Derby Day. His parents had both been ten-furlong horses, and who could be certain he would stay? Gyr, a big son of Sea-Bird, had already won the Prix Hocquart at the distance and came from France with a huge reputation. His price contracted as Nijinsky (who had colicked overnight) became easier to back.

Gyr made it a race, striking for home and going clear over two furlongs out, but he was clearly outgunned once the son of Northern Dancer had been shaken up and shown the whip. As in the Guineas, Nijinsky had two and a half lengths to spare at the finish.

Just how good was this horse? We were not going to find out at The Curragh, where the best of the opposition seemed to be colts he had beaten at Epsom. Unusually, he sweated up at the start, causing a few misgivings, but the race was as straightforward as ever. Nearly last at halfway, and only eighth at the home turn, he made rapid progress from the two-furlong marker, led at the furlong pole, and readily drew clear to win by three lengths.

10

Nijinsky

Bay colt foaled 1967
Northern Dancer - Flaming Page
Owner Charles Engelhard **Trainer** Vincent O'Brien **Jockeys**
Lester Piggott, Liam Ward **Record (Flat)** 11 wins from 13 starts

Career highlights Won 1969 Railway Stakes, Anglesey Stakes,
Beresford Stakes, Dewhurst Stakes, 1970 Gladness Stakes, 2,000
Guineas, Derby, Irish Derby, King George VI and Queen Elizabeth
Stakes, St Leger

Nijinsky and Lester Piggott after winning the Derby in 1970

We learned more about Nijinsky's merit at Ascot, where only older horses opposed him in the King George. The home-based contenders were Caliban, fresh from his victory over Park Top in the Coronation Cup, Karabas, hero of the Washington International, and Blakeney, the previous year's Derby winner. From the continent came Crepellana, heroine of the Prix de Diane and Vermeille, and Italian Derby victor Hogarth. A group of such proven international stars was entitled to test the young pretender's mettle.

Test him? He routed them. Here was a scenario that could never have been imagined, with one Derby winner emerging from a pocket, delivering a stout challenge under strong driving and gradually wearing the leaders down, while the other Derby winner, coming from further back and never off the bridle, simply loped along in his cruising gear, picking them all off at will.

Make no mistake. Blakeney ran the race of his life that day, pulling four lengths clear of the others over the final furlong. But Nijinsky humiliated him, and did so seemingly without effort.

With his unbeaten sequence now in double figures, Nijinsky was scheduled for a long rest, while Vincent O'Brien pondered over a suitable prep race for the Arc. Some rest. The colt contracted a nasty bout of ringworm and spent weeks undergoing treatment, and it soon became clear that it would be a rush job preparing him for whatever would be his next engagement.

Favourite for every race he contested, Nijinsky will always remain a favourite

The announcement that the St Leger would be the target came as a surprise to many. The trials were over, and there had been lively ante-post activity on the assumption of an open Classic staged in the absence of the season's star three-year-old. Suddenly, it was going to be a different race, potentially an historic race, with the first Triple Crown in 35 years on the cards.

We had become used to the idea that Triple Crowns belonged in the past. We were in an age of specialisation; it was no longer reasonable to expect that one colt could dominate his generation at three over a mile in the spring, over 12 furlongs in the summer, and 14 furlongs in the autumn. Moreover, this was a colt who had been precocious enough to dominate at two.

At Doncaster, on that magical September day, Nijinsky proved himself the complete racehorse – the best of 693 who had entered for the Guineas, of 667 nominated to the Derby, of 533 entries for the St Leger. And over all three distances his authority was overwhelming.

Of course, that was not the end, but perhaps it should have been. However, defeats in the Arc and Champion Stakes could not obliterate the mighty achievements that had gone before.

Favourite for every race he contested, Nijinsky will always remain a favourite. Pigs will fly before we see another champion two-year-old go on to Triple Crown glory.

nijinsky what they said

At three years old, Nijinsky ran eight times and all but two of those races were outside Ireland. He faced international competition at Newmarket, Epsom, Ascot, Doncaster, Longchamp and Newmarket again, with the Irish Derby thrown in. All in one season!

He was the first evidence of the Northern Dancer line, whose influence has been so great on European racing ever since. Nijinsky was a tremendous stallion and has proved himself a sire of sires. I count myself fortunate to have been associated with him.

I would have to rate him first or second among my horses. It is him or Sir Ivor. For brilliance: Nijinsky. For toughness: Sir Ivor. And Golden Fleece, for he was never tested – and I would have to bracket Alleged with them.

Nijinsky was a truly great racehorse and his feat of winning the English Triple Crown is a testament to his ability.

It was Charles Engelhard, Nijinsky's owner, who was so keen to go for the St Leger. He was not particularly well at the time and he felt winning the Triple Crown would mean an awful lot.

The horse had not long been home from the King George when ringworm broke out all over his body. He lost a lot of his hair. He had to recover from both the King George and the ringworm in time for Doncaster on September 12.

It was too much. Although he seemed to win the Leger easily, I do not believe he could have pulled out any more.
Vincent O'Brien, trainer

I don't usually get too emotional about individual horses, but with Nijinsky was a great, big horse and it really was love at first sight – so commanding was his presence.

I always say that Sir Ivor was the best horse overall that I rode, but I think Nijinsky on his day was the most brilliant horse I've ever ridden – he was at his best when winning the King George at Ascot.

[He] took up stud duties at Claiborne Farm in Kentucky, where I would visit him – and Sir Ivor, who was at the same stud – in later years. Even in his old age, he still gave off that sense that he knew he was something very special, which indeed he was.

Nijinsky had more sheer natural racing ability than any other horse I ever rode, and in the summer of 1970 he was indisputably one of the greatest racehorses of the century.
Lester Piggott, jockey
(Piggott's words are partly taken from his 2004 book Lester's Derbys, written with Sean Magee)

He was a horse apart and there were never any worries with him – he was an absolute steering job when I won the Irish Derby on him in 1970. You could ride him with a silver thread – pull him out and say 'Go!' and that was it.
Liam Ward, who rode Nijinsky to win the Irish Derby

A famous never-say-die determination was the

defining characteristic of Dawn Run, the only horse to win both the Champion Hurdle and the Gold Cup. A front-runner trained by Paddy Mullins, the tenacious mare broke the spirits of the opposition in lesser races – but she had to battle every inch of the way for her two greatest triumphs, which sparked unforgettable scenes at the home of jump racing.

Dawn Run was bought for a mere 5,800gns as an unbroken three-year-old at Ballsbridge by Charmian Hill, a formidable woman who possessed many of the fighting qualities of her horse. It was she who rode Dawn Run in much of her work and she who, despite being well into her 50s, partnered her to her first success, in a bumper at Tralee in June 1982.

Tony Mullins, youngest of her trainer's four sons, took over when Dawn Run went hurdling. But it was an uneasy alliance as far as Hill was concerned, and she replaced him with Jonjo O'Neill before the 1984 Champion Hurdle, in which the mare needed all of O'Neill's strength to hold off Cima by under a length. In the winner's enclosure her owner was carried shoulder-high by jubilant Irish supporters.

Mullins regained the mount when injury sidelined O'Neill and the partnership went on to take the Aintree Hurdle, the Prix La Barka and France's version of the Champion Hurdle, the Grande Course de Haies d'Auteuil. A setback after an impressive chasing debut ruled her out for a year, but she was back with a vengeance

"It wasn't just that she did it – it was the way that she did it. It was unbelievable"

in the 1985/86 season before a disastrous foray to Cheltenham's January meeting led Hill to insist O'Neill was recalled.

He excelled on her in the Gold Cup on what was only her fifth start over fences. She looked beaten at the last, but her rider somehow conjured up a last desperate effort. As she fought back, Peter O'Sullevan, commentating on the BBC, uttered those immortal words: "And the mare is beginning to get up."

She did get up – and the post-race celebrations will never be forgotten by anyone swept up in them. This time it wasn't just Hill who was lifted shoulder-high as the huge Irish contingent poured into the winner's enclosure. O'Neill was carried aloft as well, and later he lifted Tony Mullins onto his own shoulders. "That was a day in a lifetime," says O'Neill. "I suppose that it wasn't just that she did it – it was the way that she did it. Then it all started; it was unbelievable. All those years I had been riding, this was the first time I could actually feel the weight of the crowd. I remember thinking that if all that lot mobbed me, I was gone – and they almost did!"

Dawn Run had enjoyed another hurrah when she defeated Champion Chase winner Buck House in a famous match at Punchestown, but it proved to be her last. Less than three months after her Gold Cup win, she was dead, breaking her neck as she attempted to win a second French Champion Hurdle. It was the saddest of ends for such a courageous horse. "She was tough," says Mullins, "and she was a super mare, by far the best National Hunt horse I ever trained."

Michael Clower

11

Dawn Run

Bay mare foaled 1978
Deep Run - Twilight Slave
Owner Charmian Hill **Trainer** Paddy Mullins **Jockeys**
Jonjo O'Neill, Tony Mullins **Record** (jumps) 18 wins from
28 starts

Career highlights Won 1983 Page Three Handicap
Hurdle, BMW Champion Novice Hurdle, VAT Watkins
Hurdle, Christmas Hurdle, 1984 Irish Champion Hurdle,
Champion Hurdle, Aintree Hurdle, Prix La Barka, Grande
Course de Haies d'Auteuil, 1985 Punchestown Chase,
Sean P Graham Chase, 1986 Cheltenham Gold Cup,
Match (with Buck House); 2nd 1983 Sun Alliance Hurdle,
Templegate Hurdle

Dawn Run and Jonjo O'Neill after winning the Cheltenham Gold Cup in 1986

No wonder he was such a popular racehorse.

He had ability and longevity, came with quirks and character, and defied injustice and a near-death experience. That See More Business became such a chasing superstar should come as no surprise.

First and foremost, we loved See More Business – but we also appreciated him. For See More Business was good and, on his day, See More Business was very good. During the course of nine long, turbulent seasons on the track, his CV became ever more impressive. Two King George VI Chases, three Rehearsal Chases, two wins in each of the Charlie Hall Chase, the Pillar Chase and the Jim Ford Chase, plus handsome victories in the Martell Cup and Aon Chase. That list would be impressive enough, but there was also a win in the biggest contest of them all, the Gold Cup coming his way in 1999.

Yet with 'See More', there could have been so much more, even another Gold Cup. Strongly fancied for his first assault on the race, the then eight-year-old was carried out in the early stages of the contest, denied his chance through no fault of his own. There would be worse to come.

On a miserable December afternoon in 2001, we thought we had lost him. Rallying to regain a lead he had held for much of the race, he crashed out of the Rehearsal Chase at the penultimate fence. He was prone on the ground for what seemed like an eternity and stable representatives at Chepstow rushed to his side while trainer

"It was just a privilege to train him – he did more for me than any other horse"

Paul Nicholls waited and watched with anxiety from Sandown. When he got up, an entire sport breathed a sigh of relief.

Not surprisingly, there were immediate calls for the old boy to be retired. But See More Business was a racehorse who loved to race, and race on he did. And, as he got older, we loved him more. Sure, he could, and often did, throw in the odd stinker, sometimes for seemingly inexplicable reasons, but that served only to make him more of an individual and one who knew his own mind.

The ability was always there. A 40-1 outsider when a 12-year-old in the 2002 Gold Cup, See More Business gave Joe Tizzard the ride of his life to finish third behind Best Mate. There were more days like this. The veteran collected two victories at Wincanton, his local track. The last, and his last, came in the 2003 Jim Ford, leading to scenes of jubilation the like of which the track had not known for years.

"It was just a privilege to train him," says Nicholls. "He did more for my career than any other horse. He was tough and genuine, but the great thing was his soundness, which allowed him to keep going as long as he did."

See More Business kept going until a virus prompted his retirement in January 2004, just after he had turned 14. Although the illness almost killed him, See More Business was a racehorse who always came back for more, and so it proved even when his career was over. Nothing was going to keep him from the happy retirement he so thoroughly deserved. Long may it continue.

Lee Mottershead

12

See More Business

Bay gelding foaled 1990
Seymour Hicks - Miss Redlands

Owners Paul Barber, John Keighley, Sir Robert Ogden **Trainer** Paul Nicholls **Jockeys** Mick Fitzgerald (Timmy Murphy, Andrew Thornton, Joe Tizzard, Ruby Walsh) **Record (jumps)** 18 wins from 36 starts

Career highlights Won 1997 Rehearsal Chase, King George VI Chase, 1998 Pillar Property Investments Chase, Rehearsal Chase, 1999 Cheltenham Gold Cup, Charlie Hall Chase, King George VI Chase, 2000 Aon Chase, Martell Cup, Charlie Hall Chase, 2001 Pillar Property Chase, 2002 Rehearsal Chase; 3rd 2002 Cheltenham Gold Cup

See More Business (Ruby Walsh) on his way to a memorable final victory at Wincanton in February 2003

There is usually room for only one horse at a

time at the heart of the racing public's affections, but in 1971 and 1972 Mill Reef and Brigadier Gerard both earned widespread hero-worship as well as immortal fame.

Mill Reef, American-bred and -owned, was trounced by the thoroughly English Brigadier Gerard the only time they met, over the latter's ideal trip in the 2,000 Guineas, but was unbeaten thereafter, stirring our imagination with displays of supreme class during his unique sequence of victories in the Derby, Eclipse, King George and Arc.

At first it seemed scarcely credible that, only 12 months after the mighty Nijinsky, two colts should emerge who were his superior, but it gradually dawned on us that they were the greatest pair of contemporaries in racing history.

They were also remarkably consistent, versatile and durable. Mill Reef suffered only two defeats in 14 races over three seasons – the other was by a short head to champion two-year-old My Swallow in the Prix Robert Papin – was equally effective on firm and heavy ground, and was a rare all-rounder, excelling as a precocious juvenile sprinter, middle-distance Classic performer, and mature horse. He possessed superb balance and quality, and his below-average stature probably added to his appeal.

Mill Reef's stunning performances in the Eclipse and the King George were the best ever seen in those races. At Sandown he humbled champion older horse Caro by four lengths, and at Ascot he romped home six lengths clear, after which jockey

For all his brilliance, it was his courage that made our affection so abiding

Geoff Lewis said: "Daylight was second. If I'd given him one slap, the judge would have left his box before the others got there!"

He crowned his career with a scintillating three-length victory in the Arc in record time. "He was, quite simply, the best Flat horse I ever saw," says his trainer Ian Balding, perhaps not the most impartial observer, reflecting more than 30 years later.

Yet, for all Mill Reef's brilliance, it was his courage that made our affection for him so abiding. Most of his victories were demolition jobs but in the Coronation Cup, his last race, he had to battle to beat Homeric, being already afflicted by the virus that laid him low that summer and prevented a rematch with Brigadier Gerard. And when he was being readied for an autumn return, he broke a leg on the gallops and needed plenty of fortitude to survive the resulting operation and long convalescence.

His stud career added even more lustre to his glory, for he was champion sire twice, and his sons Shirley Heights and Reference Point followed him into the winner's circle after the Derby.

Mill Reef was in the public eye from his runaway debut win as a juvenile until his death 16 years later, and was a model thoroughbred in everything he did. Paul Mellon, his devoted anglophile owner-breeder, wrote and recited a sonnet in Gimcrack's honour at the annual York dinner in 1970, and the last three lines are equally applicable to his great champion: "Remember me, all men who love the Horse/If hearts and spirits flag in after days/Though small, I gave my all. I gave my heart."

John Randall

13
Mill Reef

Bay colt foaled 1968
Never Bend - Milan Mill

Owner-breeder Paul Mellon
Trainer Ian Balding **Jockey** Geoff
Lewis **Record (Flat)** 12 wins from
14 starts

Career highlights Won 1970
Coventry Stakes, Gimcrack Stakes,
Imperial Stakes, Dewhurst Stakes,
1971 Greenham Stakes, Derby,
Eclipse Stakes, King George VI and
Queen Elizabeth Stakes, Prix de l'Arc
de Triomphe, 1972 Prix Ganay,
Coronation Cup; 2nd 1971 2,000
Guineas

The 1970 Gimcrack: Mill Reef and Geoff Lewis, who rode him in every one of his 14 races

But for an unfortunate piece of timing, Best Mate

would surely have made it into the top ten of this poll. Barely a month after the final list was published in early 2004, the current star of the steeplechasing crop won his third Gold Cup. It was by no means his most brilliant success – a majestic victory at the same venue 12 months previously deserves that particular accolade – but it was undoubtedly the most memorable.

The 2004 Gold Cup did not feature a vintage field, and in beating Sir Rembrandt by merely a diminishing half-length, form experts rightly suggested that Best Mate did not achieve anything out of the ordinary on the book. However, the significance was lost on no-one and the stands at Cheltenham erupted – initially, perhaps, as much with relief as with joy – as Best Mate took his place alongside Arkle, who had completed the same Gold Cup hat-trick 38 years previously. Moreover, the success showed that Best Mate possessed courage equal to his talents.

Although Best Mate went a long way to joining the immortals that day, he had always carried himself with a distinct air of superiority. As close to a perfect jumping specimen as you could wish to find, his style of running is epitomised by the superb way in which he travels throughout his races and the matchless economy and precision of his jumping. "This horse really does think he's Arkle," said Terry Biddlecombe, one half, alongside wife Henrietta Knight, of the training partnership that has handled Best Mate so adroitly. The comment might have been fair enough

"Best Mate is not just one in a million – he's one in several million"

for a horse on the verge of racing history, but the former champion jockey was speaking in November 2000, after Best Mate had won just two novice chases!

Massive early potential was soon to become glorious achievement, the highest of expectations long since fulfilled. "Best Mate is not just one in a million . . . he's one in several million," says Knight. "He's the horse of a lifetime, such an athlete with such a wonderful, effortless action. He's good for racing."

There are those who suggest he would be even better for racing if he were not treated with such kid gloves, and his detractors have longed to see him attempt to concede weight to inferior rivals in handicap company in the manner of an Arkle, or even a Desert Orchid. However, while his appearances are few and far between, connections point to his record as justification for their patient policy and the cautious approach has seemingly done little to hurt Best Mate's standing with his fans. Indeed, 800 well-wishers sent good-luck cards to Knight's yard before his third Gold Cup.

After that race, owner Jim Lewis said he had been "ready to lose, because the dream has to come to an end some day". At the end of 2004, with another date at Cheltenham beckoning, Best Mate's crown appeared to be slipping when he was well beaten in Ireland by old rival Beef Or Salmon. A fourth Gold Cup would be a feat unparalleled in the modern era, but if the dream does have to end, Lewis is unlikely to be alone in shedding a tear.

Nicholas Godfrey

14
Best Mate

**Bay gelding foaled 1995
Un Desperado - Katday**

Owner Jim Lewis **Trainer** Henrietta Knight **Jockeys** Jim Culloty (Tony McCoy) **Record (jumps)** 14 wins from 21 starts

Career highlights Won 2000 Mersey Novices' Hurdle, 2001 Scilly Isles Novices' Chase, Haldon Gold Cup, 2002 Cheltenham Gold Cup, Peterborough Chase, King George VI Chase, 2003 Cheltenham Gold Cup, Ericsson Chase, 2004 Cheltenham Gold Cup; 2nd 2000 Supreme Novices' Hurdle, 2001 Aintree Hurdle, King George VI Chase

Best Mate at home at Henrietta Knight's stables, with the trainer looking on fondly

Wayward Lad did not stay well enough. At least,

not where it really mattered, at Cheltenham in the Gold Cup. If he had, this dashing chaser would surely have taken the final step that separates the top-class from the legendary.

Already with a supporting Oscar for his role in Michael Dickinson's 'Famous Five' in the 1983 Gold Cup – third behind Bregawn – Wayward Lad had the blue riband spotlight snatched away three years later. Surging ahead at the last, the race was his for the losing, and lose it he did as, running on empty, he faltered in the face of Dawn Run and a demonic Jonjo O'Neill. While the mare was feted as the first Champion Hurdle–Gold Cup winner, there was only bitter disappointment surrounding the horse who, taking into account the mares' allowance, was the best in the race.

But we come to praise Caesar, not to bury him. And how much there is to praise. One of the finest chasers of the 1980s, Wayward Lad possessed many outstanding qualities. He was a really handsome horse and had the performances to match his looks: when Fred Winter called him the best jumper since Pendil, the queue to disagree was not long.

While the Gold Cup may have eluded him, the King George VI Chase certainly did not. He won it three times – a record before Desert Orchid. Wayward Lad spent all his racing life – and much of his retirement – with the Dickinsons, and a first success in a novice hurdle at Leicester in 1979 was a toe in the water that would

He was a really handsome horse – and he had the performances to match

eventually see him bathing in the affection of all who admired a horse as durable as he was talented.

There were only six runners in the King George of 1982, when he won it for the first time, but they included Silver Buck, Little Owl and Night Nurse, and Wayward Lad's star was thus set among the brightest in the firmament. Twelve months later he won it again and, after a loss of form, bounced back with his record third success in 1985.

Several lacklustre performances followed that Gold Cup second, but this grand trouper bowed out in style, to undisguised delight, with a second victory in the 1987 Whitbread Gold Label Cup at Aintree. Certainly, he was one of the very best horses not to have won the Gold Cup, but as the winner of 28 of his 55 starts, his supporters never had need to dwell on his defeats.

He retired to join Michael Dickinson in the States, where he hunted before going into complete and, for him, reluctant retirement. Even shortly before he had to be put down, at the age of 28, in the autumn of 2003, he is reported to have shown an eagerness to join in when the local hunt went through the farm in Pennsylvania where he was living.

Robert Earnshaw, who won a King George on him, recalls: "He was a wonderful horse, and one of the amazing things about him was the turn of foot he had for a three-mile chaser, and he was so scopey that you never met a fence wrong."

George Ennor

15
Wayward Lad

Brown gelding foaled 1975
Royal Highway - Loughanmore

Owners Shirley Thewlis and Les Abbott **Trainers** Tony, Michael and Monica Dickinson **Jockeys** Tommy Carmody, Robert Earnshaw, Graham Bradley (John Francome, Graham McCourt) **Record (jumps)** 28 wins from 55 starts

Career highlights Won 1980 Maghull Novices' Hurdle, 1981 West of Scotland Pattern Chase, Welsh Champion Chase, Tote Silver Trophy Chase, Peterborough Chase, 1982 Lambert and Butler Premier Chase Final, Timeform Chase, Welsh Champion Chase, King George VI Chase, 1983 Charlie Hall Chase, Peterborough Chase, King George VI Chase, 1984 Edward Hanmer Memorial Chase, 1985 Whitbread Gold Label Cup (Aintree), Charlie Hall Chase, King George VI Chase, 1987 Whitbread Gold Label Cup (Aintree); 2nd 1986 Cheltenham Gold Cup; 3rd 1983 Cheltenham Gold Cup, 1984 King George VI Chase

Wayward Lad and Robert Earnshaw in the 1984 King George VI Chase at Kempton

No single hurdler stands out from all the other

champions as clearly the greatest of all time in the same way that Arkle does among steeplechasers, but Night Nurse was the best during the golden age of hurdling.

Night Nurse won the Champion Hurdle in 1976 and again in 1977, when, in the highest-quality hurdle race ever run, he proved himself superior to two other dual champions, Monksfield and Sea Pigeon (his stablemate). He later dead-heated with Monksfield in the most thrilling hurdle race of all time, and achieved the best form over fences of any Champion Hurdle winner.

Yet it was his rare combination of panache, toughness, indomitable will to win, bold front-running style and exhilarating jumping that made him a public favourite. He was a champion not only on form, but also in terms of the entertainment and excitement he provided during nine seasons over jumps, winning exactly half his 64 races.

Having been a leading juvenile hurdler, Night Nurse was unbeaten in eight races in 1975/76 including the Champion Hurdle and its equivalents in Ireland (Sweeps Hurdle), Scotland and Wales. At Cheltenham he led throughout and kept on too strongly for Birds Nest, Comedy Of Errors and Lanzarote.

He completed a run of ten consecutive hurdling victories in the autumn of 1976, and then clinched his second title when leading for most of the way in a uniquely classy renewal of the Champion Hurdle. He battled on to beat Monksfield by two lengths, with Dramatist, Sea Pigeon and Birds Nest next; each of them would have been a worthy winner in an average year.

"What made him so special was that he was a natural jumper – brilliant!"

Only 17 days later, in the Templegate Hurdle at Aintree, Night Nurse put up the greatest single performance by any hurdler in the history of the sport. He conceded 6lb to Monksfield and the pair gave their all in an epic duel which finished in a dead-heat. Red Rum's third Grand National victory, in the very next race, was almost an anti-climax.

Night Nurse lost some of his sparkle in 1977/78, finishing third to Monksfield and Sea Pigeon in the Champion Hurdle and second to Monksfield in the Templegate Hurdle. He was sent over fences the following season.

Night Nurse never won the really big steeplechase that his talents deserved but nearly became the first horse to bring off the Champion Hurdle–Cheltenham Gold Cup double. In the 1981 Gold Cup he made much of the running and was foiled only by stablemate Little Owl, who beat him by a length and a half with Silver Buck third.

He started favourite for the Gold Cup the following year but was pulled up behind Silver Buck, who triumphed in most of their encounters during a long-running and memorable rivalry.

When Night Nurse died in 1998, full of years and honours, Peter Easterby, who had trained him throughout his career, said: "What made him so special was that he was a natural jumper, brilliant from the first time we ever schooled him. He was a very, very brave horse – hard and brave."

John Randall

Night Nurse (Paddy Broderick) at Cheltenham in March 1976, on his way to his first Champion Hurdle victory

16
Night Nurse

Bay gelding foaled 1971
Falcon - Florence Nightingale

Owner Reg Spencer **Trainer** Peter Easterby **Jockeys** Paddy Broderick (Jonjo O'Neill, Ian Watkinson, Alan Brown) **Record (jumps)** 32 wins from 64 starts

Career highlights Won 1975 Free Handicap Hurdle, Fighting Fifth Hurdle, Sweeps Hurdle, 1976 Champion Hurdle, Scottish Champion Hurdle, Welsh Champion Hurdle, John Skeaping Hurdle, 1977 Champion Hurdle, Templegate Hurdle (dead-heat), Welsh Champion Hurdle, 1979 Sean Graham Trophy, Future Champions Novices' Chase, Buchanan Whisky Gold Cup, 1982 Mandarin Chase; 2nd 1981 Cheltenham Gold Cup; 3rd 1978 Champion Hurdle

Not for nothing was Giant's Causeway known

as 'The Iron Horse'. During 2000, he made history by becoming the first horse to win five Group 1 events as a three-year-old, but it was the extraordinary manner in which his successes were earned that captured the hearts of the racing public.

It was not merely his near-constant exertions that endeared him to us; it was because he appeared to like nothing more than a real dogfight. At times it looked as if Giant's Causeway, who represented the all-powerful Coolmore operation, would deliberately allow his rivals to come to him so that he could look them in the eye and then outbattle them. He was blessed with an amazingly tough constitution – he ran in nine Group 1 races that year – and it seemed as if he would rather get home by a short head after an almighty fight than win by six lengths without coming off the bridle. Not one of his five Group 1s was won by more than three-quarters of a length, and he was never outside the first two in his 13 starts.

Unbeaten in three races at two, he won the Gladness Stakes before finishing runner-up in both Guineas. While these were solid enough efforts, they gave little indication of what was to come, but trainer Aidan O'Brien and jockey Mick Kinane refused to accept this was the real Giant's Causeway and resolved to ride him more aggressively in future. The change of tactics paid off in the St James's Palace Stakes and again when George Duffield stepped in for the sidelined Kinane in the Eclipse.

He deliberately allowed rivals to come to him so he could look them in the eye

Kinane was back in the saddle for the Sussex Stakes, by which time his mount's style of racing had caught the imagination. The *Racing Post*'s front page dubbed him 'The Iron Horse' on the day of the race, and the name stuck. The horse did not let the side down, beating Dansili to record his third Group 1 success in six weeks.

The manner of his victories had not gone unnoticed by rival trainers, who were racking their brains as they tried to find ways of ensuring their horses avoided getting into a punch-up with Giant's Causeway. In the Juddmonte International, Sir Michael Stoute instructed Pat Eddery to challenge wide on Kalanisi, who had been chinned in the Eclipse, and then, in the Irish Champion Stakes, Stoute's Greek Dance came from the clouds. It made no difference: they still got beaten. "He waits for them to join him," said O'Brien, marvelling at his colt's idiosyncrasies. "He then puts his head out and battles before pricking his ears at the finish."

Finally, though, one of his opponents got it right. In the Queen Elizabeth II Stakes at Ascot, Kevin Darley and John Gosden fine-tuned the tactics and Observatory came both late and wide to mug Giant's Causeway.

However, he wasn't finished yet, and his career looked sure to finish on a triumphant note in the Breeders' Cup Classic until Kinane somehow got his whip caught up in the reins 100 yards out and was beaten a neck by the admirable Tiznow. O'Brien was adamant that Kinane's mishap had cost him the race. Still, defeat cost Giant's Causeway nothing in terms of reputation or prestige – or, for that matter, value. He was retired – and his stud fee was promptly raised by a third!

Michael Clower

Giant's Causeway (George Duffield, far side) gets the better of a fierce battle with Kalanisi in the Eclipse Stakes at Sandown in July 2000

17

Giant's Causeway

Chestnut colt foaled 1997
Storm Cat - Mariah's Storm

Owners Sue Magnier and Michael Tabor **Trainer** Aidan O'Brien **Jockeys** Mick Kinane (George Duffield) **Record (Flat)** 9 wins from 13 starts

Career highlights Won 1999 Futurity Stakes, Prix de la Salamandre, 2000 Gladness Stakes, St James's Palace Stakes, Eclipse Stakes, Sussex Stakes, Juddmonte International, Irish Champion Stakes; 2nd 2000 2,000 Guineas, Irish 2,000 Guineas, Queen Elizabeth II Stakes, Breeders' Cup Classic

Only rarely does a champion come along who

pushes the envelope, who stretches the limits of what is possible for a racehorse.

Shergar was just such a champion, for in 1981 he scored a series of spread-eagling victories in which he seemed to redefine supreme excellence in the middle-distance Thoroughbred. In particular his record-breaking triumph in the Derby, without equal at Epsom in more than two centuries, raised him to a legendary status that was, sadly, enhanced by the shock of his eventual kidnap and demise.

The Aga Khan's colt had been a high-class two-year-old, finishing second in the Futurity (now Racing Post Trophy), but no-one was prepared for the stunning impact he made when romping away with the Sandown Classic Trial by ten lengths and the Chester Vase by 12.

The Derby looked a foregone conclusion and so it proved, for Shergar was cantering just behind the leaders at Tattenham Corner and his distinctive rapid, scuttling stride carried him to an awesome ten-length triumph that remains the biggest winning distance in the race's history. The margin might have been 12 lengths or more had he not been eased in the final furlong by Walter Swinburn, who was only 19 at the time.

The latter's pre-race comment that "riding Shergar feels like riding Pegasus" was vindicated, while John Matthias, rider of runner-up Glint Of Gold, said: "I told myself I'd achieved my life's ambition. Only then did I discover there was another horse on the horizon."

His record-breaking Derby is without equal in more than two centuries

It was an epoch-making performance, though critics pointed out that the winner's only two top-class rivals, Glint Of Gold and Kalaglow, had collided and virtually put themselves out of the race early on. Even if the form was not as good as first impressions suggested, it was enough to make Shergar a great champion.

His four-length wins in the Irish Derby (under Lester Piggott, with Swinburn suspended) and the King George were less spectacular but confirmed his sky-high reputation. At Ascot he beat older horses with the same disdain he showed to his contemporaries.

The brilliance of his five consecutive victories was undimmed by the anti-climax of his last race, in the St Leger, when he was beaten before covering a mile and a half and finished a lacklustre fourth to Cut Above, whom he had humiliated in the Irish Derby.

Shergar, a prominent news-maker during his racing career, became a household name after his abduction from Ballymany Stud in Ireland in February 1983, just as he was about to start his second season at stud. He has been kept in the public eye to this day by grisly speculation about his fate, though it has long been generally accepted that he was taken by a rogue element of the IRA and killed within a matter of days.

It is sad that, for the wrong reasons, the lamented Shergar is more famous than almost any other racehorse, but at least he is remembered while other great champions are forgotten.

John Randall

18
Shergar

Bay colt foaled 1978
Great Nephew - Sharmeen

Owner-breeder Aga Khan IV **Trainer** Michael Stoute **Jockeys**
Walter Swinburn (Lester Piggott) **Record (Flat)** 6 wins from 8
starts

Career highlights Won 1981 Sandown Classic Trial, Chester
Vase, Derby, Irish Derby, King George VI and Queen Elizabeth
Diamond Stakes

Walter Swinburn takes Shergar down to the start of a famous Derby in 1981

Two-milers are usually the Cinderella horses

among the ranks of steeplechasers, but dual champion Viking Flagship changed that state of affairs temporarily in the mid-1990s by providing us with plenty of pulsating moments to cherish.

He gave many years of enthusiastic service to the sport and consistently displayed his courage against top-class rivals, especially in his first victory in the Queen Mother Champion Chase and his first in the Melling Chase at Aintree. Those two rank high among the greatest races of recent years, and in both he looked beaten but rallied to edge home in a three-horse finish.

Viking Flagship, who had started his career as a two-year-old on the Flat, showed his toughness as a novice chaser by winning twice in three days at the 1993 Punchestown Festival, and reached the top of the tree the following season via wins in the Victor Chandler, Game Spirit and Queen Mother Champion Chases.

At Cheltenham he jumped the last two fences upsides Travado and the previous year's winner, Deep Sensation. Although the first to come under pressure, he kept responding to the calls of Adrian Maguire and, in a stirring finish, beat Travado by a neck with Deep Sensation a length away third. David Nicholson said: "I've never trained a tougher horse. The amount of work that he stands would kill most people."

Viking Flagship was the champion two-mile chaser for the second time in 1994/95, when he took the Tingle Creek Trophy (beating Travado and Deep Sensation again),

"If I could come back as someone else, I'd come back as Viking Flagship"

the Queen Mother Champion Chase again (by five lengths from Deep Sensation) and the Melling Chase at the Grand National meeting.

The Melling Chase, over two and a half miles at level weights, was a dramatic, exhilarating and uplifting race in which three outstanding horses ran their hearts out. Viking Flagship, Deep Sensation and Martha's Son jumped the final fence in unison and it soon looked as if Viking Flagship was beaten. However, he and Maguire dug deep and forced their way back to beat Deep Sensation by a short head, with Martha's Son a length away.

Seldom has a race been so clearly decided by a horse and jockey's combined sheer bloody-minded refusal to accept defeat. Maguire said immediately afterwards: "When I die and if I could come back as someone else, I would come back as Viking Flagship. He just doesn't know how to stop."

He was dethroned the following season, when his Champion Chase hat-trick bid was foiled by Irish ace Klairon Davis, but he put up what was, on form, the best performance of his career when winning the Melling Chase again, romping home seven lengths clear. He was third to Martha's Son in the Champion and Melling Chases in 1997.

Viking Flagship was not a great two-mile chaser in the mould of Dunkirk and Badsworth Boy. Yet his combination of class, courage, consistency and durability, in addition to his below-average size, made him a public favourite in a way that more naturally gifted champions were not.

John Randall

19
Viking Flagship

Bay gelding foaled 1987
Viking - Fourth Degree

Owner Roach Foods Ltd **Trainer** David Nicholson **Jockeys** Adrian Maguire (Richard Dunwoody, Charlie Swan, Tony McCoy)
Record (jumps) 24 wins from 55 starts

Career highlights Won 1993 Bank of Ireland Novice Chase, 1994 Victor Chandler Chase, Game Spirit Chase, Queen Mother Champion Chase, Tingle Creek Trophy, Castleford Chase, 1995 Queen Mother Champion Chase, Melling Chase, 1996 Game Spirit Chase, Melling Chase, 1997 Haldon Gold Cup, Castleford Chase; 2nd 1996 Queen Mother Champion Chase; 3rd 1997 Queen Mother Champion Chase

Viking Flagship (Tony McCoy) wins his second Melling Chase at Aintree in 1996

Admirable staying handicap chaser though

he was, nothing that Moorcroft Boy achieved on the track can be held truly responsible for his having sneaked into the top 20. That is not to dismiss a career in which he demonstrated boundless courage over a number of seasons, notably when making a miraculous recovery from a neck injury that nearly left him for dead after a fall to come back and win the Scottish National. Rather, it is a testament to his status as the poster star of the West Sussex racehorse welfare centre to which he was gifted when his career ended, and that now bears his name.

The Moorcroft Racehorse Welfare Centre is one of three such establishments supported by the Retraining of Racehorses scheme (RoR), British horseracing's official charity for the welfare of former racehorses. RoR also supports the Thoroughbred Rehabilitation Centre – the original UK charity founded in 1991 by the redoubtable Carrie Humble and based at Nateby, near Preston – and Greatwood, which relocated to Wiltshire in 2004. Around 4,000 horses leave racing in Britain every year. The RoR scheme exists to raise funds from the racing industry to help support charitable retraining and rehoming of ex-racehorses, and to show how racehorses can flourish in a second career in alternative equine disciplines such as showing, endurance riding, eventing, polo, showjumping, dressage and hacking.

Moorcroft Boy was the sort of racehorse anyone would have loved to own. Though he won just five races, he could be relied upon to give his all, usually in the sort of

"He's an inspiration to everyone who has the privilege of working with him"

marathon slogs in the mud that suited him particularly well. His resilience was his trademark – when he was favourite for the 1994 Grand National, for example, it emerged after the race that he had broken a blood vessel after the last but still refused to cry enough, continuing to finish third to Miinnehoma.

Six months later, Moorcroft Boy suffered the only fall of his career at the same venue in the Becher Chase, when he broke three vertebrae in his neck and barely clung to life. Incredibly, thanks to the skill of vets and the patience of trainer David Nicholson, he was back on the track 14 months later to start a programme that culminated in his finest hour with victory in the Scottish National.

Nowadays, Moorcroft Boy spends his time parading and acting as a fund-raising vehicle for the centre, which rehomes an average of 30 horses a year. His exalted position in this poll is a fitting tribute to all those who take on the not insignificant responsibility of caring for ex-racehorses, and the centre's chief executive Graham Oldfield is delighted with the result.

"We were all thrilled to bits when we found out he'd made the top 20," he says. "He sees an awful lot of people and obviously he is an awful lot of people's favourite! He's an inspiration to all of us who have the privilege of working with him. He is a very genuine, kind horse and he adores people, although these days he's actually quite nervous, probably because of his injuries. But he is such a poser – he loves having his picture taken."

Nicholas Godfrey

Moorcroft Boy, at the racehorse welfare centre that bears his name in 2003

20
Moorcroft Boy

Chestnut gelding foaled 1985
Roselier - Well Mannered

Owner Ken Manley **Trainer** David Nicholson **Jockeys** Adrian Maguire (Mark Dwyer)
Record (jumps) 5 wins from 25 starts

Career highlights Won 1994 ASW Handicap Chase, Warwick National, 1996 Scottish Grand National; 2nd 1993 John Corbet Cup, 1994 Greenalls Gold Cup; 3rd 1994 Grand National, 1996 Midlands Grand National

Crisp (Richard Pitman) hurdles Becher's Brook in the 1973 Grand National

21

Crisp

Brown gelding foaled 1963
Rose Argent - Wheat Germ
Owner-breeder Sir Chester Manifold
Trainer Fred Winter **Jockeys** Richard
Pitman (Paul Kelleway) **Record (jumps)**
19 wins from 39 starts

Career highlights Won 1971
Champion Chase, 1972 Gainsborough
Chase, Coventry Pattern Chase, 1973
Geoffrey Gilbey Memorial Chase,
Hermitage Chase, Doncaster Pattern
Chase; 2nd 1973 Grand National

Why we love him One thing that really
appeals to the British public is a gallant
loser, and Crisp's uniquely exhilarating
and inspiring Grand National display in
1973 has passed into racing folklore.
Carrying top weight of 12st, he hurdled
the big fences in spectacular style, many
lengths clear of his rivals for most of the
way, but he slowed almost to a walk on
the run-in and Red Rum, receiving 23lb,
caught him close home and won by
three-quarters of a length in a time that
smashed the record by 18.3 seconds. For
Crisp, it was the most agonising of
defeats. Two years before, though, he
had won the Champion Chase by 25
lengths only five days after his debut in
Europe, and he had also started
favourite for the 1972 Cheltenham Gold
Cup. He was Australia's greatest equine
gift to Britain. **JR**

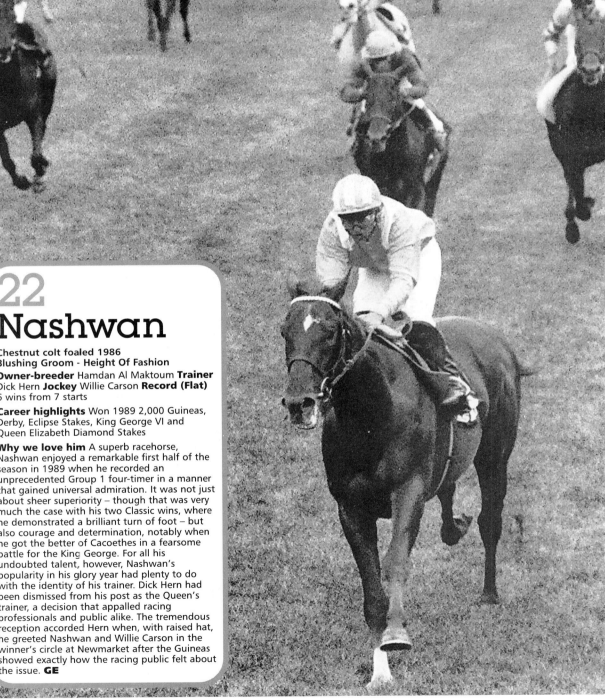

22
Nashwan

Chestnut colt foaled 1986
Blushing Groom - Height Of Fashion
Owner-breeder Hamdan Al Maktoum **Trainer**
Dick Hern **Jockey** Willie Carson **Record (Flat)**
6 wins from 7 starts

Career highlights Won 1989 2,000 Guineas,
Derby, Eclipse Stakes, King George VI and
Queen Elizabeth Diamond Stakes

Why we love him A superb racehorse,
Nashwan enjoyed a remarkable first half of the
season in 1989 when he recorded an
unprecedented Group 1 four-timer in a manner
that gained universal admiration. It was not just
about sheer superiority – though that was very
much the case with his two Classic wins, where
he demonstrated a brilliant turn of foot – but
also courage and determination, notably when
he got the better of Cacoethes in a fearsome
battle for the King George. For all his
undoubted talent, however, Nashwan's
popularity in his glory year had plenty to do
with the identity of his trainer. Dick Hern had
been dismissed from his post as the Queen's
trainer, a decision that appalled racing
professionals and public alike. The tremendous
reception accorded Hern when, with raised hat,
he greeted Nashwan and Willie Carson in the
winner's circle at Newmarket after the Guineas
showed exactly how the racing public felt about
the issue. **GE**

Nashwan (Willie Carson) completes a resounding Derby victory at Epsom in 1989

23
Danoli

Bay gelding foaled 1988
The Parson - Blaze Gold
Owner Dan O'Neill **Trainer** Tom Foley **Jockeys** Charlie Swan, Tommy Treacy (Shay Barry)
Record (jumps) 17 wins from 32 starts

Career highlights Won 1994 Deloitte and Touche Hurdle, Sun Alliance Hurdle, Aintree Hurdle, Morgiana Hurdle, Hatton's Grace Hurdle, 1995 Aintree Hurdle, 1996 Denny Gold Medal Novice Chase, 1997 Irish Hennessy Cognac Gold Cup; 2nd 1994 Irish Champion Hurdle, Christmas Hurdle (Leopardstown); 3rd 1995 Champion Hurdle, 1996 Irish Champion Hurdle

Why we love him Very talented over both hurdles and fences, Danoli was the 'people's horse' – especially, though not exclusively, as far as his native Ireland was concerned. Although he rose from relative obscurity to become a nation's favourite racehorse, his humble beginnings in a small and unfashionable yard lent his story a charming folksy feel and, by the time he took centre stage at Cheltenham to win the Sun Alliance, he was already an incredibly popular horse. Injury threatened his career after that and he was never really able to scale the heights that once looked possible, but even in defeat he was often given a more enthusiastic reception than the winner. The scenes that greeted him when he stole the limelight again in winning Leopardstown's Hennessy Cognac Gold Cup will live long in the memory. **GE**

Danoli (Charlie Swan) receives a hero's welcome at the Cheltenham Festival in 1994

Frankie Dettori plants a kiss on Lochsong after winning the King George Stakes at Goodwood in 1994

24
Lochsong

Bay mare foaled 1988
Song - Peckitts Well

Owner-breeder Jeff Smith **Trainer** Ian Balding
Jockeys Frankie Dettori (Willie Carson, Francis Arrowsmith) **Record (Flat)** 15 wins from 27 starts

Career highlights Won 1992 Stewards' Cup, Portland Handicap, Ayr Gold Cup, 1993 King George Stakes, Nunthorpe Stakes, Prix de l'Abbaye, 1994 Palace House Stakes, Temple Stakes, King's Stand Stakes, King George Stakes, Prix de l'Abbaye

Why we love her The best-loved Flat filly or mare in this survey, Lochsong was blisteringly fast from the stalls and showed speed in its rawest form in many displays of enthusiasm, courage and class. An unsound, unraced juvenile and moderate three-year-old, she made dramatic improvement to achieve a unique big-handicap treble at four, and was champion sprinter at the ages of five and six. Best at five furlongs, she was so eager to get on with the job that in her final season she lost two races by expending too much energy on her way to the start. Yet when properly harnessed, as in her two runaway victories in the Prix de l'Abbaye, her pace made her a flamboyant and charismatic speed queen. Lochsong was closely associated with Frankie Dettori's rise to the top, and shared his popularity. **JR**

25
Dubai Millennium

Bay colt foaled 1996
Seeking The Gold - Colorado Dancer
Owner Sheikh Mohammed/Godolphin **Trainer** Saeed Bin Suroor
Jockeys Frankie Dettori, Jerry Bailey **Record (Flat)** 9 wins from 10 starts
Career highlights Won 1999 Predominate Stakes, Prix Eugene

Adam, Prix Jacques le Marois, Queen Elizabeth II Stakes, 2000 Dubai World Cup, Prince of Wales's Stakes

Why we love him Europe's greatest Flat horse in the decade that preceded this poll, Dubai Millennium won by extravagant margins, was a champion at the ages of three and four, and excelled at a mile and ten furlongs and on both turf and dirt. Having suffered his only defeat in the Derby, he crushed his rivals by six lengths in both the Queen Elizabeth II Stakes and the Dubai World Cup (he was renamed with that race in mind), and by eight lengths in the Prince of Wales's Stakes at Royal Ascot. In those last two races his brilliant front-running displays were close to perfection, but he was then cruelly cut down twice – by a career-ending leg fracture on the gallops and, at the age of five, fatal grass sickness. Dubai Millennium was the apple of Sheikh Mohammed's eye – the Sheikh describes him as his favourite horse and once said he could see the "wind of heaven between his ears". The world's leading owner could spend the rest of his life trying to find another like him. **JR**

Dubai Millennium (Frankie Dettori) victorious in the Dubai World Cup in 2000

Rock Of Gibraltar powers home under Mick Kinane at Royal Ascot in 2002

26

Rock Of Gibraltar

Bay colt foaled 1999
Danehill - Offshore Boom

Owners Sir Alex Ferguson and Sue Magnier **Trainer** Aidan O'Brien **Jockeys** Mick Kinane (Johnny Murtagh) **Record (Flat)** 10 wins from 13 starts

Career highlights Won 2001 Railway Stakes, Gimcrack Stakes, Grand Criterium, Dewhurst Stakes, 2002 2,000 Guineas, Irish 2,000 Guineas, St James's Palace Stakes, Sussex Stakes, Prix du Moulin; 2nd 2002 Breeders' Cup Mile

Why we love him When it came to 'The Rock', there was style to match the substance. Blessed with abundant qualities of resilience and durability, he was a Flat-racing record-breaker, achieving the magnificent feat of going one better than the great Mill Reef by winning seven Group 1 events in a row. A stalking assassin who cruised menacingly through his races before pouncing irresistibly late, Rock Of Gibraltar crept into the public's affections, having been overshadowed both before and after his 2,000 Guineas victory by stablemate Hawk Wing. A horse who turned up anywhere and everywhere in the top mile contests, he retired leaving us with the memory of some breathtaking victories, but also one agonisingly memorable defeat, when he was a fast-finishing, luckless and unjust second in the Breeders' Cup Mile. Yet that American eclipse tarnished his reputation and popularity not one jot – sporting history shows that everyone loves a heroic loser. **LM**

27
Double Trigger

Chestnut horse foaled 1991
Ela-Mana-Mou - Solac

Owner Ron Huggins **Trainer** Mark Johnston **Jockeys** Jason Weaver, Frankie Dettori, Michael Roberts, Darryll Holland **Record (Flat)** 14 wins from 29 starts

Career highlights Won 1994 St Leger Italiano, 1995 Sagaro Stakes, Henry II Stakes, Ascot Gold Cup, Goodwood Cup, Doncaster Cup, 1996 Sagaro Stakes, Henry II Stakes, Doncaster Cup, 1997 Goodwood Cup, 1998 Goodwood Cup, Doncaster Cup; 2nd 1996 Ascot Gold Cup, 1998 Ascot Gold Cup; 3rd 1994 St Leger

Why we love him Compared to jumpers, it is relatively rare for a Flat-racer to engender true affection from the sport's followers – but no-one present for Double Trigger's third Goodwood Cup success could be in any doubt that this brave stayer was among the best-loved of recent years. As with so many popular horses, Double Trigger had his quirks, and was invariably very much in control of his own destiny. Yet when he was on a 'going' day – and there were many of those – he was the hardest of horses to pass, a point evidenced by his large number of victories in the top marathon contests. A horse to whom the racing public became attached over a number of years, Double Trigger did not figure among the very best of his era according to cold, impersonal official figures, a fact that frequently annoyed his trainer. No matter. Like Persian Punch after him, Double Trigger was a star in the public's eyes, whatever racing's number-crunchers might say. **LM**

Double Trigger (Darryll Holland) bows out with his third Doncaster Cup victory

28
Lammtarra

Chestnut colt foaled 1992
Nijinsky - Snow Bride

Owner Saeed Maktoum Al Maktoum/Godolphin **Trainers** Saeed Bin Suroor (Alex Scott) **Jockeys** Walter Swinburn, Frankie Dettori **Record (Flat)** 4 wins from 4 starts

Career highlights Won 1995 Derby, King George VI and Queen Elizabeth Diamond Stakes, Prix de l'Arc de Triomphe

Why we love him Given the brevity of Lammtarra's racing career – the shortest among the top 100, comprising just four races – this was more of a quick fling than a lasting affair. Still, you couldn't quibble with what he achieved in emulating Mill Reef with a notable treble of Europe's most prestigious middle-distance contests. Bred to be a superstar, Lammtarra was an outstanding racehorse with the courage to match, the latter attribute exemplified in his fighting back from a life-threatening lung infection to win the Derby on his seasonal debut – in record time. What followed was an epic battle for the King George and a hard-fought Arc for a horse whose brilliant, but short-lived career represented a major personal triumph for Sheikh Mohammed, his Godolphin team having nursed the chestnut back to health over the winter in Dubai before his three-year-old campaign.
NG

Lammtarra (Frankie Dettori) and trainer Saeed Bin Suroor after winning the Arc

Sea-Bird (Pat Glennon) is led in by owner Jean Ternynck after his stunning Derby win

29
Sea-Bird

Chestnut colt foaled 1962
Dan Cupid - Sicalade
Owner-breeder Jean Ternynck **Trainer** Etienne Pollet
Jockey Pat Glennon **Record (Flat)** 7 wins from 8 starts

Career highlights Won 1964 Criterium de Maisons-Laffitte, 1965 Prix Greffulhe, Prix Lupin, Derby, Grand Prix de Saint-Cloud, Prix de l'Arc de Triomphe

Why we love him The Flat Horse of the 20th Century put up the performance of the century in the 1965 Arc de Triomphe as Sea-Bird, on his final appearance, showed dazzling brilliance to crush the strongest international field ever assembled for one race. In the straight he burst clear to triumph by six lengths from Reliance (whose only defeat this was), with Diatome another five lengths away third. He raced once in Britain, when becoming the only horse in living memory to win the Derby on the bridle; the contempt he showed his rivals had to be seen to be believed. Sea-Bird, the top French-trained horse in this survey, might have challengers for the title of supreme champion, for he was beaten once at two and untested at four. But he set the standard by which all subsequent Derby and Arc winners have been measured and found wanting. **JR**

30
Mill House

Bay gelding foaled 1957
King Hal - Nas Na Riogh
Owner Bill Gollings **Trainer** Fulke Walwyn **Jockeys**
Willie Robinson (David Nicholson) **Record (jumps)** 17
wins from 36 starts

Career highlights Won 1963 Cheltenham Gold Cup,
Mandarin Chase, Hennessy Gold Cup, King George VI
Chase, 1964 Gainsborough Chase, 1965 Mandarin
Chase, Gainsborough Chase, 1966 National Hunt
Centenary Cup, 1967 Gainsborough Chase, Whitbread
Gold Cup; 2nd 1964 Cheltenham Gold Cup, Whitbread
Gold Cup, 1965 Cheltenham Gold Cup

Why we love him The unluckiest of all Cheltenham
Gold Cup winners, Mill House was a great horse in his
own right yet was foaled in the same year as Arkle, the
supreme champion who took the glory that might have
been his. When the giant horse won the Gold Cup as a
six-year-old he was hailed as the best young
steeplechaser since Golden Miller, and he then beat the
still-improving Arkle in the Hennessy, only for the pride
of Ireland to gain his revenge four times. Those
demoralising defeats, together with leg injuries, left him
only a shadow of his former self, but he did have one
last glorious and supremely popular moment in the sun,
in the 1967 Whitbread. In that inspiring victory he laid
to rest many regretful thoughts of what might have
been and seemed, in John Oaksey's words, "the spirit of
steeplechasing incarnate". **JR**

Mill House (David Nicholson) jumps the last before winning the Whitbread in 1967

31
West Tip

**Bay gelding foaled 1977
Gala Performance - Astryl
Owner** Peter Luff **Trainer**
Michael Oliver **Jockey** Richard
Dunwoody **Record (jumps)** 12
wins from 69 starts

Career highlights Won 1985
Anthony Mildmay Peter Cazalet
Memorial Chase, National Hunt
Handicap Chase, 1986 Grand
National; 2nd 1989 Grand
National; 4th 1987 Grand
National, 1988 Grand National

Why we love him West Tip
made his name thanks to his
regular efforts in the Grand
National, where his link with
the rider known as 'The Prince'
became the stuff of Aintree
legend. He ran in six Nationals
altogether, making the frame
on four occasions including
victory in 1986. (He might have
won in 1985 as well but for
falling at Becher's on the
second circuit when disputing
the lead.) Year after year he
turned up from Michael Oliver's
little stable in Worcestershire
sporting the best-known scar in
British racing, a legacy from the
days before he set foot on a
racecourse when he was
involved in a collision with a
lorry. Besides his scar, what
West Tip brought with him was
an indefatigable enthusiasm for
the job, which he demonstrated
time after time all over the
place. Aintree may have been
his favourite stage but he also
usually ran well at Cheltenham,
numbering a Festival triumph
among his wins. **GE**

Richard Dunwoody celebrates as West Tip wins the Grand National in 1986

Grundy (Pat Eddery) beats Bustino in the 1975 King George at Ascot

32
Grundy

Chestnut colt foaled 1972
Great Nephew - Word From Lundy
Owner Carlo Vittadini **Trainer** Peter Walwyn
Jockey Pat Eddery **Record (Flat)** 8 wins from 11 starts

Career highlights Won 1974 Champagne Stakes, Dewhurst Stakes, 1975 Irish 2,000 Guineas, Derby, Irish Derby, King George VI and Queen Elizabeth Diamond Stakes

Why we love him This great Derby winner will always be revered as the ultra-game victor of the 'Race of the Century' – his titanic duel with Bustino in the King George at Ascot. In a severe test of stamina and courage, he battled his way upsides his rival a furlong out and edged ahead to win by half a length in record time. A recording of the contest is etched on the memory of most racing fans, but such an enervating contest took its toll: Bustino never ran again and Grundy flopped on his only subsequent start. He had already shown plenty of spirit to recover from being kicked in the face by a stablemate at home, and proved himself an impressive dual Derby winner, scoring by three lengths at Epsom and two at The Curragh. Grundy was a champion in both the seasons he raced, and confounded the prejudice that flashy chestnuts are soft. **JR**

33
Falbrav

Bay horse foaled 1998
Fairy King - Gift Of The Night
Owners Scuderia Rencati (Teruya Yoshida) **Trainers** Luca Cumani
(Luciano d'Auria) **Jockeys** Darryll Holland, Dario Vargiu, Frankie
Dettori, Mirco Demuro **Record (Flat)** 13 wins from 26 starts

Career highlights Won 2002 Premio Presidente della
Repubblica, Gran Premio di Milano, Japan Cup, 2003
Prix d'Ispahan, Eclipse Stakes, Juddmonte International, Queen
Elizabeth II Stakes, Hong Kong Cup; 2nd 2003

Irish Champion Stakes; 3rd 2003 Breeders' Cup Turf

Why we love him A colossal warrior of a horse whose exploits
provided the most persuasive of examples for keeping older
animals in training. Although he was certainly one of the best
horses ever to come out of Italy, the tough and versatile Falbrav
did not finally grab the public imagination until a magnificent
2003 campaign that took in ten Group 1 races at a variety of
trips spread across three continents. He had already shown
high-class form from his former base, but the switch to Luca
Cumani's Newmarket yard brought five more Group 1s to
add to his tally as a five-year-old. Seldom less than convincing
at a mile and a quarter, he was also able to slam the best milers
around in the QEII, and yet was only narrowly beaten in a
three-way photo over four furlongs more in the Breeders' Cup
Turf, the race of the year. All this, plus a spectacular *coup de
grace* in Hong Kong. No wonder his trainer suggested Falbrav
was "the best horse in the world". **NG**

Falbrav (Frankie Dettori) signs off with victory in Hong Kong in 2003

Florida Pearl and Adrian Maguire win the King George VI Chase in 2001

34
Florida Pearl

Bay gelding foaled 1992
Florida Son - Ice Pearl

Owners Violet and Archie O'Leary **Trainer** Willie Mullins
Jockeys Richard Dunwoody, Paul Carberry, Ruby Walsh, Richard Johnson, Adrian Maguire, Barry Geraghty **Record (jumps)** 15 wins from 31 starts

Career highlights Won 1997 Champion Bumper, 1998 Dr PJ Moriarty Novice Chase, Royal & SunAlliance Chase, 1999 Irish Hennessy Cognac Gold Cup, James Nicholson Champion Chase (Down Royal), 2000 Irish Hennessy Cognac Gold Cup, 2001 Irish Hennessy Cognac Gold Cup, John Durkan Memorial Chase, King George VI Chase, 2002

Martell Cup, Heineken Gold Cup, 2004 Irish Hennessy Cognac Gold Cup; 2nd 2000 King George VI Chase; 3rd 1999 Cheltenham Gold Cup

Why we love him A national hero long before he was retired in July 2004, Florida Pearl may never have won the Gold Cup, but in a seven-year career he was the equine embodiment of consistency at the very highest level. Although his travails in steeplechasing's blue riband, where his stamina habitually petered out, became an unwelcome millstone around his neck, his record elsewhere spoke for itself. Florida Pearl reached the frame every time he finished a race in a period of more than five years from his debut in 1996 until the Gold Cup of 2002. More than once he was written off, but more than once he came back to silence the doubters, particularly when winning the King George in 2001 (beating Best Mate in the process) and the Irish Hennessy Cognac Gold Cup at Leopardstown in 2004 on what proved to be his final start. That victory, his fourth in Ireland's most prestigious chase, was greeted with fervour at the Dublin track. **NG**

35
High Chaparral

Bay colt foaled 1999
Sadler's Wells - Kasora

Owners Michael Tabor and Sue Magnier
Trainer Aidan O'Brien **Jockeys** Mick Kinane,
Johnny Murtagh **Record (Flat)** 10 wins from
13 starts

Career highlights Won 2001 Racing Post
Trophy, 2002 Leopardstown Derby Trial, Derby,
Irish Derby, Breeders' Cup Turf, 2003 Royal
Whip, Irish Champion Stakes, Breeders' Cup
Turf (dead-heat); 3rd 2002 Prix de l'Arc de
Triomphe, 2003 Prix de l'Arc de Triomphe

Why we love him Yet another entry in the
top 100 for Aidan O'Brien's Ballydoyle
operation, this dual Derby winner was a gifted
racehorse in 2002 when a tremendous Classic
season culminated in clinical success at the
Breeders' Cup. The welcome decision to keep
him in training as a four-year-old offered him
the chance to demonstrate other virtues, most
notably his absolute determination and
courage. While it took a while for High
Chaparral to inspire the admiration that
should have been his by right, any horse
involved in that fantastic finish to the
Breeders' Cup Turf at Santa Anita in 2003
deserved to win a place in even the hardest of
hearts. In the race of the year, he dead-heated
with US-trained Johar after a desperate battle
down the home stretch that also featured the
gallant Falbrav, whom he had previously
beaten in a controversial renewal of the Irish
Champion Stakes. **NG**

High Chaparral (Johnny Murtagh) wins the Derby in 2002

Limestone Lad (Paul Carberry) jumps the last in the 2001 Hatton's Grace Hurdle

36
Limestone Lad

Bay gelding foaled 1992
Aristocracy - Limestone Miss

Owner-trainer James Bowe **Jockeys** Shane McGovern, Paul Carberry (Barry Cash, Barry Geraghty) **Record (jumps)** 35 wins from 61 starts

Career highlights Won 1999 Morgiana Hurdle, Hatton's Grace Hurdle, Christmas Hurdle (Leopardstown), 2000 Bank Of Ireland Hurdle, Boyne Hurdle, Irish Field Novice Chase, Craddockstown Novice Chase, 2001 Bank Of Ireland Hurdle, Boyne Hurdle, Morgiana Hurdle, Hatton's Grace Hurdle, 2002 Bank Of Ireland Hurdle, Champion Stayers' Hurdle (Punchestown), Lismullen Hurdle, Morgiana Hurdle, Hatton's Grace Hurdle, Christmas Hurdle

(Leopardstown); 2nd 2000 Stayers' Hurdle, 2003 Irish Champion Hurdle; 3rd 2003 Stayers' Hurdle

Why we love him A remarkable staying hurdler, both courageous and prolific, Limestone Lad has been taken to the hearts of Irish racing enthusiasts like only a handful of horses before him. His appeal partly lies in his traits: a bold, front-running performer, he has become famous for opening up huge mid-race leads and then clinging on with guts and courage beyond the call of duty. A seemingly indefatigable individual renowned for running almost every week at the height of the season when healthy, he boasts ability to match his tenacity, having won more than half his races, many at the highest level, notably an unforgettable defeat of the outstanding Istabraq – that day a 1-7 favourite – in the 1999 Hatton's Grace Hurdle. Once an ordinary handicapper, he has risen to the top for his popular family team, horse and humans combining to epitomise the grass-roots appeal of Irish racing. Retirement beckoned at the time of writing; he will be much missed on the track. **LM**

Mtoto and Michael Roberts are greeted by trainer Alec Stewart after the King George

37
Mtoto

Bay colt foaled 1983
Busted - Amazer

Owner Sheikh Ahmed Al Maktoum **Trainer** Alec
Stewart **Jockey** Michael Roberts **Record (Flat)**
8 wins from 17 starts

Career highlights Won 1987 Brigadier Gerard
Stakes, Prince of Wales's Stakes, Eclipse Stakes,
1988 Prince of Wales's Stakes, Eclipse Stakes, King
George VI and Queen Elizabeth Diamond Stakes,
Select Stakes; 2nd 1988 Prix de l'Arc de Triomphe

Why we love him Here was a proper Flat horse:
a colt who was a late bloomer but repeatedly
showed us what he was capable of in his full
maturity, proving himself champion older horse
twice. He overcame problems with fragile feet to
become the first dual Eclipse winner in more than
60 years, getting the better of a thrilling battle with
Reference Point for his first success. Mtoto also
emulated his sire with a decisive victory in the King
George, but is perhaps best remembered for his
gallant and possibly unlucky fast-finishing second
in the Arc on his final appearance; he had to be
checked briefly early in the straight and failed by a
neck to catch Italian ace Tony Bin, who had
been third in the King George. Mtoto's career
foreshadowed the domination of racing by the
Maktoums' older horses that has become routine
via Godolphin. **JR**

Montjeu (Mick Kinane), hugely impressive in the King George

38
Montjeu

Bay colt foaled 1996
Sadler's Wells - Floripedes
Owner Michael Tabor **Trainer** John Hammond **Jockeys** Cash Asmussen, Mick Kinane **Record (Flat)** 11 wins from 16 starts

Career highlights Won 1999 Prix Greffulhe, Prix du Jockey-Club, Irish Derby, Prix Niel, Prix de l'Arc de Triomphe, 2000 Tattersalls Gold Cup, Grand Prix de Saint-Cloud, King George VI and Queen Elizabeth Diamond Stakes, Prix Foy

Why we love him This French champion displayed his greatness only once in Britain, but his afternoon stroll at Ascot in the King George as a four-year-old made an indelible impression; he scored on the bridle in an exhibition of sublime class that made him rival Nijinsky as the easiest winner in the race's 50 runnings. The previous year his wonderful turn of foot had secured a Derby double at Chantilly (by four lengths) and The Curragh (by five) and a breathtaking victory in the Arc. After the Grand Prix de Saint-Cloud, Cash Asmussen said: "The last time I went so fast, I was landing in a Concorde at New York!" The best of his epoch-making sire's offspring, Montjeu had temperamental quirks which may have contributed to the defeats he suffered in his last three races; his reputation would otherwise be even higher. **JR**

Pebbles (Steve Cauthen) strides to victory in the 1985 Eclipse Stakes

39
Pebbles

Chestnut filly foaled 1981
Sharpen Up - La Dolce

Owners Marcos Lemos, Sheikh Mohammed **Trainer**
Clive Brittain **Jockeys** Philip Robinson, Steve Cauthen,
Pat Eddery **Record (Flat)** 8 wins from 15 starts

Career highlights Won 1984 Nell Gwyn Stakes, 1,000
Guineas, 1985 Sandown Mile, Eclipse Stakes, Champion
Stakes, Breeders' Cup Turf; 2nd 1983 Cheveley Park
Stakes, 1984 Coronation Stakes, Champion Stakes

Why we love her Britain's greatest filly or mare of the
last half-century – "England's superfilly," as the
American commentator dubbed her – made a perfect
final bow in the Breeders' Cup Turf, showing instant
acceleration the moment a gap appeared, but that was
merely the culmination of her three seasons in the top
flight. Few horses make a bigger impact than a filly
who consistently beats top-class colts, and Pebbles
became the first of her sex to win the Eclipse in its
99-year history before showing the full measure of
her greatness with a devastating victory over Slip
Anchor in the Champion Stakes. She had enough
idiosyncrasies to need a travelling companion, Royal
Hunt Cup winner Come On The Blues, to keep her calm
before her races, but her talent made her the first
horse trained in Britain to earn £1 million in prize-
money. **JR**

Three-time Champion Hurdle winner Persian War (Jimmy Uttley) in action in 1968

40
Persian War

Bay gelding foaled 1963
Persian Gulf - Warning
Owner Henry Alper **Trainers** Colin Davies (Brian Swift, Arthur Pitt, Denis Rayson, Jack Gibson) **Jockey** Jimmy Uttley **Record (jumps)**
18 wins from 51 starts

Career highlights Won 1967 Challow Hurdle, Victor Ludorum Hurdle, Triumph Hurdle, 1968 Schweppes Gold Trophy, Champion Hurdle, 1969 Lonsdale Hurdle, Champion Hurdle, Welsh Champion Hurdle, 1970 Champion Hurdle, Sweeps Hurdle; 2nd 1971 Champion Hurdle; 3rd 1968 Grande Course de Haies d'Auteuil

Why we love him This triple Champion Hurdle winner ushered in the golden age of hurdlers, and some say he was the greatest of all time. He was constantly in the news because of his triumphs and travails, and what endeared him to the public was the immense toughness and resilience he showed in overcoming breathing problems, operations, and the whims of an ignorant and capricious owner who kept changing trainers and put his own interests before those of his horse. Persian War, trained by Colin Davies in his three championship seasons, raced in an era before the proliferation of weight-for-age and conditions events over jumps, and his handicap triumphs included the Schweppes under a record weight. A resolute battler, he went closer than any other triple champion to landing a fourth Champion Hurdle, for he found only Bula too good in 1971. **JR**

Daylami (Frankie Dettori) wins the 1999 Breeders' Cup Turf

41
Daylami

Grey horse foaled 1994
Doyoun - Daltawa
Owners Godolphin (Aga Khan IV)
Trainers Saeed Bin Suroor (Alain
de Royer-Dupre) **Jockeys** Frankie
Dettori (Gerald Mosse) **Record
(Flat)** 11 wins from 21 starts

Career highlights Won 1997
Poule d'Essai des Poulains, 1998
Tattersalls Gold Cup, Eclipse
Stakes, Man o' War Stakes, 1999
Coronation Cup, King George VI
and Queen Elizabeth Diamond
Stakes, Irish Champion Stakes,
Breeders' Cup Turf

Why we love him Partly
because of his light-grey coat, but
more importantly through his
rare combination of toughness
and consistency displayed over
four campaigns, and brilliance as
shown in his extravagant winning
margins. He was no more than a
routine Classic winner in France,
but his transfer to Godolphin
enabled him to blossom with age
so that he became the best horse
in the world in 1999, when he
raced in five different countries
on three continents. Having
crushed his rivals by five lengths
in the King George and nine
lengths in the Irish Champion
Stakes, Daylami ended his career
in a blaze of glory when
confirming his superiority over an
outstanding rival, Royal Anthem,
at the Breeders' Cup. This
powerful horse also showed that
the occasional lapse (he was only
ninth in the Arc) need not
diminish a champion's stature. **JR**

Edredon Bleu (Jim Culloty) enjoys his finest hour in the 2003 King George

42
Edredon Bleu

Bay gelding foaled 1992 Grand Tresor - Nuit Bleue
Owner Jim Lewis **Trainer** Henrietta Knight **Jockeys** Tony McCoy, Jim Culloty **Record (jumps)** 24 wins from 47 starts

Career highlights Won 1998 Grand Annual Chase, Peterborough Chase, 1999 Peterborough Chase, 2000 Queen Mother Champion Chase, Peterborough Chase, 2001 Championship Chase (Sandown), Peterborough Chase, 2002 Haldon Gold Cup, 2003 Desert Orchid Chase, Haldon Gold Cup, Clonmel Oils Chase, King George VI Chase; 2nd 1998 Tingle Creek Chase, 1999 Queen Mother Champion Chase, 2001 Tingle Creek Chase, 2002 Tingle Creek Chase

Why we love him After years of thrilling us at the top level, Edredon Bleu managed to endear himself even more to the jumping public by doing what perhaps even his greatest admirers thought he could not and winning the King George VI Chase in 2003. For years he had been a star, amassing a *curriculum vitae* chock-full of victories in some of the biggest steeplechases. An electric-jumping front-runner, he had thrilled us for more than half a decade even before his King George win, most memorably when emerging victorious after one of the most thrilling battles ever witnessed at the Cheltenham Festival when lifting the 2000 Champion Chase. Overshadowed for much of his career by stable companion Best Mate, his emotional Kempton triumph was one of the 2003/04 season's highlights, and one which prompted owner Jim Lewis to laugh: "Who is this Best Mate anyway?" For that day at least, the answer was that he was merely a stablemate to Edredon Bleu. **LM**

Monksfield (Dessie Hughes) clears the last before dead-heating at Aintree in 1977

43
Monksfield

Bay horse foaled 1972
Gala Performance - Regina
Owner Michael Mangan **Trainer** Des McDonogh **Jockeys** Tommy Kinane, Dessie Hughes **Record (jumps)** 14 wins from 49 starts

Career highlights Won 1976 Huzzar Hurdle, Irish Benson and Hedges Hurdle, 1977 Templegate Hurdle (dead-heat), 1978 Champion Hurdle, Templegate Hurdle, 1979 Champion Hurdle, Colt Sigma (Templegate) Hurdle, Welsh Champion Hurdle; 2nd 1976 Triumph Hurdle, 1977 Champion Hurdle,

1978 Royal Doulton Hurdle, 1979 Royal Doulton Hurdle, 1980 Irish Champion Hurdle, Champion Hurdle

Why we love him Here was a battle-hardened streetfighter from an unfashionable Irish stable, a small entire horse who possessed a heart as big as himself and became a giant in achievement. Monksfield helped to raise hurdling to heights never seen before or since in his duels with Night Nurse and Sea Pigeon; his dead-heat with the former at Aintree in 1977 was probably the most exciting hurdle race ever run, and the latter was his closest victim in both his Champion Hurdle triumphs. His fighting spirit was decisive in 1979, for Sea Pigeon challenged too soon and gave him time to hit back on the hill in an inspiring exhibition of sheer bloody-minded refusal to accept defeat. 'Monkey' disputes with Istabraq the title of Ireland's greatest hurdler, and his courage, small size and rags-to-riches story made him a favourite on both sides of the Irish Sea. **JR**

44
Burrough Hill Lad

Brown gelding foaled 1976
Richboy - Green Monkey

Owner-breeder Stan Riley **Trainer** Jenny Pitman **Jockeys** Phil Tuck, John Francome **Record (jumps)** 21 wins from 42 starts

Career highlights Won 1983 Welsh National, 1984 Anthony Mildmay Peter Cazalet Memorial Chase, Gainsborough Chase, Jim Ford Chase, Cheltenham Gold Cup, Hennessy Cognac Gold Cup, Charlie Hall Memorial Wetherby Pattern Chase, King George VI Chase, 1985 Rehearsal Chase, 1986 Gainsborough Chase (walkover)

Why we love him A great horse with a popular trainer, Burrough Hill Lad was the champion steeplechaser for three seasons. Injuries prevented his running up a sequence of victories in the Gold Cup but he did win the race once after a dramatic rise through the handicap ranks. He then defied top weight of 12st in the Hennessy, treating his rivals with disdain in the best performance of his career, and, though not ideally suited to Kempton, also won the King George. A relentless galloper, 'Buzby' was ruthless and efficient rather than flamboyant and charismatic, and that, together with his leg problems, explains why he never received the acclaim that he deserved. Only a couple of horses have stronger claims to be regarded as the best steeplechaser since Arkle. **JR**

Burrough Hill Lad (John Francome) defying a welter burden in the 1984 Hennessy

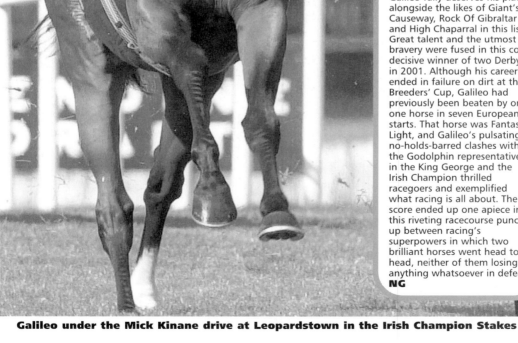

45
Galileo

Bay colt foaled 1998
Sadler's Wells - Urban Sea

Owners Sue Magnier and Michael Tabor **Trainer** Aidan O'Brien **Jockey** Mick Kinane **Record (Flat)** 6 wins from 8 starts

Career highlights Won 2001 Leopardstown Derby Trial, Derby, Irish Derby, King George VI and Queen Elizabeth Diamond Stakes; 2nd Irish Champion Stakes

Why we love him One of a multitude of top-class colts to represent Aidan O'Brien's Ballydoyle yard in recent years, Galileo fully deserves his place alongside the likes of Giant's Causeway, Rock Of Gibraltar and High Chaparral in this list. Great talent and the utmost bravery were fused in this colt, decisive winner of two Derbys in 2001. Although his career ended in failure on dirt at the Breeders' Cup, Galileo had previously been beaten by only one horse in seven European starts. That horse was Fantastic Light, and Galileo's pulsating, no-holds-barred clashes with the Godolphin representative in the King George and the Irish Champion thrilled racegoers and exemplified what racing is all about. The score ended up one apiece in this riveting racecourse punch-up between racing's superpowers in which two brilliant horses went head to head, neither of them losing anything whatsoever in defeat.
NG

Galileo under the Mick Kinane drive at Leopardstown in the Irish Champion Stakes

46
Aldaniti

Chestnut gelding foaled 1970
Derek H - Renardeau
Owners Nick Embiricos (Althea Gifford)
Trainer Josh Gifford **Jockey** Bob Champion
Record (jumps) 8 wins from 26 starts

Career highlights Won 1981 Whitbread Trial Chase, Grand National; 2nd 1979 Scottish National; 3rd 1977 Hennessy Cognac Gold Cup, 1979 Cheltenham Gold Cup

Why we love him No self-respecting publisher or film producer would have given Aldaniti's script a second glance, so fanciful would it have appeared. But this *did* happen – and Aldaniti's Grand National success was one of racing's most uplifting stories. Not only was the gelding's career threatened time after time by injuries to the extent that it was a near-miracle he even made it to Aintree, there was also his jockey Bob Champion, who returned to the most competitive of sports after suffering from testicular cancer. Trainer Josh Gifford, who stood by Champion through thick and thin, kept trying to persuade Aldaniti's owners that they were wasting their money paying training fees, but they kept the faith, to be rewarded by that unforgettable day in 1981 when the fairytale came true. To say that emotions ran high when he won the National would be underplaying it a touch – a charge that could not be levelled at the inevitable movie, *Champions*, inspired by the story. **GE**

Aldaniti and Bob Champion team up for a famous Aintree victory

L'Escargot (Tommy Carberry) crosses Becher's in the 1973 Grand National

47
L'Escargot

Chestnut gelding foaled 1963
Escart - What A Daisy

Owner Raymond Guest **Trainer** Dan Moore **Jockeys**
Tommy Carberry (Ben Hanbury) **Record (jumps)** 14 wins
from 56 starts

Career highlights Won 1969 Scalp Hurdle, Meadow
Brook Chase, 1970 Wills Premier Chase Series Final,
Cheltenham Gold Cup, 1971 Cheltenham Gold Cup, 1972
Sundew Chase, 1975 Grand National; 2nd 1969 Power
Gold Cup, 1970 Leopardstown Chase, 1972 Kerry National,
Grand National Trial, 1974 Cathcart Chase, Grand
National, Irish Grand National, 1975 Kerry National; 3rd
1971 Irish Grand National, 1973 Grand National

Why we love him L'Escargot earned our love over a ten-
year career, though for much of his decade on the track
grudging respect was the best he was accorded. 'The
Snail' was a class act on his day, the only horse other than
Golden Miller to win both the Cheltenham Gold Cup and
the Grand National. Apart from Arkle and Best Mate,
L'Escargot is the only horse to win more than one Gold
Cup since 1950, and it was great tribute to his durability
that he was able to win the National as a 12-year-old after
well over 50 races. Even if he was rather the villain of the
piece when he made the most of a weight concession to
thwart Red Rum's hat-trick at Aintree in 1975, L'Escargot
himself was so popular by then that nobody really
begrudged it. "Hail the snail" read the headlines after
Aintree, and his place in this list suggests we certainly
have. **GE**

Pendil in spectacular jumping form at Kempton in February 1973

48
Pendil

Bay gelding foaled 1965
Pendragon - Diliska

Owner Cynthia Swallow **Trainer** Fred Winter
Jockey Richard Pitman **Record (jumps)** 27
wins from 47 starts

Career highlights Won 1970 Cheltenham Trial
Hurdle, 1972 Arkle Trophy, Welsh Champion
Chase, Black & White Whisky Gold Cup, Benson
and Hedges Chase, King George VI Chase, 1973
Yellow Pages Pattern Chase, Massey-Ferguson
Gold Cup, King George VI Chase, 1974 Yellow
Pages Pattern Chase, Sandown Pattern Chase

Why we love him This great horse was a
superbly fast and fluent jumper, though in Ed
Byrne's iconic shot of him at Kempton he seems
to be launching himself into orbit, embodying
the panache and majesty of the sport at its best.
Pendil was the outstanding steeplechaser of his
time, a champion at both two and three miles,
yet is best remembered for his luckless defeats at
odds-on in his two runs in the Cheltenham Gold
Cup. He was otherwise unbeaten in his first 20
races over fences, but in the Gold Cup he
faltered in the face of deafening cheers when
beaten a short head in 1973 by The Dikler, an
inferior racehorse, and was brought down when
going easily the following year. Even if his
brilliance was never adequately rewarded, two
victories in the King George and success under
12st 7lb in the Massey-Ferguson proved he was
a giant. **JR**

Tingle Creek in typically breathtaking mode under David Mould

49
Tingle Creek

Chestnut gelding foaled 1966
Goose Creek - Martingle
Owner Helen Whitaker **Trainer** Tom Jones **Jockeys**
Ian Watkinson, David Mould, Steve Smith Eccles
(Tommy Stack, Bob Davies) **Record (jumps)** 23 wins
from 55 starts (plus 5 wins in USA)

Career highlights Won 1973 Sandown Pattern
Chase, Benson and Hedges Handicap Chase, 1977
Sandown Pattern Chase, 1978 Sandown Pattern
Chase; 2nd 1974 Champion Chase, Sandown Pattern
Chase, Benson and Hedges Handicap Chase, 1975
Sandown Pattern Chase, 1976 Sandown Pattern Chase

Why we love him One of the most spectacular
chasers of the post-war era, Tingle Creek set the
jumping world alight when he came to Britain from
America in 1972. In full flow, he could leave onlookers
spellbound with spine-tingling displays of jumping
displayed in the style of a swashbuckling front-runner.
Tingle Creek was especially at home scorching round
Sandown, the track that most played to his strengths.
Renowned for standing off his fences so far that he
could hardly have seen the wings, he used to establish
such a lead over the railway fences that his rivals, to
whom he generally gave stacks of weight, were often
run ragged. No wonder a race is named in his honour
at the Esher track, where he continued to parade long
after his retirement. Although the undulations of
Cheltenham meant that he was below form there,
Tingle Creek was a champion chaser, although he
never won the Two-Mile Champion Chase. More than
that, though, he was among the most thrilling sights
ever seen on a racecourse. **NG**

50
Triptych

Bay mare foaled 1982
Riverman - Trillion

Owners Alan Clore (Peter Brant) **Trainers** Patrick Biancone (David O'Brien, David Smaga) **Jockeys** Tony Cruz, Steve Cauthen, Christy Roche, Alain Lequeux

Record (Flat) 14 wins from 41 starts

Career highlights Won 1984 Prix Marcel Boussac, 1985 Irish 2,000 Guineas, 1986 Champion Stakes, 1987 Prix Ganay, Coronation Cup, Matchmaker International, Irish Champion Stakes, Champion Stakes, Fuji Stakes, 1988 Coronation Cup; 2nd 1985 Oaks, 1986 Coronation Cup, Eclipse Stakes, Matchmaker International

Why we love her Triptych demonstrated boundless resilience in the face of an exhausting international schedule over five seasons, during which she raced in six different countries, winning Group 1 events in England, Ireland and France. Whenever there was a Group 1 middle-distance event, you could bet that Triptych would be there. Her trainer and jockey may have changed on a regular basis – as did her owner on one occasion – but what stayed the same was her toughness, courage and ability. All the journeys and the upheavals in no way dampened Triptych's enthusiasm; she seemed incapable of running a bad race. Time after time, her determination saw her prevail, and the fact that she was as good and successful at the age of six as she had been when she was two paid handsome tribute to her relish for the task. **GE**

Steve Cauthen drives home Triptych in York's Matchmaker International in 1987

51
Further Flight

Grey gelding foaled 1986
Pharly - Flying Nelly
Owner-breeder Simon Wingfield Digby **Trainer**
Barry Hills **Jockey** Michael Hills **Record (Flat)** 24
wins from 70 starts

Career highlights Won 1990 Ebor Handicap, 1991
Goodwood Cup, Jockey Club Cup, St Simon Stakes,
1992 Goodwood Cup, Lonsdale Stakes, Doncaster Cup,
Jockey Club Cup, 1993 Lonsdale Stakes, Jockey Club
Cup, 1994 Jockey Club Cup, 1995 Jockey Club Cup

Why we love him A gutsy grey always
commands attention, and this one was unique in
winning the same European Pattern race five times.
Having graduated from the handicap ranks via an
Ebor success, he monopolised the Jockey Club Cup
from 1991 and on the occasion of his fifth victory,
when he displayed his usual zest to break the record,
the warmth of his reception from the Newmarket
crowd showed that he had become a racing
institution. He also numbered two Goodwood Cups
and a Doncaster Cup among his nine Group
successes, and was still winning at the age of 12.
Even at his best Further Flight was nearly
a stone below top class, but his grit and tenacity
consistently made him a factor in the Cup events.
Michael Hills, his regular rider for 11 seasons, said:
"He has never let me down – he's my best friend."
JR

**Further Flight
(Michael Hills)
in action at
Chester in May
1998**

52
Hawk Wing

Bay colt foaled 1999
Woodman - La Lorgnette

Owner Sue Magnier **Trainer** Aidan O'Brien **Jockey** Mick Kinane **Record (Flat)** 5 wins from 12 starts

Career highlights Won 2001 National Stakes, Futurity Stakes, 2002 Eclipse Stakes, 2003 Lockinge Stakes; 2nd 2002 2,000 Guineas, Derby, Queen Elizabeth II Stakes

Why we love him Some people do, but this section could equally well be "Why we hate him" given Hawk Wing's propensity to split opinion. For each one who marvelled at his amazing Lockinge win – visually one of the most stunning displays you could wish to see as he put 11 lengths between himself and a Group 1 field – there was another ready to accuse him of being a flashy, overly hyped horse. Those adhering to the latter theory claimed that Hawk Wing's retirement soon after an abject defeat at Royal Ascot on his only subsequent start added credence to their arguments, even though he won three Group 1 events altogether and was also runner-up in a pair of Classics. "Not a true champion," said some critics; a "stain on history" added others. So what? Votes counted in this poll and obviously this much-maligned, occasionally brilliant character left his mark. Even if you didn't rate him. **NG**

Hawk Wing (Mick Kinane) crushes his rivals in Newbury's Lockinge Stakes in 2003

53

The Dikler

Bay gelding foaled 1963
Vulgan - Coronation Day

Owner Peggy August **Trainer** Fulke Walwyn
Jockeys Ron Barry, Barry Brogan (Willie
Robinson, Stan Mellor) **Record (jumps)** 14
wins from 49 starts

Career highlights Won 1971 King George VI
Chase, 1973 Cheltenham Gold Cup, 1974
Whitbread Gold Cup; 2nd 1971 Massey-
Ferguson Gold Cup, 1974 Great Yorkshire
Chase, Cheltenham Gold Cup; 3rd 1971
Cheltenham Gold Cup, 1972 Cheltenham Gold
Cup, 1973 King George VI Chase

Why we love him Placed in four consecutive
Gold Cups, The Dikler was a regular in the top
three-mile chases of the early 1970s when his
rivalry with the great Pendil, whom he short-
headed at Cheltenham in 1973, was a
compelling feature of the jumping scene. The
Dikler may have been named after a little river
in the Cotswolds, but he was more like a
raging torrent than a quiet country stream. He
was a ferocious ride – the *enfant terrifying* of
the jumping world rather than the *enfant
terrible* – and he pulled so hard when worked
in the mornings at Lambourn that only one
person could hold him, the senior staff man
'Darkie' Deacon. But he was also a very
talented chaser: his aggressive attitude at
home very much transferred to the
racecourse. He always ran against the best
and even when he did not come out on top,
his rivals knew that they had been in a battle.
GE

The Dikler (Barry Brogan), a Gold Cup regular in action in the 1972 renewal

Mysilv (Adrian Maguire) at the head of affairs in the 1994 Triumph Hurdle

54
Mysilv

Chestnut mare foaled 1990
Bustino - Miss By Miles
Owners Million In Mind Partnership (3), Elite Racing
Club **Trainers** David Nicholson, Charlie Egerton
Jockeys Adrian Maguire, Jamie Osborne **Record
(jumps)** 11 wins from 20 starts

Career highlights Won 1993 Finale Junior Hurdle,
1994 Adonis Hurdle, Triumph Hurdle, 1995 Tote Gold
Trophy, 1996 Haydock Champion Hurdle Trial; 2nd
1996 Stayers' Hurdle, Prix La Barka, Grande Course de
Haies d'Auteuil

Why we love her Without even winning a race at
the 1996 Cheltenham Festival, Mysilv became one of
the stars of the meeting. On the Tuesday, the already
popular mare had run an eminently respectable race
in the Champion Hurdle, finishing sixth after setting a
furious pace for much of the contest. Then, two days
later, she was back, racing over an extra mile in the
Stayers' Hurdle and coming within three-quarters of a
length of a famous triumph. This was why we loved
Mysilv. She was an admirably courageous, tough little
racemare and she always ran her heart out, usually
attempting to repel all challengers from the front.
Mysilv was also very much a 'people's horse', having
raced successfully for two of Britain's best-known
ownership syndicates, which, for all her undoubted
attributes, inevitably gave her an edge over many
rivals in this poll given the extent of her potential
vote. **LM**

Sinndar (Johnny Murtagh) gets the better of Sakhee in the 2000 Derby

55
Sinndar

Bay colt foaled 1997
Grand Lodge - Sinntara

Owner Aga Khan IV **Trainer** John Oxx **Jockey** Johnny Murtagh **Record (Flat)** 7 wins from 8 starts

Career highlights Won 1999 National Stakes, 2000 Leopardstown Derby Trial, Derby, Irish Derby, Prix Niel, Prix de l'Arc de Triomphe

Why we love him Sinndar swept through the 2000 Flat season not quite like a tornado – he was more controlled than that – but certainly in a manner that left his opposition for dead. He simply got better and better throughout the season, a great tribute to the patient way in which trainer John Oxx brought him along. A near-perfect racing record of seven victories from eight starts, featuring two Derbys and an Arc (the vanquished included Sakhee and Montjeu), left no doubts as to his class. In view of the fact that he raced for only two seasons, it is quite something that he evidently managed to establish himself so firmly in public affections. That he did so may be due at least in part to his connections – the old-fashioned type of owner-breeder and trainer, and a jockey who hauled himself off racing's scrapheap to re-establish himself at the top of the pile. **GE**

Generous and Alan Munro, triumphant in the 1991 King George

56
Generous

Chestnut colt foaled 1988
Caerleon - Doff The Derby

Owner Fahd Salman **Trainer** Paul Cole **Jockeys** Richard Quinn, Alan Munro **Record (Flat)** 6 wins from 11 starts

Career highlights Won 1990 Dewhurst Stakes, 1991 Derby, Irish Derby, King George VI and Queen Elizabeth Diamond Stakes

Why we love him Those who don't will argue that in some ways Generous was a typical Flat champion: a one-season wonder who failed his biggest test and was hustled off to stud while still immature, to the frustration of the racing public. Yet such was the sublime nature of his three wide-margin victories in the summer of 1991 that he established himself as a truly great horse, for he stormed home by five lengths in the Derby, beat French ace Suave Dancer by three lengths in the Irish Derby, and crushed his rivals by seven lengths in the King George, beating the record for the biggest winning margin in the race held by Mill Reef and Dahlia. Nor was Generous one-dimensional, as he had been a precocious two-year-old and won the Dewhurst (at odds of 50-1). His dismal Arc farewell could not dim the lustre of his victories. **JR**

57
Rooster Booster

Grey gelding foaled 1994
Riverwise - Came Cottage

Owner Terry Warner **Trainers** Philip Hobbs
(Richard Mitchell) **Jockey** Richard Johnson
Record (jumps) 8 wins from 39 starts

Career highlights Won 2002 County Hurdle,
Rehabilitation of Racehorses Handicap Hurdle,
Bula Hurdle, 2003 Agfa Hurdle, Champion
Hurdle, 2004 Haydock Champion Hurdle Trial;
2nd 2001 Tote Gold Trophy, 2002 Tote Gold
Trophy, 2003 Aintree Hurdle, Christmas
Hurdle, 2004 Tote Gold Trophy, Champion
Hurdle, Aintree Hurdle, Punchestown
Champion Hurdle, Christmas Hurdle

Why we love him A remarkable hurdler,
Rooster Booster is one of the great equine
characters of recent years. The grey, who
made his name via a string of heroic efforts in
defeat under big weights in top handicaps,
earned a lasting place in our affections when
he made startling improvement to win the
Champion Hurdle as a nine-year-old. That
hugely impressive victory was achieved in
trademark fashion. Held up, he travelled
supremely well before unleashing a
devastatingly powerful gallop that crushed his
rivals and resulted in a winning margin
bettered only by Istabraq in the modern era.
On the downside, Rooster Booster's style of
running has left him vulnerable in falsely run
races, and he is by no means the most
straightforward of rides in any case, severely
testing the tactical acumen of his jockey.
Perhaps the quirks serve to add to his charms,
though a string of defeats in 2004 frustrated
his legion of followers. **NG**

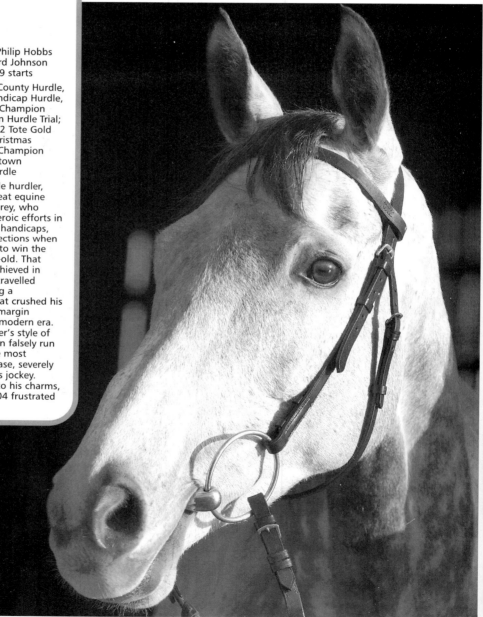

Rooster Booster at trainer Philip Hobbs's yard

58
Petite Etoile

Grey filly foaled 1956
Petition - Star Of Iran
Owners Prince Aly Khan, Aga Khan IV
Trainer Noel Murless **Jockeys** Lester
Piggott (Doug Smith) **Record (Flat)** 14
wins from 19 starts

Career highlights Won 1959 Free
Handicap, 1,000 Guineas, Oaks, Sussex
Stakes, Yorkshire Oaks, Champion Stakes,
1960 Victor Wild Stakes, Coronation Cup,
1961 Coronation Stakes (Sandown),
Coronation Cup, Rous Memorial Stakes,
Scarbrough Stakes

Why we love her This great grey filly was
the darling of racecourse crowds for most
of her four seasons. A dual Classic winner
and regular conqueror of colts, she was
wilful and highly strung, yet possessed a
brilliant turn of foot which Lester Piggott
repeatedly utilised so that she came late
and won narrowly on a tight rein. This
gave the impression that she had a large
amount in hand and enhanced her aura of
invincibility. Her slender winning margins
added to the drama of her appearances,
and though it eventually became clear that
she was a free runner who found little off
the bridle, she was game and wonderfully
consistent, never finishing out of the first
two. Petite Etoile was a prima donna who
contrived to be at the centre of attention
even in defeat, especially when second to
Aggressor in the King George, and, though
increasingly vulnerable with age, she was
never less than a celebrity. **JR**

Petite Etoile and Lester Piggott in the 1960 King George at Ascot

59
Moscow Flyer

Bay gelding foaled 1994
Moscow Society - Meelick Lady
Owner Brian Kearney **Trainer** Jessica
Harrington **Jockey** Barry Geraghty **Record
(jumps)** 23 wins from 37 starts

Career highlights Won 1999 Royal Bond
Hurdle, 2000 Punchestown Champion Novice
Hurdle, Morgiana Hurdle, December Festival
Hurdle, 2001 Shell Champion Hurdle
(Leopardstown), Denny Gold Medal Novice
Chase, 2002 Arkle Trophy, 2003 Queen
Mother Champion Chase, Tingle Creek Chase,
2004 Melling Chase, Punchestown Champion
Chase, Tingle Creek Chase

Why we love him Moscow Flyer's record
over fences is little short of incredible. If he
finishes a race, he wins it – that's how simple
it looked by the end of 2004. And that
includes when he meets fellow star two-miler
Azertyuiop, clashes between the pair having
become a highlight of the jumping scene. By
the time Moscow Flyer beat his arch-rival in a
memorable Tingle Creek showdown at
Sandown in December 2004, he had won 16
chases altogether, many of them in the
highest grade, including twice at the
Cheltenham Festival. Mind you, the stats also
tell you that he cannot be guaranteed to get
round in one piece, as became painfully
obvious when he unseated Barry Geraghty
midway through a previous clash with
Azertyuiop, in the 2004 Champion Chase.
Even allowing for his occasional mishaps,
Moscow Flyer is one of the best two-mile
chasers of recent years – and he wasn't too
shoddy over hurdles, either, having twice won
races involving the great Istabraq. **NG**

Moscow Flyer clears the final fence under Barry Geraghty in the 2002 Arkle Trophy

Silver Buck (Robert Earnshaw) over the last in the 1982 Cheltenham Gold Cup

60
Silver Buck

Brown gelding foaled 1972
Silver Cloud - Choice Archlesse
Owner Christine Feather **Trainers** Tony Dickinson,
Michael Dickinson **Jockeys** Robert Earnshaw (Tommy
Carmody) **Record (jumps)** 35 wins from 49 starts

Career highlights Won 1979 Embassy Premier Chase
Final, Edward Hanmer Memorial Chase, King George
VI Chase, 1980 Edward Hanmer Memorial Chase,
King George VI Chase, 1981 Jim Ford Chase, Edward
Hanmer Memorial Chase, 1982 Cheltenham Gold
Cup, Edward Hanmer Memorial Chase, 1984 John
Bull Chase, HS Commercial Spares Chase; 3rd 1981

Cheltenham Gold Cup, 1982 King George VI Chase

Why we love him In the top flight for most of his
lengthy career, Silver Buck was the best of the many
Dickinson champions and was the main standard-
bearer for the stable during its period of domination
of jump racing. He was versatile enough to master
both Kempton, where he won two King Georges, and
Cheltenham. After three Festival failures at the latter
venue, he beat stablemate Bregawn in the Gold Cup
and was one of his trainer's first five the following
year, finishing fourth. His rivalries included a lengthy
and memorable one with Night Nurse. 'Bucket', who
responded to the horsemanship of his young rider,
Robert Earnshaw, possessed a turn of foot rare among
staying chasers, but tended to idle in front and seldom
won by an extravagant margin. Cool and efficient, he
commanded the respect rather than the adoration of
the public, but he was game and consistent, and was
an admirable servant to the sport. **JR**

61
Sir Ivor

Bay colt foaled 1965
Sir Gaylord - Attica

Owner Raymond Guest **Trainer** Vincent O'Brien **Jockeys** Lester Piggott (Liam Ward) **Record (Flat)** 8 wins from 13 starts

Career highlights Won 1967 National Stakes, Grand Criterium, 1968 Ascot 2,000 Guineas Trial, 2,000 Guineas, Derby, Champion Stakes, Washington DC International; 2nd 1968 Prix de l'Arc de Triomphe

Why we love him This tough dual champion won races in four different countries and put up a stunning performance in the Derby for the legendary O'Brien–Piggott partnership. Held up, Sir Ivor produced a dramatic burst of speed to cut down Connaught inside the final furlong and secure his second Classic victory in a few strides. The memory of that triumph remains fresh, but his claims to greatness are compromised by the fact that, after Epsom, he lost his next four races, including the Arc, in which Vaguely Noble beat him on merit by three lengths. But his owner had the singularly American idea that the function of a racehorse is to race, and his attacking policy paid off when Sir Ivor ended his career in a blaze of glory in his native land with a victory in the Washington DC International that saw transatlantic competition come of age. **JR**

Sir Ivor (Lester Piggott) puts up an imperious performance in the 1968 Derby

El Gran Senor (Pat Eddery) wins the 2,000 Guineas in 1984

62
El Gran Senor

Bay colt foaled 1981
Northern Dancer - Sex
Appeal
Owner Robert Sangster
Trainer Vincent O'Brien
Jockey Pat Eddery **Record
(Flat)** 7 wins from 8 starts

Career highlights Won
1983 Railway Stakes,
National Stakes, Dewhurst
Stakes, 1984 Gladness
Stakes, 2,000 Guineas, Irish
Derby; 2nd 1984 Derby

Why we love him El Gran
Senor ran only once at a
mile, so he might seem an
unlikely contender for the
title 'best miler since
Brigadier Gerard', but his
majestic 2,000 Guineas
victory was of such
superlative quality that his
claims are hard to deny. In a
vintage Classic, the colt
showed a spectacular turn of
foot to sprint clear up the hill
and beat Chief Singer by two
and a half lengths, with Lear
Fan, Rainbow Quest and
others spreadeagled far
behind. El Gran Senor was no
one-race wonder, as he
proved a champion in both
his seasons and was a short
head away from retiring
unbeaten. He snatched
defeat from the jaws of
victory when touched off by
Secreto in a controversial
finish to the Derby – people
still debate whether pilot
error or shortage of stamina
was to blame – but made
partial amends on his
farewell at The Curragh. **JR**

63
Morley Street

**Chestnut gelding foaled 1984
Deep Run - High Board**

Owner Michael Jackson **Trainer** Toby Balding **Jockeys** Jimmy Frost, Graham Bradley (Richard Dunwoody, Tony Charlton) **Record (jumps)** 20 wins from 37 starts

Career highlights Won 1989 Mumm Prize Novices' Hurdle, Mercury Communications Hurdle, 1990 Aintree Hurdle, Breeders' Cup Chase, Ascot Hurdle, 1991 Champion Hurdle, Aintree Hurdle, Breeders' Cup Chase, Ascot Hurdle, 1992 Aintree Hurdle, 1993 Aintree Hurdle; 2nd 1992 Irish Champion Hurdle

Why we love him Like Olivier and Gielgud, Morley Street was blessed with the most astonishing theatrical timing. A superb physical specimen in possession of rare levels of natural ability, he was almost impossible to ride, becoming more difficult with each and every season that passed. A Champion Hurdle winner twice voted America's leading steeplechaser thanks to two Breeders' Cup triumphs, Morley Street had to be ridden with incomparable levels of finesse. Although his cruising speed was lethal, he would come to a halt almost as soon as his head hit the front, a trait that could make his jockeys look either extremely stupid or superbly gifted. Teaming up with Morley Street for his fourth Aintree Hurdle victory, the weighing room's supreme artist Graham Bradley was hailed a hero, oozing confidence as he delayed his winning challenge until 50 yards from home. Drama and Morley Street went together like eggs and bacon. **LM**

Morley Street (Jimmy Frost) in the 1990 Aintree Hurdle

64
Strong Promise

Bay/brown gelding foaled 1991
Strong Gale - Let's Compromise
Owner-trainer Geoff Hubbard (Chris Kinane, trainer)
Jockeys Kieran Gaule, Norman Williamson **Record (jumps)** 8 wins from 35 starts

Career highlights Won 1996 First National Bank Gold Cup, 1997 Comet Chase, Faucets Showers Silver Cup Chase; 2nd 1996 Tolworth Hurdle, Aintree Hurdle, Murphy's Gold Cup, 1997 Melling Chase, 1998 Comet And Sony (Ascot) Chase, Jim Ford Chase, Cheltenham

Gold Cup; 3rd 1998 Melling Chase, 2000 Mitsubishi Shogun Ascot Chase, Cheltenham Gold Cup.

Why we love him At his brilliant best, Strong Promise could be a glorious sight; tanking on the bridle, galloping seemingly without effort, the assassin just waiting to pounce. Campaigned with limitless ambition by his lower-league connections, he almost overcame a lack of stamina to win the Gold Cup, most notably when just edged out by Cool Dawn in 1998. Yet, despite some high-profile successes – including a defeat of One Man in the 1997 Comet Chase – it is impossible to argue otherwise than that such a high rank in this list was a little unexpected. The most magnificent of specimens, Strong Promise was a star chaser who never quite got what he deserved, and certainly not the end he deserved. On a miserable day at Aintree in 2000, he suffered a fatal fall in the Martell Cup, aged just nine. **LM**

Strong Promise (Norman Williamson) on the road to Comet Chase victory in 1997

Miesque (Freddie Head) stretches clear to win the 1,000 Guineas

65
Miesque

Bay filly foaled 1984
Nureyev - Pasadoble

Owner Stavros Niarchos **Trainer** Francois Boutin **Jockey** Freddie Head **Record (Flat)** 12 wins from 16 starts

Career highlights Won 1986 Prix de la Salamandre, Prix Marcel Boussac, 1987 1,000 Guineas, Poule d'Essai des Pouliches, Prix Jacques le Marois, Prix du Moulin, Breeders' Cup Mile, 1988 Prix d'Ispahan, Prix Jacques le Marois, Breeders' Cup Mile; 2nd 1987 Prix de Diane, Queen Elizabeth II Stakes, 1988 Prix du Moulin; 3rd 1986 Prix Morny

Why we love her It is testament to Miesque's quite outstanding ability that she became one of ours, even though she was really one of theirs. One of the all-time great French racehorses, Miesque was rarely less than sensational over a mile, and she proved it on the biggest stage of all, turning British and Irish racefans into true Europeans as we cheered her home for consecutive triumphs in America at the Breeders' Cup. Neither victory came as a surprise, for this supremely talented filly had proved herself on more familiar soil, becoming almost unbeatable once reaching her splendid pomp. Heroine of both the 1,000 Guineas and the French equivalent before going on, at three and four, to thump both older and younger rivals, Miesque oozed class and greatness. She hardly ever ran outside Group 1 company and finished out of the first two just once in 16 runs. And even then she was third! **LM**

Mr Frisk (Marcus Armytage) bounding round Aintree in the 1990 Grand National

66
Mr Frisk

Chestnut gelding foaled 1979
Bivouac - Jenny Frisk

Owner Lois Duffey **Trainer** Kim Bailey
Jockeys Marcus Armytage (Alan Jones, Paul
Croucher) **Record (jumps)** 18 wins from 40
starts

Career highlights Won 1989 Anthony
Mildmay Peter Cazalet Memorial Chase, 1990
Grand National, Whitbread Gold Cup; 3rd
1988 Racing Post Chase, Hennessy Cognac
Gold Cup, 1989 Hennessy Cognac Gold Cup

Why we love him Although he was a
talented staying handicap chaser, Mr Frisk
finds himself in this list purely because of his
performance in one event. The Grand
National is the one horserace that can be
guaranteed to generate significant levels of
interest on a national scale beyond the
confines of the sport itself. It fully deserves its
billing as the world's most famous
steeplechase – and it has had few more
flamboyant or exciting winners than Mr Frisk.
Bounding across the big Aintree fences with
astonishing enthusiasm and jumping with a
boldness that simply thrilled, he covered the
four and a half miles faster than any horse
before him. Then, for good measure, he did
what no other horse had ever done by
following up in the Whitbread. A handful at
home, where he required an unusually
dedicated training regime, Mr Frisk loved to
race and we loved to watch him. **LM**

Ardross lands the Henry II Stakes under Lester Piggott at Sandown in 1982

67
Ardross

Bay horse foaled 1976
Run The Gantlet - Le Melody

Owners Charles St George (Paddy Prendergast) **Trainers** Henry Cecil (Paddy Prendergast, Kevin Prendergast) **Jockeys** Lester Piggott (Christy Roche) **Record (Flat)** 14 wins from 24 starts

Career highlights Won 1979 Gallinule Stakes, 1980 Jockey Club Cup, 1981 Yorkshire Cup, Ascot Gold Cup, Goodwood Cup, Geoffrey Freer Stakes, Prix Royal-Oak, 1982 Jockey Club Stakes, Yorkshire Cup, Henry II Stakes, Ascot Gold Cup, Geoffrey Freer Stakes, Doncaster Cup;

2nd 1980 Ascot Gold Cup, Goodwood Cup, Doncaster Cup, 1982 Prix de l'Arc de Triomphe

Why we love him Here was the last of a dying breed – a magnificent stayer with a superb turn of foot who nearly won the Arc. In the three main Cup races in 1980, Ardross just lost to Le Moss in the closest and most exciting series of duels ever seen at the top level in Britain, being beaten an aggregate of little more than a length after a total of seven miles three furlongs. After changing stables and maturing with age, he strolled home in the next two Gold Cups, gave Lester Piggott his 4,000th domestic Flat victory, equalled Brigadier Gerard's record of 13 European Pattern wins, and went within a head of landing the Arc at the age of six. Ardross was a tough, game and durable champion during a golden age for stayers that will never return, for potential stayers with his speed are nowadays, for commercial reasons, kept to middle distances. **JR**

Dayjur (Willie Carson) in typically blistering form in the Prix de l'Abbaye

68
Dayjur

Brown colt foaled 1987
Danzig - Gold Beauty
Owner Hamdan Al Maktoum **Trainer** Dick
Hern **Jockey** Willie Carson **Record (Flat)** 7
wins from 11 starts

Career highlights Won 1990 Temple
Stakes, King's Stand Stakes, Nunthorpe
Stakes, Haydock Sprint Cup, Prix de
l'Abbaye; 2nd Breeders' Cup Sprint

Why we love him Dayjur was all about
speed, pure and simple. Blistering from the
stalls, he established a mark unrivalled by
any sprinter since as he blitzed his way
through the division as a three-year-old in
1990. None of Dayjur's rivals could touch
him. Indeed, such was his superiority that
he was sent off at odds as short as
1-10 to win the Prix de l'Abbaye, where a
characteristic display of raw power saw him
burst from the gate, burn off the field by
halfway and finish the race eased well
before the line for yet another emphatic
victory, his fifth of the year. Even his final
defeat added to his renown as it was
caused by one of the most famous
incidents in recent racing history when he
jumped a shadow near the line at Belmont,
forfeiting the Breeders' Cup Sprint in the
process. He may have lost the race, but it
added to his lustre – only a freakishly gifted
horse like Dayjur could have made the
crack US dirt specialists look slow. **NG**

69
Ribot

Bay colt foaled 1952
Tenerani - Romanella

Owner Marchese Mario Incisa della Rocchetta **Trainer** Ugo Penco **Jockey** Enrico Camici **Record (Flat)** 16 wins from 16 starts

Career highlights Won 1954 Criterium Nazionale, Gran Criterium, 1955 Premio Emanuele Filiberto, Prix de l'Arc de Triomphe, Premio del Jockey Club, 1956 Gran Premio di Milano, King George VI and Queen Elizabeth Stakes, Prix de l'Arc de Triomphe

Why we love him This Italian world-beater retired undefeated in 16 races including two renewals of the Arc, and his legend grows with the passing years. The masterpiece of breeding genius Federico Tesio, Ribot raced only once in Britain, the land of his birth, and, even in one of his less impressive victories, took the King George by five lengths. In his second Arc he put up a dazzling exhibition of supreme class as he relentlessly galloped further and further away from a top-quality international field and scored by an official margin of six lengths from British champion Talgo, though photographs show the verdict should have been eight or nine lengths. Invincible in three campaigns and in three countries in all conditions, and at distances from five to 15 furlongs, Ribot was one of the greatest racehorses of the 20th century. He also became champion sire three times. **JR**

Ribot (Enrico Camici) extends his unbeaten record in the 1956 King George

Captain Christy (Bobby Beasley) leads The Dikler over the last in the 1974 Gold Cup

70
Captain Christy

Bay gelding foaled 1967
Mon Capitaine - Christy's Bow

Owner Jane Samuel **Trainer** Pat Taaffe **Jockeys** Bobby Beasley, Bobby Coonan, Gerry Newman **Record (jumps)** 18 wins from 40 starts

Career highlights Won 1972 Sweeps Hurdle, 1973 Scalp Hurdle, Scottish Champion Hurdle, 1974 PZ Mower Chase, Cheltenham Gold Cup, Power Gold Cup, King George VI Chase, 1975 PZ Mower Chase (dead-heat), Prix du Velay, Punchestown Chase, King George VI Chase; 2nd 1975 Whitbread Gold Cup, Grand Steeple-Chase de Paris; 3rd 1973 Champion Hurdle

Why we love him This wayward but brilliant talent was a top-class hurdler who became the champion steeplechaser for three seasons. In his early days Captain Christy proved a tearaway who was just as likely to demolish the obstacles as to clear them, and the drama of his appearances was typified when he became the last novice to win the Cheltenham Gold Cup, for he made a wholesale blunder at the final fence before scampering up the hill to score decisively and complete jockey Bobby Beasley's comeback from alcoholism. He led all the way in both his King George VI Chase triumphs, beating Pendil by eight lengths and then Bula by 30 in a breathtaking performance as he jumped and galloped his rivals into submission. Spectacular and erratic, unpredictable and capable of sulking and pulling himself up, Captain Christy would have provided us with even more stirring memories had he not broken down. **JR**

71
Golden Miller

Bay gelding foaled 1927
Goldcourt - Miller's Pride

Owner Dorothy Paget **Trainers** Basil Briscoe (Owen Anthony) **Jockeys** Gerry Wilson (Ted Leader, Billy Stott, Evan Williams) **Record (jumps)** 29 wins from 52 starts

Career highlights Won 1932 Cheltenham Gold Cup, 1933 Troytown Chase, Cheltenham Gold Cup, 1934 Cheltenham Gold Cup, Grand National, 1935 Grand International Chase, Cheltenham Gold Cup, 1936 Cheltenham Gold Cup, 1938 Prince's Chase

Why we love him Golden Miller is the sole pre-war champion in this survey and few, if any, of the voters can have seen him race, yet his name echoes down the years. He remains the only horse to win the Cheltenham Gold Cup five times, and the only one to achieve the Gold Cup-Grand National double in the same season, defying 12st 2lb at Aintree to score in record time. The following year he just beat Thomond in a thrilling Gold Cup duel, emphasising the fact that, in spite of his estimable record, his margin of superiority over his contemporaries was slender. Golden Miller had to overcome an eccentric owner, an inexperienced trainer, and frequent changes of jockey, but he possessed rare soundness and durability, and did more than any other individual to raise the status of jump racing between the wars. One journalist called him "a god on four legs". **JR**

Pre-war champion Golden Miller with his eccentric owner Dorothy Paget

72
Lady Rebecca

Bay mare foaled 1992
Rolfe - Needwood Fortune
Owner Kinnersley Optimists **Trainer** Venetia Williams **Jockeys** Norman Williamson (Shane Kelly) **Record (jumps)** 13 wins from 19 starts

Career highlights Won 1999 Cleeve Hurdle, 2000 Cleeve Hurdle, 2001 Cleeve Hurdle; 3rd 1999 Stayers' Hurdle, 2000 Champion Stayers' Hurdle

Why we love her One of the most successful bargain-basement buys in racing history, Lady Rebecca was the ultimate 'littl'un with a big heart'. The mare was light of frame and small of build – she looked like a puff of wind would blow her over – and she did not race all that often. But she was as tough as old boots, and her opponents always knew they had been in a real fight. The mare particularly loved Cheltenham, where she made a speciality of winning the Cleeve Hurdle at the January meeting, recording a hat-trick in the race. Besides her slender frame, Lady Rebecca also had problems with her feet, which also affected the number of times she could race, and in the end she had to retire to stud after developing a leg infection. By then she had won nearly £162,000 for her owners, who had paid only 400gns for her in the first place. **GE**

Lady Rebecca (Norman Williamson) en route to her third Cleeve Hurdle in 2001

An exuberant leap from Looks Like Trouble (Richard Johnson) in the 2000 Gold Cup

73

Looks Like Trouble

Bay gelding foaled 1992
Zaffaran - Lavengaddy

Owner Tim Collins **Trainer** Noel Chance **Jockeys** Richard Johnson (Paul Carberry, Norman Williamson) **Record (jumps)** 8 wins from 17 starts

Career highlights Won 1999 Royal & SunAlliance Novices' Chase, 2000 Pillar Property Chase, Cheltenham Gold Cup, James Nicholson Wine Merchant Champion Chase, 2002 John Bull Chase

Why we love him Here was a horse who achieved the rare Cheltenham Festival double of the Royal & SunAlliance Novices' Chase (by a distance) and the Gold Cup, but never received the credit he deserved because those triumphs were overshadowed by the falls of Nick Dundee and Gloria Victis respectively. The latter was killed at the second-last in the Gold Cup, leaving Looks Like Trouble to gallop up the hill for a five-length victory over Florida Pearl, with Strong Promise, See More Business and Dorans Pride further behind. In terms of quality it was a vintage Gold Cup, giving a popular trainer his second success in the race and ranking the winner superior to many champions, but after his reappearance that autumn at Down Royal (he beat Dorans Pride and Florida Pearl again) he was found to have a serious injury and he was never the same again. **JR**

74
Corbiere

Chestnut gelding foaled 1975
Harwell - Ballycashin

Owner Brian Burrough **Trainer** Jenny Pitman **Jockeys** Ben de Haan (Peter Scudamore, Bryan Smart) **Record (jumps)** 12 wins from 63 starts

Career highlights Won 1982 Welsh National, 1983 Grand National; 2nd 1981 Sun Alliance Chase, 1983 National Hunt Handicap Chase, 1986 Scottish National; 3rd 1984 Grand National, 1985 Grand National

Why we love him Corbiere has his place in the history books of racing as the first winner of the Grand National to be trained by a woman, and he played a major part in establishing Jenny Pitman at the top of her profession and her being crowned the 'Queen of Aintree'. Although Corbiere loved the Liverpool track, where he was third in two other Nationals and his abundant stamina and determination served him so well, he was just as good away from those big fences, as he showed when winning the Welsh National and running well time after time in the major staying handicaps. Despite being described as "cantankerous" at home, Corbiere was the gamest horse you could ever hope to encounter on the racecourse, where he never gave up. His trainer, who selected him as her own personal favourite, is by no means alone in "loving him to bits", as she put it. **GE**

Corbiere (Ben de Haan), the first Grand National winner trained by a woman

75
Mandarin

Bay gelding foaled 1951
Deux Pour Cent - Manada
Owner Peggy Hennessy **Trainer** Fulke Walwyn **Jockeys**
Gerry Madden, Fred Winter (Michael Scudamore, Willie
Robinson) **Record (jumps)** 19 wins from 52 starts

Career highlights Won 1957 Broadway Novices' Chase,
Hennessy Gold Cup, King George VI Chase, 1958 Golden
Miller Chase, 1959 King George VI Chase, 1961 Hennessy
Gold Cup, 1962 Cheltenham Gold Cup, Grand Steeple-
Chase de Paris; 2nd 1957 Whitbread Gold Cup, 1958
Whitbread Gold Cup, 1959 Whitbread Gold Cup, Grand

Steeple-Chase de Paris; 3rd 1961 Cheltenham Gold Cup

Why we love him Mandarin achieved legendary status
in his last race, when he triumphed under Fred Winter in
the Grand Steeple-Chase de Paris by overcoming an
impossible handicap, having neither brakes nor steering
for nearly four miles after his bit had snapped. For good
measure he also broke down in the closing stages and
needed all his courage to hold on in a photo-finish. It
was the pinnacle in the careers of Britain's greatest jockey
and greatest trainer over jumps. In eight seasons the
French-bred had already proved a multiple champion in
Britain, winning two Hennessys and two King George VI
Chases and coming good in the Cheltenham Gold Cup at
the third attempt, though he had become even more
popular through his battling defeats. The bravest of the
brave, Mandarin overcame his unimpressive physique,
clumsy jumping and injuries, and on that hot summer
day in Paris he became one of the immortals. **JR**

Mandarin and Fred Winter team up for an unlikely victory in Paris in 1962

Flagship Uberalles (Richard Johnson) in the 2004 Champion Chase

76
Flagship Uberalles

Brown gelding foaled 1994
Accordion - Fourth Degree

Owners Elizabeth Gutner and Michael Krysztofiak, J P McManus **Trainers** Philip Hobbs, Paul Nicholls, Noel Chance **Jockeys** Richard Johnson, Joe Tizzard **Record (jumps)** 12 wins from 29 starts

Career highlights Won 1999 Arkle Trophy, Maghull Novices' Chase, Haldon Gold Cup, Tingle Creek Chase, 2000 Tingle Creek Chase, 2001 Tingle Creek Chase, 2002 Queen Mother Champion Chase, 2003 BMW Chase

Why we love him Season after season a regular in the top two-mile chases, Flagship Uberalles has earned our respect over the years for his ability to turn what looked to be hopelessly lost causes into winning ones. Although at one stage, after leaving Ireland for Britain, he had a run of never being out of the first two in 12 starts, he can give his nearest and dearest serious cause for concern. More than once he has dropped so far out of contention to have seemingly forfeited all chance before so often responding to the determined driving of his jockey to retrieve the situation. Though he was runner-up in the 2004 Champion Chase, by the end of the year it seemed younger horses clearly had his number, but he retained a place in our affections for more than half a decade at the top level. **GE**

77
Dorans Pride

Chestnut gelding foaled 1989
Orchestra - Marians Pride
Owner Tom Doran **Trainer** Michael Hourigan **Jockeys** Shane Broderick, Richard Dunwoody (Paul Carberry, Paul Hourigan) **Record (jumps)** 27 wins from 62 starts

Career highlights Won 1995 Stayers' Hurdle, Hatton's Grace Hurdle, 1996 Drinmore Novice Chase, 1997 Power Gold Cup, Hot Power Chase, 1998 Irish Hennessy Cognac Gold Cup, Ericsson Chase, 2000 Leopardstown November Handicap (Flat); 3rd 1997 Cheltenham Gold Cup, 1998 Cheltenham Gold Cup, 2001 Queen Alexandra Stakes (Flat)

Why we love him Top class over both hurdles and fences, Dorans Pride became an old friend in his capacity as a Cheltenham Festival stalwart. Although his seven runs at the meeting produced only one win, in the Stayers' Hurdle, he was twice third in the Gold Cup – the first time as a novice, the second as favourite after triumphing in the Irish version by 15 lengths. The most popular steeplechaser of his time in Ireland, evergreen Dorans Pride was a doughty stayer with the speed to be placed at Royal Ascot as a 12-year-old, and there was universal sadness (and some anger) when he suffered a fatal fall at Cheltenham after being brought out of retirement at the age of 14. Also poignant are the memories of his partnership with Shane Broderick, who was paralysed in a fall from another horse. **JR**

Dorans Pride (Richard Dunwoody) en route to finishing third in the 1998 Gold Cup

Birds Nest (Andy Turnell) in action at Ayr in the 1977 Scottish Champion Hurdle

78
Birds Nest

Chestnut gelding foaled 1970
Entanglement - Fair Sabrina

Owner Ian Scott **Trainer** Bob Turnell **Jockeys** Andy Turnell (Steve Knight) **Record (jumps)** 19 wins from 62 starts

Career highlights Won 1976 Fighting Fifth Hurdle, 1977 Oteley Hurdle, Fighting Fifth Hurdle, Bula Hurdle, 1978 Bula Hurdle, 1979 Scottish Champion Hurdle, Fighting Fifth Hurdle, Christmas Hurdle, 1980 Scottish Champion Hurdle, Bula Hurdle; 2nd 1976 Champion Hurdle; 3rd 1980 Champion Hurdle

Why we love him He was such a frustrating horse that it is almost a shock to find him in a list of people's favourites. Yet he was a horse of considerable ability who, on his day, was able to hold his own against the top hurdlers during what is regarded as the golden age. His exploits against champions like Sea Pigeon, Night Nurse and Monksfield left no doubt of his talent, showing what Birds Nest could do when the mood took him – but you could not always tell when that would be. It was certainly never at Cheltenham in March, although he ran in the Champion Hurdle no fewer than six times and was twice placed. At one time he became so infuriating that Timeform allotted him their dreaded squiggle, the mark the Halifax sages put beside the name of horses who cannot be trusted. In a perverse sort of way, however, this was part of his appeal: Birds Nest was almost the horse we loved to hate. **GE**

79
Time Charter

Bay filly foaled 1979
Saritamer - Centrocon
Owner-breeder Robert Barnett **Trainer** Henry Candy
Jockeys Billy Newnes, Joe Mercer (Steve Cauthen)
Record (Flat) 9 wins from 20 starts

Career highlights Won 1982 Masaka Stakes, Oaks, Sun Chariot Stakes, Champion Stakes, 1983 King George VI and Queen Elizabeth Diamond Stakes, Prix Foy, 1984 Coronation Cup; 2nd 1982 1,000 Guineas, 1984 Eclipse Stakes

Why we love her Time Charter was a rare filly who regularly beat high-class colts, a dual champion who delighted racecourse crowds until the age of five and set a new British prize-money record. She was an apprentice-ridden Oaks winner who romped home by seven lengths in the Champion Stakes and kept her form wonderfully well with age. She defeated all her male rivals in both the King George and the Arc, though in the latter (for which she started favourite) she was herself beaten by three other fillies; and in her last season she strolled home in the Coronation Cup and was within a neck of becoming the first of her sex to win the Eclipse. Time Charter's turn of foot was a formidable weapon in the very best company, and since she retired only Pebbles and Lochsong have emulated her by becoming a female champion older horse. **JR**

Time Charter (Billy Newnes) goes down to the start of the Oaks in 1982

80
Reference Point

Bay colt foaled 1984
Mill Reef - Home On The Range
Owner Louis Freedman **Trainer** Henry Cecil **Jockey** Steve Cauthen **Record (Flat)** 7 wins from 10 starts

Career highlights Won 1986 William Hill Futurity, 1987 Dante Stakes, Derby, King George VI and Queen Elizabeth Diamond Stakes, Great Voltigeur Stakes, St Leger; 2nd 1987 Eclipse Stakes

Why we love him Reference Point was a real star, a top two-year-old who more than delivered the goods in his Classic season. The colt won a lasting place in our affections in fighting back from an illness so severe it looked odds-against his ever returning to the track, let alone winning the most prestigious races in the calendar. A relentless galloping style became Reference Point's trademark thereafter, and few horses could withstand his power (though one in particular, Mtoto, managed it in a great Eclipse). He had the perfect rider to exploit his talents in Steve Cauthen, the popular American who revolutionised British race-riding in the 1980s with his expertise from the front, which has not been equalled since in Europe. The partnership between Cauthen and Henry Cecil had legions of followers – and the fact that Reference Point was British-owned and -bred to boot probably helped to earn him an even bigger place in some hearts. **NG**

Reference Point (Steve Cauthen) adds the St Leger to his Classic haul in 1987

Carvill's Hill (Peter Scudamore) in Chepstow's Rehearsal Chase in 1991

81
Carvill's Hill

Bay gelding foaled 1982
Roselier - Suir Valley

Owners Maeve McMorrow, Paul Green **Trainers**
Jim Dreaper, Martin Pipe **Jockeys** Ken Morgan,
Peter Scudamore **Record (jumps)** 17 wins from
25 starts

Career highlights Won 1988 Sean Graham
Hurdle, 1989 Irish Gold Cup, Power Gold Cup,
Tattersalls Gold Cup, 1990 Leopardstown Chase,
Punchestown Chase, 1991 Rehearsal Chase, Welsh
National, 1992 Irish Hennessy Cognac Gold Cup

Why we love him Newsworthy throughout his

roller-coaster career, Carvill's Hill consistently
provoked debate with his brilliant victories and
comprehensive failures. He was the Irish contender
who became the British champion and, though
flawed, was touched by greatness during his
stunning all-the-way victory under top weight in
the Welsh National. He is best remembered for his
controversial 1992 Gold Cup defeat, when he
jumped poorly and finished last after being taken
on for the lead by the alleged 'spoiler' Golden
Freeze, though he had twice won the Irish version,
the first time as a novice. Carvill's Hill divided
public opinion and was much maligned in some
quarters as a soft horse who crumpled under
pressure, but his failings were more physical than
mental, as he was a big, long-striding horse who
struggled with back problems and was not a fluent
jumper. For good or ill, he made a lasting
impression. **JR**

Lester Piggott takes The Minstrel down to the start of the 1977 Derby

82
The Minstrel

Chestnut colt foaled 1974
Northern Dancer - Fleur

Owner Robert Sangster **Trainer** Vincent O'Brien **Jockey** Lester Piggott **Record (Flat)** 7 wins from 9 starts

Career highlights Won 1976 Dewhurst Stakes, 1977 Derby, Irish Derby, King George VI and Queen Elizabeth Diamond Stakes; 2nd Irish 2,000 Guineas; 3rd 2,000 Guineas

Why we love him The Minstrel was one of the very best in the golden era for the O'Brien/Piggott/Sangster team. A deeply ingrained racing prejudice suggests you shouldn't trust chestnuts — and, according to the old sages, there was another no-no as far as The Minstrel was concerned in that he also possessed four white socks. How wrong they were. Not only did The Minstrel possess abundant talent, what set him apart was his remarkable courage to come back for more after some incredibly hard races, including a kitchen-sink job from Lester Piggott in an unforgettable Derby duel that saw him just prevail from Hot Grove. After winning the Irish Derby, he beat Orange Bay (by a short head) in a King George battle that nearly rivalled Grundy and Bustino. They simply don't come any tougher than The Minstrel. He was taken to the brink — and always came back for more. Or at least he did until he was shipped off to America for stud duties. **GE**

83
Earth Summit

Bay gelding foaled 1988
Celtic Cone - Win Green Hill

Owner The Summit Partnership **Trainer** Nigel Twiston-Davies **Jockeys** Carl Llewellyn, Tom Jenks (David Bridgwater) **Record (jumps)** 10 wins from 41 starts

Career highlights Won 1994 Scottish Grand National, Steel Plate and Sections Young Chasers' Final, 1995 Peter Marsh Chase, 1997 Welsh National, 1998 Grand National, Becher Chase

Why we love him There is surely no finer quality in a racehorse than courage, the in-bred willingness to go beyond the pain barrier, to fight hardest when it hurts the most. Earth Summit was blessed with such a quality. Never was it more evident than on the first Saturday in April 1998 when he became one of the bravest winners of the world's most famous steeplechase. This was a Grand National like few others, run on ground so impossibly testing that only six horses completed the four and a half miles, and only five of them without needing to be remounted. Already successful in a Scottish National and a Welsh National, he ran his rivals into the atrocious ground, finishing almost at a walk, but also finishing a hero. Earth Summit earned his popularity through grit and determination. He may be one of the slowest horses in this list, but he is also one of the most admirable. **LM**

Earth Summit and Carl Llewellyn, No. 1 at Aintree in the 1998 Grand National

Baracouda (Thierry Doumen), a real professional over hurdles at Newbury in 2003

84
Baracouda

Bay gelding foaled 1995
Alesso - Peche Aubar
Owners J P McManus (Roger Barby) **Trainer** Francois Doumen **Jockey** Thierry Doumen (Tony McCoy) **Record (jumps)** 18 wins from 24 starts

Career highlights Won 2000 Long Walk Hurdle, 2001 Distance Championship Hurdle (Sandown), Ascot Hurdle, Long Walk Hurdle, 2002 Rendlesham Hurdle, Stayers' Hurdle, Ascot Hurdle, 2003 Stayers' Hurdle, Long Distance Hurdle, Long Walk Hurdle, 2004 Sandown Hurdle, Long Distance Hurdle, Long Walk Hurdle; 2nd 2004 Stayers' Hurdle

Why we love him The best winner in the history of the Stayers' Hurdle, Baracouda has done more than any other horse to raise the status of long-distance hurdlers. The quality of his performances at Cheltenham meant that this regular French raider could be rated superior to the best two-milers, and therefore the overall hurdling champion, for two seasons. Not an easy ride, the tactics adopted on him add drama and excitement to his appearances, for he is habitually held up well off the pace to come with an irresistible late run so that he has no opportunity to idle in front. Baracouda compiled a sequence of 14 victories in 15 starts up to his defeat by Iris's Gift at Cheltenham in 2004, and his legacy was to make it a foregone conclusion that the Stayers' Hurdle (renamed the World Hurdle) would be the centrepiece of the extra day at the Festival from 2005. **JR**

85
Pilsudski

Bay horse foaled 1992
Polish Precedent - Cocotte

Owner-breeders Lord Weinstock and Simon Weinstock
Trainer Michael Stoute **Jockeys** Walter Swinburn, Mick Kinane **Record (Flat)** 10 wins from 22 starts

Career highlights Won 1996 Brigadier Gerard Stakes, Grosser Preis von Baden, Breeders' Cup Turf, 1997 Eclipse Stakes, Irish Champion Stakes, Champion Stakes, Japan Cup; 2nd 1996 Prix de l'Arc de Triomphe, 1997 King George VI and Queen Elizabeth Diamond Stakes, Prix de l'Arc de Triomphe

Why we love him Pilsudski was a mature globetrotting star who put most Classic winners in the shade, a progressive sort who graduated from the handicap ranks to become a champion as a five-year-old. A game horse with an iron constitution, he won Group/Grade 1 races in five countries – Germany, Canada (Breeders' Cup Turf), Britain, Ireland and Japan – and was unlucky to come up against two great champions, Helissio and Peintre Celebre, on his two runs in the Arc. His Breeders' Cup victory from stablemate Singspiel was particularly memorable because it showcased their trainer's supreme skill with late-developing horses, and set the seal on jockey Walter Swinburn's comeback from serious injury. However, it was tinged with sadness following the untimely death of Simon Weinstock, who had arranged the matings that produced him and many of his family's other horses, including Troy. **JR**

Pilsudski and Mick Kinane collect the Champion Stakes at Newmarket in 1997

Troy (Willie Carson) after the King George in 1979

86
Troy

Bay colt foaled 1976
Petingo - La Milo

Owner-breeder Sir Michael Sobell **Trainer** Dick Hern **Jockey** Willie Carson **Record (Flat)** 8 wins from 11 starts

Career highlights Won 1978 Lanson Champagne Stakes, 1979 Sandown Classic Trial, Predominate Stakes, Derby, Irish Derby, King George VI and Queen Elizabeth Diamond Stakes, Benson & Hedges Gold Cup

Why we love him The 200th Derby would have been special even with a routine winner, but Troy gave the historic occasion a worthy climax. This great champion was in an apparently hopeless 12th position on the rails at Tattenham Corner, yet when switched to the outside he produced a stunning burst to win going away by seven lengths. He created one of the sport's defining moments and gave his hugely respected trainer a first victory in the race; the fact that Sir Gordon Richards was the owner's racing manager added to the winner's popularity. Troy completed a unique Group 1 four-timer at Epsom, The Curragh, Ascot and York, though with ever-decreasing margins, before being beaten in the Arc when over the top. A thoroughly Anglo-Irish champion in an era dominated by horses with US pedigrees, Troy gave traditionalists hope that the Derby might still be the world's greatest race. **JR**

87
Katy Nowaitee

Bay filly foaled 1996
Komaite - Cold Blow

Owner The Stable Maites **Trainer** Peter Harris **Jockey** John Reid (Tony Beech)
Record (Flat) 5 wins from 11 starts

Career highlights Won 2000 Doncaster Spring Mile, Cambridgeshire, Severals Stakes

Why we love her Er, to be truthful we're not entirely sure. All right, some punters might remember Katy Nowaitee fondly after she landed a fair old gamble in the Cambridgeshire, but her inclusion must be regarded as the most surprising on the list. Trainer Peter Harris agrees. "Frankly, I was astonished," he says. "Of course, I am pleased she made it, but I have to admit I was surprised." It is not as if she was particularly sweet-natured at home, either. "She was actually very miserable, pinning her ears back and looking as if she wanted to kill you," says Harris. "But she would never touch you, and maybe people remembered her because her owners were on Channel 4 quite a lot." Having said that, Harris denies any block vote from her syndicate owners, so it remains a mystery how she made the Top 100. Whatever, Katy Nowaitee was an admirable racehorse who only three times finished out of the first two in her career, and quite a few people clearly remember her fondly. **NG**

Katy Nowaitee (John Reid) wins Newmarket's Severals Stakes in October 2000

The Fellow (Adam Kondrat) jumps ahead in the 1991 King George VI Chase

88
The Fellow

Bay gelding foaled 1985
Italic - L'Oranaise

Owner Marquesa de Moratalla **Trainer** Francois Doumen
Jockeys Adam Kondrat (Dominique Vincent) **Record
(jumps)** 15 wins from 51 starts

Career highlights Won 1990 Prix La Haye Jousselin, 1991
Prix Millionnaire II, Grand Steeple-Chase de Paris, King
George VI Chase, 1992 Prix Heros XII, King George VI
Chase, 1994 Cheltenham Gold Cup, Prix Millionnaire II; 2nd
1991 Cheltenham Gold Cup, 1992 Cheltenham Gold Cup

Why we love him French horses are seldom popular in
Britain, but The Fellow became an honorary Brit through his
exploits in the Cheltenham Gold Cup and his trainer's Gallic
charm. This hardy non-thoroughbred seemed fated to be
remembered as a gallant loser after being beaten a short
head in the race by both Garrison Savannah and Cool
Ground and then finishing fourth, but he finally came good
when dethroning Jodami in 1994 (bizarrely, the two old
rivals are separated by only one place in this survey). He thus
followed Mandarin as only the second horse to win both the
Gold Cup and its French equivalent, the Grand Steeple-Chase
de Paris. The Fellow was equally at home at Cheltenham,
Auteuil, Kempton (two King George VI Chase victories) and
Aintree, and was one of the three musketeers who
dominated French jump racing for several years, the others
being his stablemates Ucello and Ubu. **JR**

Jodami (Mark Dwyer) collars Rushing Wild in the 1993 Cheltenham Gold Cup

89
Jodami

Bay gelding foaled 1985
Crash Course - Masterstown Lucy
Owner John Yeadon **Trainer** Peter Beaumont **Jockeys** Mark Dwyer (Anthea Farrell, Patrick Farrell) **Record (jumps)** 18 wins from 39 starts

Career highlights Won 1992 West of Scotland Pattern Novices' Chase, 1993 Mandarin Chase, Peter Marsh Chase, Irish Hennessy Cognac Gold Cup, Cheltenham Gold Cup, Edward Hanmer Memorial Chase, 1994 Irish Hennessy Cognac Gold Cup, 1995 Irish Hennessy Cognac Gold Cup, 1997 Peter Marsh Chase; 2nd 1994 Cheltenham Gold Cup

Why we love him Jodami proved that a family horse can still beat the big battalions and become a champion, at any rate over jumps. From a small northern yard, this big, old-fashioned type of chaser was ridden by the trainer's daughter or son-in-law in his early races and proved a consummate professional, a good jumper with plenty of stamina who developed into a worthy Cheltenham Gold Cup winner in 1993. Indeed, he nearly repeated the dose 12 months later, being foiled only by The Fellow. He won the Irish equivalent three consecutive times, remained in the top flight until the age of 12, and, unlike most subsequent champions, regularly put his reputation on the line in handicaps. Although not one of the greats, Jodami embodied many of the virtues of the winter game. **JR**

90
Chaplins Club

**Chestnut gelding foaled 1980
Parade Of Stars - Nautical Rose**

Owner Peter Savill **Trainer** David
Chapman **Jockeys** Kevin Darley,
David Nicholls **Record (Flat)** 24
wins from 160 starts

Career highlights Won nine
handicaps in a season twice, in
1985 and 1988; on second occasion
won seven races in 19 days,
including Tote Bookmakers' Sprint
Trophy at Ayr

Why we love him Renowned for
his supreme toughness and
resilience, this prolific sprinter
gained an enormous fan club in the
process of winning a remarkable
nine handicaps in a single season in
the 1980s. The feat had not been
achieved for 111 years – and he did
it not once, but twice, in 1985 and
again as a veteran in 1988. At the
end of his four-year-old season,
Chaplins Club was given a Timeform
rating of just 59, hardly the sort of
mark that you would expect to lead
to inclusion in this august list. Yet
such was his progress that 12
months later his rating had gone up
by about two and a half stones. "He
saves his effort until it's needed,"
said his trainer. "Before the race, he
walks around the paddock like an
old hunter chaser." Such a laid-back
outlook allowed Chaplins Club to
continue to race until the age of 12,
when in July 1992 on his 160th
outing, he won his final start at
Redcar. **GE**

Chaplins Club (Kevin Darley) scores at Haydock to record his ninth win of 1988

Rondetto (Johnny Haine) holds off Fort Leney at the Cheltenham Festival in 1965

91
Rondetto

Chestnut gelding foaled 1956
Caporetto - Roundandround
Owner Albert Mitchell **Trainer** Bob Turnell
Jockeys Jeff King (Bill Rees, Johnny Haine)
Record (jumps) 21 wins from 82 starts

Career highlights Won 1964 Jerry M Chase,
1965 Stone's Ginger Wine Chase, National
Hunt Handicap Chase, 1967 Hennessy Gold
Cup; 3rd 1969 Grand National

Why we love him Rondetto put in ten

seasons of faithful service to the Turnell
stable and was a reliable supporting actor in
some of the dramas of the golden age of
steeplechasing in the 1960s, occasionally
seizing the starring role for himself. He beat
subsequent champion Fort Leney at the
Cheltenham Festival in 1965, separated Arkle
and Mill House in the Gallaher Gold Cup at
Sandown, and held off Stalbridge Colonist and
What A Myth in a spine-tingling finish to the
Hennessy. However, he derived his support
mainly from his status as a Grand National
regular who fell five out when going strongly
in the lead in 1965, was a victim of the pile-up
in Foinavon's year, and finished a thoroughly
deserving third at the age of 13. Rondetto is
the oldest horse to be placed in the National
in the last 80 years. **JR**

Amrullah schools at home under Rachel Bridger, daughter of trainer John

92
Amrullah

Brown gelding foaled 1980
High Top - Ravenshead
Owner Terry Thorn **Trainer** John Bridger
Jockey Gary Moore **Record (jumps)** 0 wins
from 74 starts

Career highlights Got within 30 lengths of
two-mile champion Barnbrook Again when
2nd of three in a novices' chase at Ascot in
1988; 3rd (of three) behind Remittance Man
in 1990 Wayward Lad Novices' Chase

Why we love him Everyone loves a winner,
but there is ample evidence to suggest

racing folk are pretty fond of serial losers as
well. In the 1990s the hapless Quixall
Crossett, the 'Sultan of Slow', became
famous for failing to win in 103 outings
over jumps, while similar records devoid of
achievement have earned Zippy Chippy and
Haruurara lasting fame in America and
Japan respectively. Amrullah was the
prototype Quixall Crossett, and this lifelong
novice chaser's failure to win even a single
race became the stuff of racing legend in
the 1980s. Although he had a semblance of
ability, it was his absolute bloody-minded
determination never to put his head in front
that earned him celebrity status, with even
News At Ten featuring his efforts – or lack
of them – at one stage. He died in 2003 at
John Bridger's farm. "He was a crafty
character, but I feel a bit sick I couldn't get
him to win," said the trainer. **NG**

93
Singspiel

Bay horse foaled 1992
In The Wings - Glorious Song

Owner Sheikh Mohammed **Trainer** Michael Stoute
Jockeys Frankie Dettori (Mick Kinane, Gary Stevens,
Jerry Bailey) **Record (Flat)** 9 wins from 20 starts

Career highlights Won 1996 Canadian International,
Japan Cup, 1997 Dubai World Cup, Coronation Cup,
Juddmonte International; 2nd 1995 Grand Prix de Paris,
Eclipse Stakes, 1996 Coronation Cup, Breeders' Cup Turf

Why we love him Singspiel trotted the globe in the
style of an equine superstar, developing into a top-class
international performer as a four- and five-year-old. After
his juvenile debut, he made the frame in every one of his
19 subsequent outings, most of which – in his last two
seasons at least – came in the world's premier middle-
distance contests. The older he got, the better he
became, winning Group 1 events on three different
continents, among them the 1997 Dubai World Cup, a
'home' victory for Sheikh Mohammed that sparked
memorable scenes at Nad Al Sheba. Although beaten by
stablemate Pilsudski in a memorable one-two for
Michael Stoute at the Breeders' Cup in 1996, he was
regarded as a banker to go one better the following
season until an 11th-hour injury ended his career in the
morning mist at Hollywood Park. It was the saddest of
ends. **NG**

Singspiel receives a pat from Frankie Dettori after winning the 1997 Coronation Cup

94

Hatton's Grace

Bay gelding foaled 1940
His Grace - Hatton

Owner Moya Keogh **Trainer** Vincent O'Brien
Jockeys (jumps) Aubrey Brabazon, Tim Molony
(Morny Wing, Martin Molony on Flat) **Record (Flat)**
6 wins from 20 starts; **(jumps)** 12 wins from 32
starts

Career highlights Won 1949 Champion Hurdle,
Irish Lincolnshire, Irish Cesarewitch, 1950 Champion
Hurdle, Irish Cesarewitch, 1951 Champion Hurdle

Why we love him An ugly duckling who became
one of the immortals of the Turf, Hatton's Grace was
the first horse to win the Champion Hurdle three
times, and helped to start the Vincent O'Brien
legend. This remarkable dual-purpose performer was
the Irish equivalent of Sea Pigeon, winning top-class
handicaps on the Flat whilst proving himself a
champion over jumps. He was small and
unimposing, but his appearance enhanced his
popularity and he proved a David capable of slaying
Goliaths at both The Curragh and Cheltenham,
where his Flat-race speed was devastating up the
final hill. The first 11-year-old to win the Champion
Hurdle, he was the horse who did most to make that
race a true championship event, and he might have
won it even more often had he been trained by
O'Brien throughout his career instead of only from
the age of eight. **JR**

Hatton's Grace (Tim Molony, left) wins the 1951 Champion Hurdle as National Spirit falls

Go Ballistic winning under Mick Fitzgerald at Ascot in April 1996

95
Go Ballistic

Brown gelding foaled 1989
Celtic Cone - National Clover
Owner Sheila Lockhart **Trainers** John O'Shea, David Nicholson, Henrietta Knight, Richard Phillips **Jockeys** Richard Johnson (Mick Fitzgerald, Tony Dobbin) **Record (jumps)** 9 wins from 57 starts

Career highlights Won 1996 Betterware Cup, 1998 Jim Ford Chase; 2nd 1999 Cheltenham Gold Cup, King George VI Chase, 2001 Tote Gold Trophy Chase; 3rd 1994 Festival Bumper

Why we love him It was partly because he seemed to be around forever that we treasured Go Ballistic. Perhaps the greatest appeal of jumping is that its stars return season after season, and this gelding became famous on that score, at the highest level and at the most precious place of all. Cheltenham and Go Ballistic went together like fish and chips. He may have changed trainers on a regular basis, but he was a constant at the Festival, appearing nine times altogether and running in five consecutive Gold Cups, almost winning the 1999 renewal when a 66-1 second to See More Business after a titanic battle up the hill. Then again, gallant defeat summed up Go Ballistic. Second in a King George and third in a Festival Bumper, he was short-headed by Marlborough in Sandown's 2001 substitute Gold Cup. A real trier who defied long-term wind problems to make his mark, Go Ballistic was a fine chaser but, more than that, he was a old friend. **LM**

Remittance Man (Richard Dunwoody) gives a Newbury fence plenty of air in 1991

96
Remittance Man

Bay gelding foaled 1984
Prince Regent - Mittens

Owner Tim Collins **Trainer** Nicky Henderson
Jockeys Richard Dunwoody (Jamie Osborne)
Record (jumps) 16 wins from 29 starts

Career highlights Won 1991 Arkle Trophy,
1992 Arlington Premier Chase Final, Queen
Mother Champion Chase, Melling Chase, Desert
Orchid South Western Pattern Chase,
Peterborough Chase

Why we love him An outstanding two-mile
chaser, Remittance Man was a rare champion
novice who fulfilled his promise in open
competition. He was wonderfully consistent,
running up a Pendil-like sequence of 13 wins in
his first 14 races over fences before injury
compromised his career. In that time his sole
defeat came on his only attempt at three miles,
in the King George VI Chase, which suggests
that he would not have developed into a Gold
Cup horse, but as he was only eight when
injuring a tendon we can only ponder what
might have been. He had already earned many
fans with his fast and accurate jumping, and his
victory over Katabatic and Waterloo Boy in a
vintage renewal of the Queen Mother
Champion Chase lingers long in the memory.
Remittance Man had his idiosyncrasies and was
accompanied everywhere by his best friend,
Nobby the sheep. **JR**

Spanish Steps clears Becher's Brook under Philip Blacker in the 1973 Grand National

97
Spanish Steps

Bay gelding foaled 1963
Flush Royal - Tiberetta

Owner-breeder-trainer Edward Courage **Jockeys** John Cook (John Buckingham, Geordie Mawson, Bill Smith, Philip Blacker) **Record (jumps)** 16 wins from 78 starts

Career highlights Won 1968 Black & White Gold Cup, 1969 Totalisator Champion Novices' Chase, Hennessy Gold Cup, Benson & Hedges Gold Cup, 1970 Gainsborough Chase, 1971 Stone's Ginger Wine Chase, SGB Chase; 2nd 1971 King George VI Chase; 3rd 1970 Cheltenham Gold Cup, 1975 Grand National; 4th 1973 Grand National, 1974 Grand National

Why we love him Thanks to his gameness, splendid jumping and cast-iron constitution – and the popularity of his small sporting stable – Spanish Steps became one of racing's best-loved old friends during his ten campaigns. He looked a title contender when running out a 15-length winner of both the Totalisator Champion Novices' (now Royal & SunAlliance) Chase and the Hennessy as a six-year-old but he did not quite fulfil that promise, always seeming to find one or two too good for him when it mattered most. Once he had lost some of his speed he became a Grand National regular, and his sure-footedness enabled him to emulate his dam by finishing in the frame three consecutive times; he might have triumphed had that not been the golden age of Red Rum, Crisp and L'Escargot. The pleasure Spanish Steps brought to many thousands ensured that he is not forgotten. **JR**

98
See You Then

Brown gelding foaled 1980
Royal Palace - Melodina
Owner Stype Wood Stud **Trainers**
Nicky Henderson (Con Collins) **Jockeys**
Steve Smith Eccles (Tommy Carmody,
John Francome) **Record (jumps)** 10
wins from 19 starts

Career highlights Won 1984 Corsa di
Siepi dei Quattro Anni, HSS Hire Shops
Hurdle, 1985 Champion Hurdle, 1986
Oteley Hurdle, Champion Hurdle, 1987
De Vere Hotels Hurdle, Champion
Hurdle; 2nd 1984 Triumph Hurdle

Why we love him As one of the five
horses to win the Champion Hurdle
three times, See You Then might have
been expected to rank more highly in
this survey, but he ran so seldom (only
twice in his last championship season)
that he acquired the disparaging
nickname 'See You When'. The reason
for his status as an invisible champion
was his fragile legs, and his trainer did
wonders to nurse him effectively for so
long. The fact that he raced in a non-
vintage era for hurdlers also prevented
his becoming a public favourite. He
was lucky that Browne's Gazette
presented him with his first Champion
Hurdle, but he won the next two
renewals of the race on merit thanks to
a turn of foot consistent with his
Classic pedigree, and he was a worthy
champion. If only he had been more
robust. **JR**

See You Then (Steve Smith Eccles) jumps the last in the 1985 Champion Hurdle

99
Norton's Coin

Chestnut gelding foaled 1981
Mount Cassino - Grove Chance

Owner-trainer Sirrell Griffiths **Jockeys** Graham McCourt (Richard Dunwoody) **Record (jumps)** 6 wins from 32 starts

Career highlights Won 1989 South Wales Showers Silver Trophy, 1990 Cheltenham Gold Cup, 1991 South Wales Showers Silver Trophy

Why we love him Everyone loves an underdog and there haven't been many bigger than Norton's Coin, who earned his place in racing folklore when producing the biggest upset in Gold Cup history with 100-1 success in 1990. With the odds-on Desert Orchid having finished only third, the front-page headline in the following day's *Racing Post* hailed the result as the "Shock of the century!" The gelding's humble antecedents lent his Cheltenham victory a fairytale air. His trainer Sirrell Griffiths was a bald 50-year-old Welsh farmer who handled just three horses under permit and, despite his weighing in at 15st 7lb, rode Norton's Coin out every morning after milking his cattle. Explaining the secret of the gelding's success, Griffiths pointed to some unusual stablemates. "The chickens used to perch on his back in his box and their company helped build up his confidence," he explained. You couldn't make it up. **NG**

Norton's Coin (Graham McCourt) en route to the biggest Gold Cup shock in history

100
Bula

Brown gelding foaled 1965
Raincheck - Pongo's Fancy

Owner Bill Edwards-Heathcote **Trainer** Fred Winter
Jockeys Paul Kelleway, John Francome (Richard
Pitman) **Record (jumps)** 34 wins from 51 starts

Career highlights Won 1970 Gloucestershire
Hurdle (Div 2), Benson & Hedges Hurdle, 1971
Champion Hurdle, Welsh Champion Hurdle,
Ackermann Skeaping Trophy, 1972 Champion Hurdle,
Cheltenham Trial Hurdle, 1973 Black & White Whisky
Gold Cup, 1975 Blue Circle Cement Chase, 1976
Gainsborough Chase

Why we love him A remarkably consistent, versatile
and durable jumper, this great champion was in the
top flight for each of his eight seasons and carried the
flag for the Winter stable throughout its golden years
at the top of the sport. Bula's superb turn of foot
enabled him to win his first 13 races, notably when
dethroning Persian War to notch the first of his two
wide-margin Champion Hurdle victories, and the fact
that he was usually held up for a powerful late run
enhanced the drama of his appearances. With a little
more luck he might have become the first to complete
the Champion Hurdle–Gold Cup double, for in the
latter event he finished third on impossibly heavy
ground in 1975 and started favourite the following
year. There was universal sadness when the injuries
he sustained at Cheltenham in 1977 proved fatal. **JR**

Bula (Paul Kelleway) over the last flight in the 1971 Champion Hurdle

the α-z of nominees

A TOTAL of 967 horses received at least one third-place vote in our ballot to identify racing's favourite horse. Various other figures were mentioned at the time. They were inaccurate; a final count-up ahead of this book produced what we hope is the correct figure.

Here we name every one of them, grouped by letter in descending order depending on how many votes they received. Thus, among horses beginning with the letter 'A', Arkle received more votes than Aldaniti, who in turn bettered Ardross and so on.

Horses beginning with the same letter with the same number of votes are named in alphabetical order. Thus, among the 'A's, although Atours, Avalanche and Avro Anson each received just one third-choice vote, Atours's name appears before Avalanche, and the latter appears before Avro Anson.

Although some of the horses named here were ineligible for the poll, in that they never raced in either Britain or Ireland, they are all named in this comprehensive list of horses who received votes.

a

Arkle, Aldaniti, Ardross, Amrullah, Arazi, Alamshar, Alderbrook, Alverton, Audacter, Anaglogs Daughter, Alexander Banquet, Alleged, Ajdal, Arctic Owl, African Chimes, Alsina, American Cousin, American Swinger, Andrew's First, Annie Cares, Aquarius, Ask Tom, Atavus, Acatenango, Airborne, Airwave, Alborada, Amberleigh House, Aramram, Attivo, Adobe, Affirmed, Alakdar, Allinson's Mate, Al Moulouki, Alycidon, Among Dreams, Anglo, Armida, Astral Charmer, Atours, Avalanche, Avro Anson (43)

b

Brigadier Gerard, Best Mate, Burrough Hill Lad, Birds Nest, Baracouda, Bula, Bosra Sham, Barton Bank, Behrajan, Bradbury Star, Brown Lad, Balanchine, Buona notte, Benny The Dip, Bregawn, Bindaree, Badsworth Boy, Be Friendly, Barnbrook Again, Bonanza Boy, Barathea, Baronet, Beat Hollow, Beef Or Salmon, Barton, Brother Joe, Bachelor's Hall, Borgia, Bond Boy, Baulking Green, Ben Nevis, Banks Hill, Baron Allfours, Baron Blakeney, Bean Dreams, Beau, Belljinks, Be My Native, Blakeney, Blowing Wind, Blue Reef, Bob, Bobby Socks, Bolkonski, Branston Abby, Brown Jack, Bruni,

Burlington Boy, Ballymoss, Banbury, Barbason, Bassenhally, Be Hopeful, Belmez, Bengal Boy, Bertie Wooster, Better Times Ahead, Big Brown Bear, Blue Charm, Blue Velvet, Bobby Grant, Bob Major, Boom Docker, Border Incident, Brevity, Brondesbury, Babodana, Back In Front, Balthus, Bannow Bay, Bartlemy Boy, Bash Street Kid, Beech Road, Bells Life, Berge, Biloxi Blues, Bionic, Bishops Court, Black Baize, Black Secret, Blazing Walker, Blueberry King, Bobbyjo, Boldboy, Bollin Eric, Brave Highlander, Brown Chamberlin, Buck House, Busted (89)

c

Crisp, Captain Christy, Corbiere, Carvill's Hill, Chaplins Club, Celtic Swing, Comedy Of Errors, Commander In Chief, Chief Singer, Colonist, Commanche Court, Cool Dawn, Cool Ground, Cyfor Malta, Cadeaux Genereux, Cavalero, Central Park, Charlie Potheen, Combs Ditch, Commanche Run, Cap Juluca, Captain's Treasure, Carib Royal, Cartwright, Caunton, Celestial Choir, Champagne Prince, Chief's Song, Chickawicka, Choisty, Chorus, Classic Millennium, Clay County, Cloudwalker, Commander Collins, Country Retreat, Cahervillahow, Cantoris, Captain O'Neill, Call Collect, Cheeney Basin, Chesham Squire, Claptrap, Cosmo Jack, Credo's Daughter, Crepello, Crimson Embers,

Camus, Captain Moonlight, Carrickbeg, Carry On Katie, Cenkos, Charlottown, Cherry Kind, Chicmond, Choisir, Chovey Down, Chrysaor, Cider Apple, Cigar, Cinnamon Court, Clever Folly, Colt Bridge, Connaught Ranger, Cormorant Wood, Cornish Rebel, Cottstown Boy, Coulton, Crash Course, Crusoe, Culture Vulture, Cyborgo (72)

d

Desert Orchid, Dancing Brave, Dawn Run, Danoli, Dubai Millennium, Double Trigger, Daylami, Dayjur, Dorans Pride, Deano's Beeno, Detention, Direct Route, Dublin Flyer, Dunkirk, Dahlia, Dalakhani, Davy Lad, Diamond Edge, Dizzy, Docklands Express, Dramatist, Dubai Destination, Danakil, Dee Ell, Delmoss, Diamond Way, Double Blue, Dom Samourai, Dr Devious, Dromhale Lady, Duke Of Milan, Dundonald, Deadly Dudley, Deep Sensation, Diminuendo, Don Puccini, Don't Forget Me, Double Splendour, Durham Edition, Daring Destiny, Derring Valley, Diplomatist, Dispol Evita, Double Dash, Double Thriller, Dunfermline (46)

e

Edredon Bleu, El Gran Senor, Earth Summit, Ei Ei, Ekbalco, Easter Ogil, Erhaab, Ezzoud, Eclipse, Ellens Lad,

En Vacances, Escalus, El Viejo, Epervier Bleu, Escartefigue, Even Keel, Ebony Jane, Eimear's Pride, Elmhurst, Enzeli (20)

f

Falbrav, Florida Pearl, Further Flight, Flagship Uberalles, Flyingbolt, French Holly, Fantastic Light, Foinavon, Floyd, Forgive'N Forget, Flakey Dove, Fujiyama Crest, Freddie, Fruits Of Love, Flying Ace, Flying Wild, Fly To The End, Fort Devon, Frederick James, Frenchman's Cove, Fylde Flyer, Fabulous, Far Too Young, First Gold, Flaked Oats, Flaming East, Folly Road, Fabroy, Fadalko, Fasliyev, Father Hayes, Father Krismas, Federal Trooper, Final Deed, First Island, Flashing Steel, Flint River, Florida Coast, Fredcoteri, Fred The Tread (40)

g

Giant's Causeway, Grundy, Galileo, Generous, Golden Miller, Go Ballistic, Gunner B, Golden Cygnet, Garrison Savannah, Gloria Victis, Grand Lodge, Green Green Desert, Galcador, Garliestown, Gay Spartan, Germano, Get Real, Gilderdale, Glint Of Gold, Go Red, Gralmano, Greenwich Bambi, Grey Desire, Grey Kingdom, Gymcrak Premiere, Galmoy, Gaye Brief, Gay Trip, Gee-A, General Bunching, Golden Fleece, Grandera, Gypsy Castle, Gali, Gallant Buck, Gallows Corner, Gay Kildare, General Wolfe, Glanford Brigg, Golan, Golden Fire, Golden Panda, Gossamer, Green 'N' Gold, Grey Power, Grundy Lane, Gunther McBride (47)

h

High Chaparral, Hawk Wing, Hatton's Grace, Hopscotch, Hard To Figure, Hyperion, Halling, Hasta La Vista, Heighlin, Highborn, Hugs Dancer, Harmonic Way, Happy Victorious, Hard Frost, Hardi Guichois, Harry Flatman, Hatoof, Hallo Dandy, High Estate, High Grade, High Line, Hotcallie Legend, Humorist, Hurricane Lamp, Hurricane Floyd, Helissio, High Edge Grey, Highflying, Hit The

Deck, Holy Orders, Honey Trap, Hamers Flame, Harbour Pilot, Hethersett, Hever Golf Rose, Hey Cottage, H Harrison, Horsford Henry, Hors La Loi, How's The Boss (40)

i

Istabraq, In The Groove, Islington, I Cried For You, Ibn Bey, Indian Skimmer, Ice Cracker, Imperial Call, Irish Fashion, Its A Snip, Ile de Bourbon, Indian Yeldah, Ivor's Flutter, Idris, Ile de Chypre, I'm A Driver, Imagine, I'm Happy, Iran Scam, Iris Royal, Iris's Gift, Italian Symphony, Ivory's Grab Hire (23)

j

Jodami, Just So, Johannesburg, Jair du Cochet, Joveworth, Jalmood, John Jacques, Jacmar, Jamaican Flight, Jo Mell, Jamesmead, Jawani, Just James, Just Martin (14)

k

Katy Nowaitee, Kris, Katabatic, Knockroe, Kris Kin, Kahyasi, Killiney, Kincsem, Kribensis, Kingscliff, Klairon Davis, Kyllachy, Kildimo, King's Best, Kalanisi, Kalaglow, Kent, Kif Kif, Kilbrittain Castle, Kind Emperor, King's Fountain, Knock Knock, Kadastrof, Karinska, Katies, Kelso, Kerstin, Kings Rhapsody, Knock Hard, Killeshin, Killick, King Flyer, King Of Kings, Kinoko, Kybo (35)

l

Lochsong, Lammtarra, Limestone Lad, L'Escargot, Lady Rebecca, Looks Like Trouble, Lyric Fantasy, Lanzarote, Lean Ar Aghaidh, Large Action, Lady Cricket, Lakota Brave, Lift And Load, Le Garcon d'Or, Love Legend, Lygeton Lad, Lord Gyllene, Lake Verdi, Land Afar, Latalomne, Laurel Queen, Le Pretendant, Loppylugs, Loving Words, Lucedeo, Lady McNair, Lalindi, Lear Spear, Lemon Souffle, Lennox, Lumiere d'Espoire, Lunar Leo, Lacson,

Lambourn Raja, Land Lark, Ledham, Listen Timmy, Little Polveir, Livius, Lord Of The Turf, Luso (41)

m

Mill Reef, Moorcroft Boy, Mill House, Mtoto, Montjeu, Monksfield, Mysilv, Moscow Flyer, Morley Street, Miesque, Mr Frisk, Mandarin, Monty's Pass, Monsignor, Micko's Dream, Master Oats, Morse, Make A Stand, Mac Vidi, Maylane, Mellottie, Marling, Martha's Son, Mole Board, Mighty Mogul, Misternando, Maori Venture, Mister Baileys, Morston, Mitcham, Marwell, Mr Mulligan, Miinnehoma, Milk It Mick, Madam Gay, Manor Mieo, Marlborough, Mayotte, McGillycuddy Reeks, Mehmaas, Midnight Court, Mighty Fine, Mister Ed, Moonax, Mr Cool, Mr What, Mudahim, Mumuqa, Muse, Madame Jones, Majestic Bay, Mandalay Prince, Marabar, Mark Of Esteem, Markree Castle, Mayfair Bill, Moon Ballad, Mutamam, Male-Ana-Mou, Marakabei, Marlingford, Master Butcher, Master Smudge, Media Puzzle, Mind Games, Mighty Marine, Mischievous Jack, Miss Assertive, Miss Orchestra, Monsieur Le Cure, Morton The Hatter, Mr Snaggle, Mr Streaky, Mujahid, My Henry, Mystiko (76)

n

Nijinsky, Night Nurse, Nashwan, Norton's Coin, Noddy's Ryde, Nayef, Northern Dancer, Nice One Clare, Nickel Coin, New Seeker, Nick Dundee, Nearco, New Colonist, New Halen, Nick The Brief, Night City, Noholme, Norse Dancer, Nasrullah, Native Upmanship, Nearly An Eye, Night Dance, Nureyev, Nagnagnag, Niche, Nineofus, Noble Locks, Nobody's Sweetheart, Nobody Told Me, No Submission (30)

o

One Man, Oh So Sharp, Ormonde, Out Of The Gloom, O I Oyston, On The House, Otter Way, One For Me, Out Line, Observe, Ocean Link, Old

the a-z of **nominees**

Vic, Olivia Grace, Olveston, On Edge, Operatic Society (16)

p

Persian Punch, Pebbles, Persian War, Pendil, Petite Etoile, Pilsudski, Phantom Turtle, Pentire, Papillon, Pearlyman, Party Politics, Peintre Celebre, Playschool, Pretty Polly, Pinza, Pas Seul, Peaty Sandy, Prospectors Cove, Pegwell Bay, Provideo, Panto Prince, Poppy Carew, Pagan Prince, Painted Warrior, Pedro Jack, Perryston View, Pretty Young Thing, Proud Sun, Psidium, Paris Pike, Pasternak, Persian Bold, Peruvian Chief, Pipalong, Plausible, Plum Jam, Posse, Pridwell, Prince Regent, Prow, Palacegate Touch, Pappageno's Cottage, Park Top, Petit Palais, Pontenuovo, Princeful, Professor Plum, Proud Native, Prominent, Proud Tarquin (50)

q

Quixall Crossett, Quito, Qattara, Queen's Logic (4)

r

Red Rum, Rock Of Gibraltar, Rooster Booster, Ribot, Reference Point, Rondetto, Remittance Man, Rough Quest, Red Marauder, Relkeel, Rhyme 'N' Reason, Royal Palace, Rainbow Quest, Running Stag, Ridgewood Pearl, Red Alligator, Run And Skip, Rheingold, Royal Academy, Royal Gait, Rince Ri, Risk Of Thunder, Raffingora, Rodrigo de Triano, Rock Hopper, Rhinestone Cowboy, Ragusa, Raymylette, Right Job, Ringmoor Down, Rith Dubh, Roberto, Round Robin, Royal Athlete, Royal Flush, Royal Judgement, Rabble Rouser, Rathbawn Prince, Red Robbo, Redundant Pal, Red Wine, Repertory, Repton, Revenge, Right Tack, River Bay, River North, Robellino, Rockforce, Royal Anthem, Royal Applause, Run Over, Rag Trade, Rambo's Hall, Rami, Rapscallion, Rex To The Rescue, Rev Counter, Rob Leach, Rock Roi, Roi Estate, Roman Dawn,

Romney, Royal Rebel, Ryalux (65)

s

Sea Pigeon, See More Business, Shergar, Sea-Bird, Sinndar, Silver Buck, Sir Ivor, Strong Promise, Singspiel, Spanish Steps, See You Then, Star Rage, Sadler's Wells, Sakhee, Sabin du Loir, Spindrifter, Soba, Salsabil, Suny Bay, Shahrastani, Sprowston Boy, Santa Claus, Swain, Stormez, Silver Patriarch, Senor El Betrutti, Sceptre, Stalbridge Colonist, Sir Harry Lewis, Sonny Somers, Salse, Silver Wedge, Spartan Missile, Seagram, Strong Flow, Soviet Song, Samlee, Sabrehill, Sir Ken, Sandy Lady, Saxon King, Scimitarra, Scallywag, Schwartzhalle, Scots Grey, Sea Spice, Shady Deal, Shujan, Silver Fling, Sir Desmond, Sky Quest, Solerina, Silver Grey Lady, Son Of Sharp Shot, Sparky Gayle, Star Appeal, Stearsby, Sugarfoot, Sugar Palm, Sultana, Sundew, Supermaster, Susarma, Swift Silver, Sabaki River, Sagaro, Sandy Abbot, Saphila, Sausalito Bay, Sausalito Boy, Selhurstpark Flyer, Shannon Spray, Silly Season, Simply Dashing, Skara Brae, Slick Cherry, Snurge, So Careful, Sovereign Bill, Space Agent, Spectroscope, Stanerra, Stravinsky, Stormyfairweather, Stromness, Summer Recluse, Summerville, Saifan, Sandhurst Prince, Saxon Farm, Sayyedati, Scottish Memories, Shackle Pin, Siege Perilous, Silver God, Six Perfections, Skipping Tim, Slap Shot, Slip Anchor, Sneak Preview, Snow Ridge, Sounds Cool, Stormy Passage, Stray Harmony, Superfine, Superlative, Sweet Charmer (107)

t

Tingle Creek, Triptych, The Dikler, Time Charter, The Minstrel, Troy, The Fellow, Teeton Mill, Terimon, Top Cees, Tulyar, Tied Cottage, Titus Oates, Trelawney, Taufan Boy, Ten Plus, Trainglot, The Last Fling, The Pilgarlic, The Laird, The Thinker, Toto Toscato, Traverse, Treble Bob, Twin Oaks, Tap On Wood, Tawafij, Tawny Way, Tedburrow, Thornton Gate, Topsham Bay, Toulouse Lautrec, The

Calvados Kid, The Wiley Kalmuck, They All Forgot Me, Three Star, Travel Mystery, Tristan, True Lad, Tudor Minstrel, Turn-to, Typhoon Ginger, Teleprompter, Theatreworld, The Awkward Horse, The Elk, The Little Ferret, The Next Waltz, Therealbandit, The Tystan, Tillerman, Tomahawk, Trade Dispute, Tree Poppy, Tropical Lake, Trillium (56)

u

User Friendly, Ubedizzy, Ultra Bandem, Urgent Request (4)

v

Viking Flagship, Vinnie Roe, Vintage Crop, Vaguely Noble, Venn Ottery, Vilprano, Vindaloo, Vakil-ul-Mulk, Volant, Very Promising, Vintage Tipple, Vodkatini (12)

w

Wayward Lad, West Tip, What's Up Boys, Willsford, Willie Wumpkins, Warning, Wollow, Waterloo Boy, Wingspan, Walnut Wonder, Walter Plunge, Wave Of Optimism, Wave Rock, Well To Do, What A Buck, Winter Fair, Wither Or Which, Welsh Lion, What A Myth, Whereareyounow, Whitechapel, White Heart, White Muzzle, Windward Ariom, Winnie The Witch, Woodford Gale, Woodland Nymph, Wonder Man (28)

x

(0)

y

Young Hustler, Young Kenny, Yavana's Pace, Yangtse-Kiang, Yeats, Young Spartacus, Yorkshire Gale (7)

z

Zafonic, Zagreb (2)

the **favourites of 2004**: there but for the grace of a few months . . .

IF a week is a long time in politics, then a year must be eternity. It is certainly a long enough time in horseracing: if the 100 Favourite Racehorses poll had taken place 12 months later, we might have found some quite different results.

No doubt Arkle, Desert Orchid and Red Rum would still have been returned the 1-2-3. But Best Mate (below) would surely have made the top ten if the vote had taken place after, and not before, his third Gold Cup success, while, lower down the scale, Moscow Flyer would probably have featured higher than 59.

There are other horses who missed out altogether who might have made the list if a few more months had passed. Taking high rank among them must be Vinnie Roe, close to making the original 100 even before strengthening his claims on the public's hearts with a remarkable fourth consecutive victory in the Irish St Leger, in September 2004, and then finishing runner-up in the Melbourne Cup. Ouija Board, who scooped a handful of Horse of the Year awards at the end of 2004, had not made her name at the time of the poll, while Attraction, though a champion two-year-old in 2003, had similarly yet to cast her spell.

In the next few pages, we feature a handful of horses who missed out – but probably wouldn't have done if the poll had been held at the end of 2004 instead of at the start.

Amberleigh House (Graham Lee) on the way to winning the Grand National

Amberleigh House

Brown gelding foaled 1992
Buckskin - Chancy Gal

Owner Halewood International Ltd **Trainers** Ginger McCain (Michael Hourigan) **Jockeys** Graham Lee (Warren Marston, Paul Hourigan) **Record (jumps)** 9 wins from 62 starts

Career highlights Won 2000 Kinloch Brae Chase, Emo Oil Handicap Chase, 2001 Becher Chase, 2004 Grand National; 2nd 2002 Becher Chase, 2003 Becher Chase; 3rd 2003 Grand National

Why we love him For one reason, and one reason only – his fairytale victory in the 2004 Grand National for Ginger McCain, the trainer dubbed 'Mr Aintree' after his exploits with the legendary Red Rum. Amberleigh House earned his own lasting place in racing folklore when defying advancing years for an emotionally charged success in the world's most famous steeplechase, 27 years after his illustrious predecessor's third win in the race. With barely a dry eye in the house, McCain said: "I'm just an old, broken-down taxi driver who got lucky in the National – again." Amberleigh House has become one of those Aintree specialists loved by the public, a regular over the big fences whose record bears close inspection. At the time of writing, a tilt at the 2005 National was beckoning – at the age of 13. **NG**

Attraction

Bay filly foaled 2001
Efisio - Flirtation
Owner The 10th Duke of Roxburghe **Trainer** Mark Johnston **Jockey** Kevin Darley **Record (Flat)** 9 wins from 12 starts

Career highlights Won 2003 Queen Mary Stakes, Cherry Hinton Stakes, 2004 1,000 Guineas, Irish 1,000 Guineas, Coronation Stakes, Sun Chariot Stakes; 2nd Falmouth Stakes, Matron Stakes

Why we love her Attraction earned the utmost respect in 2004 when becoming the first filly in history to complete the English-Irish Guineas double, then routing her opposition at Royal Ascot and adding another Group 1 event to her tally in the autumn. But while she is an outstanding filly – you don't win four Group 1 events in a single season if you're anything less, and she was invincible against her age and gender – there were other reasons why she gained such a special place in the public's affections. Attraction endeared herself with a bold, front-running style of racing allied to seemingly boundless reserves of courage and tenacity. With forelegs splayed out sideways and the most ungainly of gallops, Attraction was by no means the most attractive of fillies in terms of looks – or indeed pedigree, for that matter. If anything, that only added to her popularity, for alongside her relatively humble antecedents came a heart the size of a house. **NG**

Attraction (Kevin Darley) adds the Coronation Stakes at Royal Ascot to two Classic wins

Azertyuiop (Ruby Walsh) jumps the last before winning the Champion Chase

Azertyuiop

Bay gelding foaled 1997
Baby Turk - Temara
Owner John Hales **Trainers** Paul Nicholls
(Guillaume Macaire) **Jockeys** Ruby Walsh
(Timmy Murphy, Adrian Maguire) **Record**
(jumps) 10 wins from 19 starts

Career highlights Won 2001 Kingwell
Hurdle, Elite Hurdle, 2002 November
Novices' Chase, 2003 Arkle Trophy, 2004
Game Spirit Chase, Queen Mother
Champion Chase, Haldon Gold Cup; 2nd
2003 Tingle Creek Chase, 2004 Victor
Chandler Chase, Tingle Creek Chase; 3rd
2004 King George VI Chase

Why we love him There aren't many
sights as thrilling as a top two-mile chaser
hurtling round the track, and few in recent
years have graced the division like
Azertyuiop, the ex-French jumper with the
near-unpronounceable name. A talented
hurdler, he found his true calling when
sent over fences, evincing speed and agility
in a manner reminiscent of a sports car on
cruise control. Azertyuiop pointedly
demonstrated his class in a pair of zestful
victories at the Festival in 2003 and 2004,
while his courage was there for all to see
when he narrowly failed to give stacks of
weight away to Isio in a pulsating finish to
the Victor Chandler Chase. Having said
that, his nine-length Champion Chase
success was achieved only after chief rival
Moscow Flyer unseated his rider four out,
and Azertyuiop's crown was slightly
tarnished in the first half of 2004/05 when
that outstanding Irish performer gained
the second of two convincing victories over
him in the Tingle Creek. **NG**

Ouija Board (Kieren Fallon) wins the Breeders' Cup Filly & Mare Turf in Texas

Ouija Board

Bay filly foaled 2001
Cape Cross - Selection Board

Owner 19th Earl of Derby **Trainer** Ed Dunlop **Jockey** Kieren Fallon **Record (Flat)** 5 wins from 8 starts

Career highlights Won 2004 Pretty Polly Stakes (Newmarket), Oaks, Irish Oaks, Breeders' Cup Filly & Mare Turf; 3rd 2004 Prix de l'Arc de Triomphe

Why we love her Fillies largely outshone their male counterparts on the Flat in 2004, and foremost among them was Ouija Board, the only member of a one-horse string sporting the famous colours of a popular aristocratic owner, one of whose forebears gave his name to Britain's premier Classic. Ouija Board earned her own place in history with a resounding victory in the Oaks that was followed up five weeks later in the Irish equivalent. But it was in the autumn that she etched her name indelibly on our hearts, specifically when crushing her rivals at the Breeders' Cup. The Americans treated her like a superstar and she ran like one. Ouija Board won a handful of end-of-season gongs – an Eclipse award in the States, and was named Horse of the Year by *Racing Post* readers, the BHB and at the Cartier awards. **NG**

Solerina (Gary Hutchinson) en route to victory at Navan in November 2004

Solerina

Bay mare foaled 1997
Toulon - Deep Peace
Owner John Bowe **Trainer** James Bowe
Jockeys Gary Hutchinson (Paul
Carberry) **Record (jumps)** 15 wins
from 25 starts

Career highlights Won 2002 Future
Champions Novice Hurdle, 2003 Golden
Cygnet Novice Hurdle, Deloitte and
Touche Novice Hurdle, Hatton's Grace
Hurdle, Tara Hurdle, 2004 Bank of
Ireland Hurdle, John James McManus
Memorial Hurdle, Lismullen Hurdle, Tara
Hurdle; 2nd 2004 Irish Cesarewitch

Why we love her How could we do
anything but love Solerina, a totally
admirable mare from a near-identical
mould to her esteemed stablemate
Limestone Lad, who has done so much
to put his tiny stable in the spotlight in
recent seasons. The similarities between
the pair are uncanny. Like Limestone
Lad, Solerina is a tough front-runner,
both prolific and versatile. Indefatigable
almost to a fault, she thrives on her
racing, having run seemingly every other
week since her debut in 2002 at a
variety of trips, winning a string of good
races in Ireland from two miles to three
miles. That's not all, either. As if she had
not done enough already over jumps,
she was tried on the Flat in 2004, a
move that brought a couple of victories
and second place in the Irish
Cesarewitch! **NG**

Soviet Song (Johnny Murtagh) beats Attraction in the Falmouth Stakes in July 2004

Soviet Song

Bay filly foaled 2000
Marju - Kalinka
Owner Elite Racing Club **Trainer** James Fanshawe
Jockeys Johnny Murtagh (Oscar Urbina) **Record (Flat)**
7 wins from 15 starts

Career highlights Won 2002 Ascot Fillies' Mile, 2004
Falmouth Stakes, Sussex Stakes, Matron Stakes,
Ridgewood Pearl Stakes; 2nd 2003 Coronation Stakes,
2004 Queen Anne Stakes

Why we love her Soviet Song, a top two-year-old filly,
returned to her best in 2004 when her two clashes with
Attraction were among the highlights of the summer.
Attraction's customary fondness for making the running
meant that to some extent she was a sitting duck
against Soviet Song and the latter's decisive finishing
burst twice saw off the people's favourite, convincingly
at Newmarket in the Falmouth and then a shade cheekily
at Leopardstown in the Matron. Also scoring in between
in the Sussex Stakes, when she beat some of the best
mile colts in training, Soviet Song has won four times
altogether in the top grade, much to the delight of her
15,000-strong owners, the Elite Racing Club. If the poll
had been held a few months later, their votes alone
would have ensured high rank for her. **NG**

Vinnie Roe (Pat Smullen) wins at Leopardstown in August 2002

Vinnie Roe

Bay/brown horse foaled 1998
Definite Article - Kayu
Owner Jim Sheridan **Trainer** Dermot Weld **Jockey** Pat
Smullen **Record (Flat)** 12 wins from 24 starts

Career highlights Won 2001 Irish St Leger, Prix Royal-Oak,
2002 Irish St Leger, 2003 Irish St Leger, 2004 Irish St Leger;
2nd 2002 Ascot Gold Cup, 2004 Melbourne Cup

Why we love him A high-class performer over a number of
seasons, Vinnie Roe emerged as the most popular horse in
training on the Flat in Ireland at the time of the poll in
February 2004, only just missing out on making the Top 100
proper. But although he scored just a single victory in the
campaign that followed, that alone would probably have
been enough to justify his inclusion as it was the fourth year
in succession that he had landed the Irish St Leger, a Classic
he has made his own. Connections wondered if advancing
years had blunted his speed, but a memorable victory was in
no doubt from the moment he was produced to challenge
powerfully two furlongs out. Subsequently he came close to
embellishing Dermot Weld's fantastic record in the
Melbourne Cup when finishing a superb second to the locally
trained favourite Makybe Diva. **NG**

how they voted in the **ultimate poll**
by Nicholas Godfrey

AS IT usually was on the racecourse, Arkle's victory in the *Racing Post* poll to identify the 100 favourite racehorses of all time in Britain and Ireland was emphatic.

The question was not which horse readers considered to be the greatest in the history of racing; rather, they were asked to vote for their personal favourites. In the end, though, it made no difference. The steeplechaser universally regarded as the greatest ever is also the best-loved.

It was a long, hard battle, but there could be only one winner, and it was the horse known to many simply as 'Himself'. After eight weeks of voting that started at Christmas 2003, Arkle was voted racing's favourite horse, the most popular in the history of the sport in Britain and Ireland, with 21.9 per cent of the vote.

Readers had been asked to choose between the ten horses who polled the highest in an initial vote that identified the top 100. They were given two weeks to vote on the top ten, by telephone, email or on the *Racing Post* website. Although the first round of voting had produced a varied list, the top-ten ballot started with four horses – the quartet who eventually filled the top four places in the final poll – forming a breakaway group. While bookmakers made Desert Orchid the odds-on favourite, it was immediately obvious there would be no clear-cut winner. Istabraq's challenge faltered

at the halfway stage, at which point Arkle was just nosing ahead of Red Rum, with Desert Orchid in third. It was a lead he maintained, mainly via the phone poll as the great grey actually topped both the email and internet ballot.

Strangely, the second week's voting was more concentrated between the two principals, but Desert Orchid could make no inroads into Arkle's lead, although he passed Red Rum for second. In the end, Desert Orchid polled 19.1 per cent of the vote, still nearly three per cent adrift of the winner.

Arkle's nonpareil status is all the more marked considering that he finished racing in 1966, which means that you needed to be in your late 40s to remember seeing him live. March 2004 marked the 40th anniversary of his first Gold Cup, when he beat the much-revered Mill House (himself No.30 in this poll); the event was celebrated in entirely appropriate fashion when modern-day chasing king Best Mate emulated his feat by winning his third in a row.

To win what was in effect a popularity contest so many years after retirement amply demonstrated the enormous affection in which Arkle is still held. His groom Johnny Lumley was delighted with the news. "His fame has never faded, which is quite remarkable after all these years," he said.

Flyingbolt: often described as second-best chaser of all time

how they voted in the **ultimate poll**

"People ask me about him all the time, wanting to know about his character. Who'd have thought a horse would come out top in a vote almost 40 years after he last ran?"

Desert Orchid, unquestionably the most popular horse ever trained in Britain, got closest to Arkle, but even the support of one in five voters was not enough.

One man who was far from surprised, and certainly not despondent at coming second, was the grey legend's trainer David Elsworth. "I must admit, I did have a serious bet on Arkle because I reckoned there would be a massive patriotic vote from Ireland," he said, speaking just after the result was announced. "Finishing runner-up to Arkle is a huge honour, be it in a race or in a poll such as this, which, I know, has given people lots of fun and entertainment."

Next in the poll with 13.6 per cent of the vote was Red Rum, the horse who earned a place in the nation's hearts with his barely credible record on the sport's biggest stage.

If Arkle was 'Himself' and Desert Orchid was 'Dessie', then Red Rum was simply 'Rummy'. His trainer Ginger McCain was not overjoyed to learn the Aintree legend had finished 'only' third. "I thought Red Rum would finish second to Arkle, not third," said McCain, who, remarkably, saddled another Grand National winner in Amberleigh House just a few weeks after the conclusion of the poll.

"I don't mean to be disrespectful because Desert Orchid was a grand chaser, but would he have pulled in crowds of 10,000 or more, as was the case when Red Rum appeared at Southport Town Hall? This was a popularity poll, and our horse had more charisma than Desert Orchid – when Red Rum died, he was on the front of every national newspaper apart from the *Financial Times*!"

Arkle, Desert Orchid and Red Rum were the only horses to reach double figures in percentage terms in the final vote, in which triple Champion Hurdle winner Istabraq took fourth with 8.9 per cent. In fifth came Brigadier Gerard, making him the most popular Flat horse of all time.

Looking at the top 100 list in its entirety, there are several statistics that the reader may find interesting:

○ It contains 58 jumpers compared to 42 Flat-racers. Sea Pigeon and Hatton's Grace are adjudged to have straddled the divide and contribute a half-point to each section!

○ Five-time Gold Cup winner Golden Miller is the only pre-war horse

○ It includes six greys (Desert Orchid, One Man, Day lami, Further Flight, Rooster Booster and Petite Etoile)

Soba: flying filly only just failed to make the cut

how they voted in the **ultimate poll**

Top 10
Jumpers

1 ARKLE
2 Desert Orchid
3 Red Rum
4 Istabraq
5 One Man
6 Sea Pigeon
7 Dawn Run
8 See More Business
9 Best Mate
10 Wayward Lad

Top 10
Irish-trained

1 ARKLE
2 Istabraq
3 Nijinsky
4 Dawn Run
5 Giant's Causeway
6 Danoli
7 Rock Of Gibraltar
8 Florida Pearl
9 High Chaparral
10 Limestone Lad

Top 10
Still racing at time of poll

1 PERSIAN PUNCH
2 Best Mate
3 Florida Pearl
4 Limestone Lad
5 Edredon Bleu
6 Rooster Booster
7 Moscow Flyer
8 Flagship Uberalles
9 Baracouda
10 Deano's Beeno

Share of the vote

1 ARKLE	21.9%
2 Desert Orchid	19.1%
3 Red Rum	13.6%
4 Istabraq	8.9%
5 Brigadier Gerard	8.2%
6 One Man	8.0%
7 Persian Punch	5.7%
8 Dancing Brave	5.5%
9 Sea Pigeon	5.4%
10 Nijinsky	3.7%

Top 10
Fillies and mares

1 DAWN RUN
2 Lochsong
3 Pebbles
4 Triptych
5 Mysilv
6 Petite Etoile
7 Miesque
8 Lady Rebecca
9 Time Charter
10 Katy Nowaitee

Top 10
Flat horses

1 BRIGADIER GERARD
2 Persian Punch
3 Dancing Brave
4 Nijinsky
5 Mill Reef
6 Giant's Causeway
7 Shergar
8 Nashwan
9 Lochsong
10 Dubai Millennium
Sea Pigeon omitted

how they voted in the **ultimate poll**

○ At the time the final poll was published in February 2003, it featured nine horses who were still in training, with Persian Punch achieving the highest position at seven

○ No.1 horse Arkle was one of 23 Irish-trained horses in the list, compared to 68 (and a half) from Britain

○ Ireland also provided the highest-placed filly or mare in Dawn Run at No.11, one of ten of her sex to make the list

○ Lammtarra had fewest races (four)

○ Ribot and Lammtarra were the only unbeaten horses

Although you probably could have guessed those at the very top of the list of 100 favourite racehorses, there were still names to raise the odd eyebrow lower down, among them Moorcroft Boy at No.20. His high rank owes everything to his status as the flagship of the racehorse rehabilitation centre that bears his name, while the retirement of See More Business (No.12) midway through the poll and the unforgettable King George win of Edredon Bleu (No.42) at its start probably did no harm to their respective causes. Lower down, Amrullah actually managed to come home in front for the first time in his life, winning the battle of the nearly useless by making the charts at No.92, leaving that other famous non-

winner Quixall Crossett to fail miserably yet again.

The final list also threw up many anomalies. Recent equine heroes held a clear advantage, which explains why a horse such as Flyingbolt missed out – despite his often being described as the second-best steeplechaser in history behind his stablemate Arkle. Flyingbolt would have made the next ten; ditto star sprinter Soba, unsighted here, but so popular in her heyday.

Top two-mile chasers such as Badsworth Boy and Barnbrook Again, unstoppable in the 1980s, didn't make it either, but Remittance Man and Viking Flagship, of slightly newer vintage, did.

What did Looks Like Trouble (No.73) have to recommend him above other recent Gold Cup winners such as Master Oats or Imperial Call? Why did Galileo make the top 50, yet his old rival Fantastic Light, who had a much longer career, not do so? How come Lammtarra is in the top 30 while Sakhee, a more recent Godolphin star, missed out? And most surprising of all, how on earth did the 2000 Cambridgeshire winner Katy Nowaitee (No.87) get into the top 100?

We don't know. We just counted the votes. Readers had only themselves to blame.

How the top 100 breaks down

JUMPS	58
Flat	42
MALE	90
Female	10
EX-RACEHORSES	91
Still racing at time of poll	9
PRE-WAR	1
Post-war	99
BAY	61.5*
Brown	9.5*
Chestnut	23
Grey	6

Strong Promise was listed as bay or brown

Where they were trained

BRITAIN	68.5*
Ireland	23
France	6.5
Italy	1.5*
UAE	0.5*

Many horses in the list were trained in more than one country; we have used the country in which they were based for their major successes for the purposes of this poll, awarding a half-point when, like Ardross, they achieved notable success from two different national bases

the whiff of scandal **ballot rigging**

by Nicholas Godfrey

THE FIRST vote in the *Racing Post*'s 100 Favourite Racehorses series was registered at just after 9am on December 20, 2003. It went to Dancing Brave.

A couple of thousand more followed, all of them diligently logged before the definitive list was produced. And the high-tech counting machine that kept abreast of all developments ahead of compiling the final chart? That'll be me then. Or rather, me armed with a big pad and a couple of ball-point pens.

I was chief invigilator, vote-counter and returning officer. It was a weighty responsibility – and it did not take long after the opening of the polls for the worrying lessons of history to loom large in my thinking, in particular those offered us by the likes of Bob Nudd, Belle and Sebastian and George W Bush. All of them featured at the centre of alleged vote-rigging scandals, though as we are talking about merely the BBC Sports Personality of the Year (100,000 votes for angler Bob Nudd were thrown out), the Brits best newcomer award (the Scottish popsters won it fair and square, despite Pete Waterman's suggesting otherwise when they defeated the legendary Steps) and the US presidency (ask brother Jeb in Florida), it was not as if any real harm could be done. Certainly, nothing as serious as attempting to rig a public poll designed to identify the 100 most popular racehorses of all time. There was betting on it, for goodness sake.

The rules seemed so simple: one reader, one vote. But close scrutiny suggested that there was more than a hint of the odd attempt to skew the ballot, if not distort it completely.

Every day brought a new potential outrage. If it wasn't that old chancer Amrullah, for whom some votes emanated from suspiciously similar email accounts, then it was the 'Hatton's inquiry' that nearly resulted in disqualification for triple Champion Hurdle winner Hatton's Grace after ten votes were registered, all from people named Mike or Michael, in the space of one Sunday morning. Still, even if the Hatton's Grace vote was a little sexed-up, he still received enough to make the 100. Just.

My colleague Alastair Down went as far as threatening bodily violence to any of his close acquaintances who failed to vote for his old favourite Rondetto; someone called 'Razzer' apologised for hitting his send button a few times too many to vote for Jamie Osborne's Morse; Lammtarra attracted emailed votes from addresses identical but for one letter; Katy Nowaitee seemed to have more fans than any mere Cambridgeshire winner had any right to expect; two votes arrived on the same day on rather nice postcards depicting the works of Monet. They were both for Hugs Dancer, Summitville and Double Trigger. Only one of them was counted.

The Moorcroft Racehorse Welfare Centre's block vote for their hero got him into the top 20, and the same body failed only narrowly to capture a place in the lower reaches of the 100 for Star Rage.

The Jischa family's attempts to do something similar for Austria's finest, Phantom Turtle – eligible because she was once trained in Ireland, she won the 2003 Central European Breeders' Cup Sprint at Kincsem Park, apparently – could not dent the charts. She is, though, "a nice filly, always ready to play a joke on you if you don't have something to eat for her". Or so I was told on making discreet inquiries into how she obtained so many votes.

However, the most suspicious voting pattern of all concerned a mysterious, obviously orchestrated turnout from the Galway area

the whiff of scandal **ballot rigging**

for a Paul Roche-trained maiden hurdler named Detention, a horse of whom I had never heard.

Every vote for this syndicate-owned horse came via email, so I hit the 'reply' button to a couple of them in a bid to find out why Detention had been chosen. The initial response was less than satisfactory – "He showed promise over Christmas on his last run," it read. Fair enough if you are looking for a punt, but your favourite horse ever? Come on now...

Thankfully, 28-year-old accountant Jack Ryan responded to pleas for enlightenment, confessing via email that he knew some of those involved in the syndicate that owns Detention, who, seemingly, has become a cult hero at the University of Galway, where his wife Stephanie is based.

"Me and a good few friends of mine like our betting and our horses," said Ryan. "I'm from a place called Castlegar in Galway and a group of guys I know are involved in the syndicate, all National Hunt enthusiasts. They've had horses previously, all with careers as glittering as Detention!

"However, we don't let results get in the way of fun. So, we take an interest in

Star Rage: star turn at equine welfare centre

the horse and all go down and have a big day out when he runs.

"It has spread amongst our friends and family and that's where the college connection comes in. One of the lads has a brother doing physics there, and he got all his mates to come on the trip to the races and they were hooked, with the result that Detention became part of the social scene. So, when the poll came out, everyone felt that Detention deserved a mention – if not for his Arkle-like ability then at the very least for the contribution he has made to the racecourse bars when he has run and the number of sore heads and missed projects he has caused!"

So it was all down to those wacky students – but, sadly for them, the arcane points system we used worked against Detention. Horses with supporting letters received slightly more than those who did not – Detention's followers were seldom moved to explain their choice – while horses named without a second and third choice, like nearly all of his votes, were also marked down. Detention didn't quite make the cut.

Close, but no cigar, my student friends. Thanks for taking part, though, and better luck next time.

why I voted for
Mill Reef
by Ian Balding

I IMAGINE it is not difficult for anyone to understand why I would vote for Mill Reef as my favourite racehorse. If such a distinguished man as Paul Mellon would like to be remembered more than anything else for being the owner-breeder of Mill Reef, as he once confided to me, then I think I would be more than happy also to be thought of as having been this great horse's trainer.

Mill Reef looked a superstar from the day he arrived at Kingsclere and, amazingly, went on to be just that both as a racehorse and as a stallion. Most Derby winners become favourites, but I suspect that it was only when he became the first English-trained horse for 23 years to win the Prix de l'Arc de Triomphe that he truly sealed his immense popularity with the racing public. That first Sunday of October in 1971 was certainly the most memorable day of my training career.

In my obviously biased opinion, I am still convinced that he is the best all-round Flat horse that I have ever seen – and he is my favourite horse because he possessed every virtue that endears a horse to his trainer.

First of all, he was small in stature and that somehow is always more appealing than a big horse. But he also had enormous courage, as he first showed us in the Prix Robert Papin as a two-year-old when, after various setbacks, he was beaten just a short head by My Swallow.

Two seasons later, he again showed immense bravery in his final race. Then, he held on to win the Coronation Cup, when he was later found to have been suffering from the ghastly respiratory virus rhinopneumonitis at the time.

Finally, and most tellingly, when he broke his near foreleg he demonstrated tremendous guts at many different stages both before and after the crucial operation.

For the whole of the three years he was here in training I cannot recall a single occasion when he looked unwilling to do what we asked of him. Furthermore, he frequently used to lead the string wherever we went, which is something a trainer only ever asks his most sensible horse to do. In the stable he was always kind and amenable and had a wonderful relationship with his lad John Hallum.

However, Mill Reef took so little notice of the fillies that we wondered how he would fare in that respect when he went to the National Stud as a stallion!

It was only after his operation and the pain and discomfort he endured during his recuperation that he became irritable and bad-tempered.

The choice of Arkle as my second favourite is simply because I considered he was the greatest racehorse of all time and feel privileged to have seen him race. He knew it as much as any of his admirers, which I suspect is why he was always known as 'Himself'. His presence in public was regal to say the least.

My third choice is Lochsong because I became as fond of her as of any filly I had in my 39 years as a trainer. She was an amazing character with very much a mind of her own. She became a flying machine, but not until after she had overcome all sorts of leg problems and a mindless trainer who took three years to discover her best distance!

1 Mill Reef **2** Arkle **3** Lochsong

why I voted for
Urgent Request
by Richard Birch

I STILL remember the conversation as if it had taken place yesterday. A November night in 1993 at Wimbledon dogs. Chatting to a fellow greyhound owner, who also had horses with Reg Akehurst.

"I was playing golf with Reg this morning and he told me about this horse he's got. The owner bought it against Reg's advice. Reg was furious. It made a noise; something wrong with it. So he sent it to his vet, who found muck in his lungs. Three days later they galloped it, and the thing took off. Reg says it's a Group horse, and it will win its first handicap next year from here to Billericay. I think he said it was called Urgent Address."

Seven months later, Urgent Request ran in the Northern Dancer Handicap at Epsom. The coup I'd been plotting all winter and all spring; all day and all night.

Urgent Request had 9st 6lb, and Richard Quinn, my favourite jockey, was riding. He was 16-1 in the Pricewise tables after some scare stories had conveniently emerged. "He's not fit enough," said one source. "Worked like a pig the other day," said another.

I wasn't fooled. At 10.15am I walked into Hills in Morden and had £200 at 16-1. A friend simultaneously placed another £200 on his account for me.

At 10.25am, a pal rang. "Birchy," he said, "Urgent Request is going through the floor. The 'Reg men' are having their lives on it."

"Can you get me another £300 at 16s?"

"I'll try."

Ten minutes later he was on again. "£300 at 14s. You're on."

Urgent Request started 8-1. The race was over a mile and a half, but after 100 yards I knew he'd won. No nerves at all. 'Quinnie' looked over his shoulder two furlongs out, and the pair coasted home by seven lengths. I went ballistic, and jumped on a table at *The Times* – where I was freelancing that day – shocking some rather distinguished, serious-looking people with my antics.

Next day I picked up £3,200 in cash from Hills. Later that night, I got a cheque for £3,200. The following week I met my pal outside Bethnal Green station. Pocketed an envelope full of £50s totalling £4,200. "Reggie is king; Quinnie for Prime Minister," we used to say.

Out of the £10,600 winnings, I spent £1,400 on some automatic garage doors. It became a standing joke at the *Racing Post*. Urgent Request became known as "garage doors", and to this day every time anyone gets wind of a decent punt I might have had, the words 'garage doors' are never far away.

It had to be Urgent Request: who else was I going to vote for? Perhaps Red Robbo, responsible for a welcome case of *déjà vu* in the Hunt Cup. 33-1 into 16-1. Olivier Peslier for Reg. Different jockey. Same result.

And then there's Reference Point. 'Herbie'. Dear Herbie. I was at Sussex University, and everyone wanted to know what would win the Derby. Everyone, including a very pretty girl, whom I secretly adored. "How much should I bet, Rich?" "Whatever. He'll win." She invested a fiver; the first bet of her life. Reference Point made all. The local bookie's in Falmer was packed 40-deep with screaming students. Later that night I went on a date.

1 Urgent Request **2** Red Robbo **3** Reference Point

why I voted for
Titus Oates
by Graham Dench

I AM not certain that I ever even saw him in the flesh, and if I backed him it would have been only for pennies. Yet Titus Oates remains my favourite racehorse more than 30 years after he was last in action.

I was at an impressionable age when Titus Oates was in his prime, and he was the first horse truly to capture my imagination. I would eagerly await each appearance and watch him on television at home, usually with my father, the pair of us fighting over the *Sporting Life* and a well-thumbed *Timeform Black Book*.

Titus Oates was never quite the best of his era, but he was a formidable three-mile chaser on his day and a real character.

He was also one of those horses who you are immediately drawn to as a spectator. He was a bold-jumping front-runner of striking appearance, and he took a fierce hold, often seemingly taking charge even of horsemen as strong as Stan Mellor and Ron Barry, the two riders with whom he was principally associated. He had a most distinctive head carriage too, for his nose would often be almost on the ground as he tanked along between fences, his broad-blazed head straining against the reins.

He never won at the Cheltenham Festival, but in those days the jump season was defined just as much by a series of classic handicap chases – races like the Mackeson, the Hennessy, the Massey-Ferguson and the Whitbread.

Titus Oates had the class to win a King George VI Chase – he beat the great Flyingbolt, admittedly no longer in his pomp, in 1969,

with The Laird, Gay Trip and Larbawn further behind – but I've always loved the big handicaps, and it is for his weight-carrying performances that I remember him best.

The 1969 Massey-Ferguson, for example, when he turned around the previous month's Mackeson form and beat Gay Trip so bravely. The same season's Coventry Pattern Chase, the forerunner of the Racing Post Chase, in which he put The Dikler in his place, giving him 8lb and scoring by a neck after an epic struggle. And above all the following season's Whitbread, when he defied a monstrous 11st 13lb and gave that classy mare Young Ash Leaf 22lb and a beating.

It would be unfair to say that it was all downhill after that famous win in the Whitbread, for there were many more wins, yet Titus Oates never quite hit the high spots again. The unthinkable happened when Young Ash Leaf turned him over at level weights just months later, and in that season's King George he could manage only third behind The Dikler and Spanish Steps.

Titus Oates was trained by the late Gordon Richards, whose son Nicky, now a trainer himself, enjoyed an unforgettable thrill as a mere 17-year-old when partnering the horse to his final success in an amateur riders' chase.

I often wondered how Titus Oates spent his retirement and Nicky Richards was happy to fill me in. I couldn't imagine a horse who exhibited so much energy and exuberance spending his dotage turned out in a field, and it was good to hear that Titus Oates was hunted regularly to a ripe old age. That must have been quite a sight.

1 Titus Oates **2** Summerville **3** Birds Nest

why I voted for
Rondetto
by Alastair Down

RACING is about winning, yet winning isn't everything.

In a lengthening career pursuing a passion, it has been my privilege to see many incontrovertible greats – horses under both codes who have illuminated racing's self-regarding stage through sheer brilliance, courage or character. But tucked away in the private treasury of the mind is one moment that still means as much to me as when I watched it through distinctly watery eyes more than 35 years ago.

And the horse in question didn't even win the race. He was third, beaten 13 lengths, but if ever there was victory and vindication in defeat it came that March afternoon in 1969 when a boot-tough old character called Rondetto finished third to Highland Wedding in the Grand National. He was 13 years old and so was I. And I loved him dearly with that unquestioning, uncomplicated and loyal love that is the prerogative of the very young and very old, those two periods of life that remain immune to the pressure to be cynical.

The record books will tell you that Rondetto had finer hours than his National third but the record books lie. Mind you, the 1967 Hennessy was a special moment. My involvement in world events at prep school – on this occasion captaining the 2nd XI football team – meant the race could not be viewed on the box. But after the game as the crowds drifted away (both of them), one racing-mad master with a memory like the bloke in *The Thirty-Nine Steps* arrived with the news from Newbury. He wouldn't tell me the result, but instead gave me a

fence-by-fence commentary that would have done credit to the finest close-up man in the land. It must have made for a strange sight in the dying light of that November afternoon as, some 90 miles from Newbury, a small figure in football boots leapt up and down in paroxysms of excitement as he listened 'live' to the victory of Rondetto which had been achieved an hour and a half earlier.

The Hennessy was great, but what I desperately wanted the old boy to win was the National. To one young lad who followed his every move it was the greatest injustice in the world that he didn't win all five Nationals he ran in. In 1967, he was the only horse other than Foinavon to get over the 23rd but, having jumped about seven others and the fence from a hopeless angle and with no momentum, he unseated Johnny Haine on the landing side. When he finally got round in third, staying on like the old trier he was behind Highland Wedding, it seemed to me a glorious ending to the career of an indomitable battler who scaled some heights but had the peak denied him.

I have hoarded the moment ever since, bringing it out of the lumber room of memory and dusting it down whenever the superficialities, greeds and idiocies of the game have left me in need of cheering up.

To many, Rondetto was just a horse, albeit a good one. But to me he was, and remains, *the* horse – an enduring encapsulation of endeavour, durability and the will to win.

One day, perhaps, my memories of the old warrior will cease to move me and that will be the signal to move on, the time to go.

1 Rondetto **2** Willie Wumpkins **3** Brigadier Gerard

why I voted for
Saxon King
by Sir Clement Freud

ONE is torn. Some of me would select Alycidon, winner of the Ascot Gold Cup in 1949, but only because he beat Benny Lynch, whom I had laid at 100-1 to a customer of the hotel I managed, and on the broadcast it sounded as if the pacemaker was going to make it . . . and cost me 22 years' wages.

Yet my favourite horse of all time is Saxon King. If you nod sagely it is either because you were a follower of fourth-rate Irish bumpers in the 1960s, or you have an ailment that causes you to nod at regular intervals.

Saxon King was the first horse I rode in public; he was owned by Joe Hehir, who made his fortune from a company called Kilkenny Retread Tyres. I knew Joe from Cheltenham, where, more years than not, I was asked by Toby Balding, who trained for us both, to help carry Joe to his car after racing.

No trouble. He was light on his feet and easy to sling over your shoulder: the drink was so evenly distributed, filled every nook and cranny, that lifting him was akin to carrying a filled waterbed.

When I got a licence from the Irish Turf Club, and talked of this on Gay Byrne's *Late Late Show*, Joe telephoned the television company to offer me a ride in the following Saturday's bumper at Naas.

I spent several nights in a sauna; I tried on boots and had trouble until someone said you wear them over silk stockings. I walked the course, over and over. I inspected the churchyard adjoining the racetrack. I read John Hislop on tactics, and practised switching the whip from left to right hand. I admit that it did not occur to me to meet Saxon King, without whom I would have gone to Naas as a punter.

We met in the parade ring, gave each other cursory glances. He was brown, looked pretty much like the other horses, failed to notice I did not look remotely like the other jockeys, who included a very young Dermot Weld and even younger Mouse Morris and Arthur Moore.

What shall I do if I canter to the start and he doesn't stop, I asked the trainer. "Aim him at the other horses, he's a gregarious brute," said the man. We got to the start. He stopped. The starter dropped his flag. He started, galloped, and I sat on his back – actually stood in my stirrups above him – practised switching the whip and, when I looked round after half a mile, I was in front.

Hislop had written about riding tactically and pointed out the problems of "making the pace" so, at halfway, I let a horse come past, then another, then some more.

With a couple of furlongs to go, Saxon King found a second wind and, instead of finishing last, we were 12th of 20. What in racing parlance is called 'beat a few'.

Joe Hehir told me he would have done no better had he been ridden by a proper jockey, then passed out. Saxon King stood there like the star he was: quietly watching me try to take the saddle off and nuzzling my arm. Not a word of complaint, though he must have known that of all the crap jockeys riding that afternoon, I was the crappiest.

1 Saxon King **2** Winter Fair **3** Nagnagnag

why I voted for
Salse

by Peter Gomm

CHOOSE a two-year-old from Raceform's *Horses In Training*, named or unnamed, and follow the course of their career. It just might change your life. It did mine.

In 1987 when I was in my teens I selected, at random, an unnamed two-year-old at the behest of a friend whose casual interest in the sport mirrored my own.

My horse was number 99 in Henry Cecil's list, a bay colt foaled on February 24 by Topsider out of Carnival Princess, and owned by Sheikh Mohammed.

That is where it all started. Afterwards I followed the colt's career, from his racecourse debut when he won at Yarmouth in August 1987 – by which time he was named Salse – through to his Group 1 triumph in the Prix de la Foret at Longchamp, and then his tenure at stud, where I was fortunate enough to visit him many times. And I have followed the myriad runners he went on to sire, including those who are themselves now stallions – Classic Cliche, Luso, Timboroa and the tragically short-lived Air Express, responsible for brilliant filly Airwave – and the lesser lights, whose exploits I follow avidly to this day, irrespective of their ability.

No high was higher than seeing Salse run well, as he always did. Beaten by Warning twice, perhaps, but still brave in defeat, or taking on the best of the rest and putting them in their places. He was a seven-furlong specialist who won eight times and was never out of the first three in a racing career that spanned just two seasons; I was always there when circumstances allowed.

Then, accompanied by my father and armed with Polo mints and camera, it was off to Side Hill Stud in Newmarket for the regular visits. Born with a fire in his belly, a trait he passed on to the best of his offspring, Salse would have few qualms about taking a bite out of a misplaced hand or item of clothing, but with stallion man Peter Wight catering for his every need, he was always the perfect gentleman in our presence.

Yet none of the above can encompass what Salse, who died in 2001, aged only 16, really meant to me. I now work as a sub-editor on the *Racing Post*, via the *Sporting Life*, a fact I can directly attribute to the horse and the passion for racing he instilled in me. Anyone who knows me knows of my infatuation – and no, that is not too strong a word.

I really *do* have Salse-emblazoned T-shirts, baseball caps, mugs, you name it. And then there were the times I had 'SALSE' stencilled (since faded out) into my hair (now fallen out).

Armed with this knowledge, it will come as no surprise to anyone that, when given the opportunity to vote for my favourite racehorse, there was only one choice.

Sadly, though, my request to place Salse first, second and third was given short shrift, so I did the next best thing. My number two, Moyglare Stud Stakes winner Lemon Souffle, was her sire's first big-race heroine – no prizes for guessing her sire's name! – while Luso's first win at the International meeting in Hong Kong brings back particularly fond recollections of a birthday well and truly enjoyed.

Thank you, Salse.

Thank you for your life.

---

1 Salse **2** Lemon Souffle **3** Luso

why I voted for
Brigadier Gerard
by Paul Haigh

ONLY one horse I've known ever got three cheers from the entire Newmarket crowd. The cheers were for the Brigadier after his last race – the 18th of his career, his 17th victory, and his second in the Champion Stakes. It was a wonderful moment: an expression of gratitude as much as anything else. What amazed me then was that somewhere along the line this superhero horse had somehow managed to lose one. More than three decades later it amazes me still.

How it happened no-one knows. Somehow the Panamanian Braulio Baeza coaxed a performance out of Roberto that surpassed anything he'd achieved before or was to achieve afterwards. Somehow, perhaps, the Brigadier ran a little flat after the extraordinary effort that saw him win the King George at a distance that was at least two furlongs beyond him, and four furlongs beyond the mile that was his optimum – at which trip no horse who ever raced in Britain, not Tudor Minstrel, not Nijinsky, not El Gran Senor, not Dancing Brave, could possibly have lived with him.

It says something about the Brigadier, though, that the racing world should have been so stunned that a Derby winner (who, though we didn't know it then, had beaten a subsequent Arc winner), ridden by a masterly judge of pace, and running in conditions that suited him to perfection, should have been able to break the champion's unbeaten record. It says even more that someone felt it necessary to invent the bee-sting theory – Roberto ran like that because

he'd been stung – to explain it, and that the theory should still have its adherents even to this day.

I wasn't always a Brigadier Gerard fan. In fact, just before the 2,000 Guineas in 1971, I sat solemnly with a select bunch of fellow racing enthusiasts in a university junior common room and made a brief but, I believe, moving statement to the effect that if Mill Reef got beaten in this race, I would never, ever have another bet on a horse.

Always ignore fools who make such pronouncements. My own resolution lasted only as long as it took the Brigadier to sweep past the favourite and the brilliant My Swallow, who would have been a Guineas winner in almost any other Classic year.

That stunning victory was the start not just of my adulation but of what was probably the greatest rivalry the British Turf has known. By the end of it, in spite of the magnitude of their idol's other achievements, Mill Reef fans were forced to acknowledge the Brigadier's almost certain supremacy at any distance shorter than ten furlongs, and a strong possibility that he might have been too good even at that trip too.

There is great irony in the fact that it was in the race then called the Benson and Hedges Gold Cup – actually invented so that the two could meet again – that the Brigadier met his one, to some quite inexplicable, defeat.

But still the memory that glows is not of that horrific moment but of the majestic triumphs, culminating as they did in those three cheers for the Brigadier. How could I ever have dreamt of voting any other way?

1 Brigadier Gerard **2** Arkle **3** Wayward Lad

why I voted for
Cloudwalker
by Marten Julian

I'VE been lucky enough to see most of the great horses to have raced in the course of my career. Why then, you may wonder, have I opted for a little-known grey called Cloudwalker as my all-time favourite racehorse?

The answer is quite simple. This horse changed the course of my life. Treasured experiences and memories of crazy days will forever be locked into his racing career – places visited for the first time, people I met and, of course, coups landed.

Had it not been for Cloudwalker, my family and I would never have moved to the Lake District. I'm fairly sure that my two youngest daughters wouldn't have been born and, for certain, my eldest daughter would not have met her future husband and provided me with a grandson.

Interesting things always seemed to happen when Cloudwalker was around. I managed him on behalf of a handful of friends who included Mel Smith, then enjoying public acclaim through the satirical TV programme *Not The Nine O'Clock News*. Soon afterwards the talented actor and impressionist Enn Reitel, who was to become a lifelong friend, acquired a share.

Cloudwalker, for a reason that never became totally clear to any of us, soon acquired the nickname 'Norman'. He was a bit of a weaver and I'll never forget the trouble he caused by passing on that strange, head-rolling trait to his nearby stablemates most of whom, by chance, also happened to be greys!

I should add, by the way, that Cloudwalker was also quite a good racehorse. He won twice on the Flat, seven times over hurdles and once over fences. At his best he was able to produce a telling turn of foot, which often made for exciting viewing from the stands.

Cloudwalker took me to all points of the compass. He had a great record in Scotland, winning races at Ayr and Perth. However, his greatest moments came at Cartmel, where he won three times during the 1982/83 season.

I'd never heard of the place until my trainer rang me one day to say he'd entered him to run there. On a burning hot, busy August Bank Holiday I made the long journey from south-east Kent to the southern Lakes. On arriving, I was greeted by the smiling countenance of the racecourse chairman, entertained liberally and became so enamoured of the place that within a couple of years I had bought a house just a mile or so from the course.

Shortly afterwards my family and I relocated there full-time. Cloudwalker brought me into contact with some of racing's greatest names. One of my lasting memories is the sight of the late Fulke Walwyn, who trained him at the start of his final season, cheering him home from the stands at Wincanton as he strode away to win his first chase.

Later that season, he took off a stride too soon at a fence down the far side at Market Rasen. Sustaining terrible injuries, there was an empty stable in his yard that night. Even now, there is rarely a day when I don't think of him.

1 Cloudwalker **2** Park Top **3** My Henry

why I voted for
Ridgewood Pearl
by Jon Lees

BREEDERS' Cup victories must be regarded as ten a penny these days. Surely that can be the only reason that Ridgewood Pearl failed to garner enough votes to claim a place in the 100 Favourite Racehorses list. Indeed, of 65 horses beginning with the letter 'R' she was only 15th, behind Red Rum but in front of Red Alligator.

I must declare an interest here. Through a family connection I can be found guilty of bias, but that should not prevent an examination of the merits of one of Europe's best fillies of recent times.

Everyone has a soft spot for fillies. We were all in awe of Attraction in 2004, and it was she who lowered Ridgewood Pearl's longstanding track record over the Ascot round mile when she won the Coronation Stakes at the Royal meeting.

Like Attraction, Ridgewood Pearl had won the Irish 1,000 Guineas, but the John Oxx-trained filly went on to prove herself against both her elders and colts.

Bred by Sean Coughlan, my wife's uncle, and raced in the colours of his wife Anne, Ridgewood Pearl won six of her eight starts. By Indian Ridge, whom the Coughlans had also raced, she won a Group 3 prize at two but came into her own at three. Having underlined her credentials with a seven-length win in the Listed Athasi Stakes, she then ran away with the Irish 1,000 Guineas by beating Warning Shadows by four lengths. Britain's Classic heroine Harayir, the 11-10 favourite, was only fifth.

Punters forgave Harayir's performance at The Curragh and she again started favourite for the Coronation Stakes. But while she narrowed the gap, she couldn't get closer than third to a filly who set a record time that would last for nine years.

Ridgewood Pearl's victory at Ascot helped introduce her jockey Johnny Murtagh, then relatively unknown outside Ireland, to British racegoers and usher the studious John Oxx on to an international stage he now occupies with regularity. With the precision planning for which he is now renowned, Oxx then brought her back from a three-month break to beat colts in the Prix du Moulin.

The extent to which tactics were responsible for her defeat next time out in the Queen Elizabeth II Stakes is open to debate, but Willie Carson's decision to steer a solitary course on Bahri along a route under the trees was rewarded by a six-length victory.

However, it didn't halt Ridgewood Pearl, who bounced back at Belmont Park, New York, to claim the Breeders' Cup Mile, an emotional occasion for both connections and this correspondent, on hand to report the celebrations. The filly had been cast in her box the night before and Coughlan was indebted to the staff of Godolphin, whose prompt reactions helped ensure her participation went ahead. She recorded Europe's only win at the meeting that year.

She died in May 2003 of a haemorrhage. Oxx described her as "exceptional", adding that she was "definitely the best filly" he'd ever trained.

Ridgewood Pearl will not be forgotten in Ireland, where a statue of her was unveiled this year at The Curragh, nor by me. She was a rare gem.

1 Ridgewood Pearl **2** Rambo's Hall **3** Desert Orchid

why I voted for
Ekbalco
by Bruce Millington

WHILE some of my peers were getting their addictive teenage kicks from narcotics, I got myself hooked on racing.

My fix probably cost me as much as theirs did (it takes time to get the hang of betting) but I had heroes instead, and none bigger than Ekbalco.

When you first immerse yourself in racing, you view the horses at the top of the tree at the time as legends, regardless of how truly great they are when compared to other generations.

Ekbalco, in the grand scheme of things, was not a great hurdler in the purest sense of the word – but I have never felt the same way about a racehorse as I did about him.

Why? Funnily enough, it wasn't the fact that during his golden year of 1982 he kept winning and I kept backing him. Nice though it was that the Guntrips credit account my pal's dad had opened for us was being swollen by the horse's victories, my love of Ekbalco was based on more than just punting profitability.

To a kid from south London, there was something mystical about this beast from deepest Cumbria, trained by Roger Fisher and ridden, in his early races, by 'Gipsy' David Goulding, a jockey renowned for dropping his horses right out at the back before driving them past their flagging rivals on the run for home.

If younger readers thought Liam Cooper was a master of the patient use of waiting tactics, they should have seen Goulding, Cooper's uncle.

He helped Ekbalco, owned by Tawfik Fakhouri, establish himself as one of the most formidable hurdlers of the early 1980s, but as time wore on the horse became the mount of Jonjo O'Neill.

The son of Deep Run served notice that he was really top notch when winning the 1981 Fighting Fifth Hurdle at Newcastle. Two months later he ran a stormer to go down by a whisker to Donegal Prince in the Schweppes despite having to lug top weight around muddy Newbury.

Champion Hurdle glory proved elusive in 1982 as For Auction and Broadsword got the better of him up the hill. But before the year was out he had landed the Welsh equivalent and then, having fallen when trying to win the Fighting Fifth again, he stormed to the head of the 1983 Champion Hurdle market with a Bula Hurdle victory over his Cheltenham conquerors, followed by a Christmas Hurdle success that confirmed his superiority over Broadsword. It was not to be, though. Gaye Brief and three others were too good for him in March, when he was sent off 3-1 joint-favourite.

After Ekbalco had failed to prove himself the very best over hurdles, I expected him to kick some butt in the chasing division, but, tragically, he never got the chance.

The following season he had another crack at the Fighting Fifth and I was so confident of victory I went to watch the other love of my life, Crystal Palace. I got home, put on Ceefax, saw the main headline, "Ekbalco killed in fall at Newcastle", and cried my eyes out.

1 Ekbalco **2** Wayward Lad **3** Dancing Brave

why I voted for
Desert Orchid
by Lee Mottershead

IT IS a treasured possession, inexpensive yet priceless: a video cassette, purchased as a 14-year-old, picked up from the sports section of the Blackburn branch of WH Smith. On a shelf it now proudly sits, the spine bearing the words, *Desert Orchid – The Video*. Played countless times, the pictures, the sounds, the emotions remain as vivid as they ever did. So many precious moments, so many precious memories.

There will never be another racehorse like Desert Orchid, for there never could be. To a teenager with an increasingly insatiable appetite for the Sport of Kings, he was like a gift from the gods. A horse to latch on to, a horse you could call your own but happily share with everyone else, for everyone felt the same. Everyone loved him.

The tape tells the story. The early days, runaway wins at Kempton, Ascot, Sandown, over hurdles, then over fences, different races, the same method – bold, flamboyant and courageous, this was the ultimate competitor. No horse knew what it was to win better than Desert Orchid did.

He was a racehorse who raced, the best sort of racehorse. He appeared when you might not have expected him to, like that day at Ascot in April 1987. The Peregrine Handicap Chase was special only because Desert Orchid was there. He made it an occasion, thrilling and enthralling his people. Conceding an astonishing 28lb to Gold Bearer, he carried 12st 4lb to victory, finishing so weary it still hurts to watch, though not as much as it must have hurt him.

There are two favourite bits. First there's the 1988 Whitbread. Nine fences from home, the front-running Dessie stands off from outside the wing of the 16th obstacle, putting in so astonishing a leap that John Oaksey's cry of incredulity can be heard over the background of Graham Goode's commentary. Then the charge up the hill, the Sandown faithful making unprecedented noise as the whitening grey shrugs off Kildimo, sending 'GG' into rapture. "I have never, *ever*," – such emphasis on the 'ever' – "heard the crowd warm to a horse like they've warmed to Desert Orchid," he declares. He was – he is – right.

And my favourite moment, so wondrous it can never be equalled. The Cheltenham Gold Cup of 1989. The finest horserace I have ever seen, won by my favourite-ever horse, supported by the greatest commentary I have ever heard. Peter O'Sullevan's words still send a chill down my spine. "Desert Orchid's beginning to get up," he screams, confirming what the eye sees, Dessie fighting through the detested mud to claw back Yahoo in the race that mattered above all others. "There's a tremendous cheer from the crowd, as Desert Orchid is gonna win it. Desert Orchid has won the Gold Cup . . . Dessie has done it!"

I never saw Desert Orchid race in the flesh but, 13 years after his retirement, I saw him grazing in a Hampshire field. Happy as a hero should be. Another precious moment. Another precious memory.

1 Desert Orchid **2** Corbiere **3** Rooster Booster

why I voted for
Pas Seul
by John Oaksey

PUTTING Pas Seul above Arkle obviously doesn't strictly reflect their ability, but I do think he was about the only horse I ever saw who, at his best, could have given 'Himself' a race.

However, given that he was foaled about two miles from where I live, and that I was riding out regularly with his trainer Bob Turnell at the time Pas Seul was in the stable, it is not surprising that he is my personal favourite.

In England, don't forget, we had not even heard of Arkle in 1960, the year Pas Seul won the Cheltenham Gold Cup. Then, Arkle was still just an unknown Irish three-year-old, named after a Scottish mountain.

In 1960, my only reason for going to Hurst Park in the middle of December was to ride a horse called Loppylugs, on whom Ginger Dennistoun was kind enough to put me up. But it turned out to be one of the least forgettable meetings of my life.

Hurst Park is a housing estate nowadays but it was a favourite course of Bob's – especially when, for whatever reason, he wanted a horse to have a nice easy race. The apple of Bob's eye at that time – and, I believe, for the rest of his life – was Pas Seul.

Less easy to understand was Bob's choice of the two-mile Westminster Handicap Chase for Pas Seul's return to active service after his Gold Cup season. Having his first race of the season, Pas Seul was set to carry 12st 7lb, giving weight to specialist two-mile chasers. Ridden by Dave Dick, he was giving 22lb to one top two-mile chaser, Quick

Approach, and 6lb to an even better one, Blue Dolphin. Not surprisingly, Pas Seul, quite unfancied, started at 100-8! But the race taught all of us who saw it an unforgettable lesson. Because, with Dave never moving a muscle, Pas Seul was pulling double throughout. He jumped like a stag inspired and passed the post still virtually on a tight rein.

So, why, you may very well ask, did Pas Seul not win that season's Gold Cup at Cheltenham, where he was second to Saffron Tartan? The answer can be given in two words. Fred Winter.

Fred had one trump card. For part of his genius was knowledge of the horse he was riding, its weaknesses as well as its strengths. He knew, for instance, that Saffron Tartan did not *quite* stay the Gold Cup distance, especially at Cheltenham with its uphill finish. So now, after driving into the last fence for all he was worth – and gaining a priceless length in the air – Fred just sat, holding the big horse together, lifting him up the hill.

It took this masterpiece of strong tactical jockeyship to beat Pas Seul that year, and when Fred walked into the changing room, all the other jockeys stood up and cheered. What a man.

I was, just once, allowed to sit on Pas Seul myself, for a slow canter up a steepish hill. I just managed to hold him, but could feel, all too clearly, what Bob and the others meant when they talked about 'Rolls Royces'. No wonder I can name him as my favourite.

1 Pas Seul **2** Arkle **3** Proud Tarquin

why I voted for
Susarma
by Bill O'Gorman

HOW can you truly identify a favourite horse when every one represents a separate thread in the fabric of your life? Faded names from my career as a trainer stand as much as monuments to friendships and rivalries that ebbed and flowed through the passing years as to the horses themselves.

Brigadier Gerard and Arkle are the two racehorses who have made an outstanding impression on me from relatively afar. However, when voting for my own personal favourite, I had to choose one to whom I was much closer. I may not be the most sentimental of characters where horses in my stable are concerned – I generally regard it as a professional attachment – but Susarma was a horse who I looked after myself and often rode two or three times every day. I have fond memories of him as a racehorse and as a friend.

He appeared at the sales as a six-year-old from Scobie Breasley's yard, apparently sound apart from making a noise, but having lost his form completely. I bought him for 2,600gns thinking that, even if he wouldn't run, he would do as a lead horse.

This highly scientific approach led to Susarma becoming my regular ride. There was no question about his musical bent, but he could certainly run – and because he was so thick-winded he often went out two or three lots in the morning.

It didn't do him any harm. In his first run at Doncaster he probably just needed the race, finishing fourth with a big weight. After Doncaster he was flying with horses like Milk Of The Barley and Sayyaf, who were running

extremely well. I thought him sure to win the Field Marshal Stakes. He was last.

Sheepdog triallers say that if a dog disappoints you, you should remember that it's still the same dog. But unfortunately, when the BBA offered a good profit for him to go to South Africa as a stallion, I overlooked that maxim and sold him on the understanding that he could run for me until he went into quarantine. The rest, as they say, is history. He won at Chester with 10st, and then won a good race at York with 10st 2lb. He never ran again.

Although I was lucky enough to train several more high-profile horses, he remains the one horse that I'd most like a chance to do it all over again with. I wish that I'd had him earlier, or that I had him still.

There are many others I could mention, like our first Group winner Mummy's Game, Fayruz, who won six races in 23 racing days, and Provideo, a plain horse with a heart like a lion. To win 16 races as a two-year-old was like running the four-minute mile!

However, my second choice is Superlative, certainly the most able horse I ever had and a thorough gentleman in every way, but lazy. He never really achieved on the racecourse what he had shown at home.

And although he only won claiming races and cheap handicaps, Berge was another horse for whom I always had a soft spot. If this were an award for racing spirit, he would win. Although he was severely compromised by his knees, which required surgery on several occasions, he still managed to win 12 races.

1 Susarma **2** Superlative **3** Berge

why I voted for
Nijinsky
by Rachel Pagones

I NEVER saw Nijinsky, but his name has been etched across my mental tableau for almost as long as I can remember. Not that anyone else in my American-based family had the slightest interest in horses, or even knew there was a horse named Nijinsky, but our house was full of books, and one of them, a dog-eared white paperback on a bottom shelf, was called simply *Nijinsky*.

It was about a dancer, not a horse. My older sister was a dancer, and there were a lot of books about ballet on our shelves. I took ballet lessons, too, and although there was nothing mysterious about *pliés* and *tendus*, the ballets themselves were wrapped in mystery, a shrouded glimpse into the world of adults. It wasn't a happy world – the world portrayed through classical ballet, that is, with its heavy dose of Russian tragedy, and Nijinsky was no exception. A brilliant dancer who appeared to hover in midair, he descended into madness.

All this I learned from the back of the book. I never saw Nijinsky the dancer either, but my ballet teachers spoke of him with awe. He was a legend.

Around the same time, I became aware of racing. That was thanks to Secretariat, the big red colt who thundered across America's collective consciousness in 1973. I devoted a whole scrapbook to him, and pricked my ears every time the radio presenter rumbled: "Secretaryofstate . . ." For this reason I still associate 'Big Red' with Henry Kissinger.

At some point not long after – probably through another book – I became aware there was a horse named Nijinsky. Dancer and horse became inextricably linked in my mind.

The horse, they said, was a legend, and he was trained in a place as mysterious and foreign as Nijinsky the dancer's St Petersburg – Ireland's Ballydoyle. The timeline wasn't clear to me, and for all I knew the equine Nijinsky had been around as long as the dancer. But I knew he was awesome, almost ethereal in his athleticism yet touched somehow with tragedy.

Years later, I saw a great video. It was simply named *A Horse Called Nijinsky*, and I was pleased (but not surprised) to find that the horse was everything I had known he was. He was great: he sizzled past the fastest two-year-olds, dominated the 2,000 Guineas and stayed the Derby and St Leger, usually winning on the bridle with ears pricked. He was mysterious: the inscrutable Lester Piggott was his regular rider, laconic Vincent O'Brien his trainer, misty Ireland his adopted homeland and the larger-than-life Charles Engelhard his owner.

He was also touched by tragedy, in two ways. Engelhard was not to live long, and the once invincible Nijinsky lost his last two races. Not by much, admittedly, but it wrought obvious agony on his connections, who turned themselves inside out looking for an explanation. To me, a connoisseur of *National Velvet*, it was natural that love of a horse could bring such suffering on people.

So Nijinsky is more than a great racehorse to me. A marvellous athlete and an influential sire, he also represented to my child's mind the mystery and awe of everything I suspected was out there. And, to my great relief, although sometimes coated in muck, it is.

1 Nijinsky **2** Abernant **3** Sea-Bird

why I voted for
Arkle
by John Randall

ANY self-respecting racing anorak will tell you that 'favourite horse' ought to be synonymous with 'greatest horse', and that Arkle is therefore the only possible choice in this survey.

Childhood heroes stay with you for life, and Arkle was the horse most responsible for nurturing the interest in the sport of this budding anorak as a schoolboy, starting with the first of his three Cheltenham Gold Cups.

If you idolise people or horses and put them on a pedestal, you nearly always find that they have feet of clay, but in Arkle's case hero-worship and mature judgement coincide. Indeed, that five-length triumph over Mill House would have made him the greatest steeplechaser of all time even if he had never run again.

The 1964 Gold Cup – run on a Saturday and therefore accessible to this ten-year-old viewer – was a defining moment in racing history, marking the exact instant when a great champion was dethroned by the supreme paragon. At the time I was unaware of the Ireland v England aspect of Arkle's rivalry with Mill House, but already realised that to witness greatness is the most inspiring and comforting experience that any sporting event can offer. In any case, the awesome Dreaper-Taaffe champion transcended national loyalties.

Little did any of us know that his performance graph was still on a steep upward curve that in the next two years would take him into realms previously undreamt of.

Arkle's near-unbroken sequence of triumphs would have become tedious, except that watching perfection is never boring. He regularly carried top weight of up to 12st 10lb in handicaps and never ducked a challenge. It was cruel luck that injury ended his career while he was still in his prime.

Superlatives became inadequate as, in majestic, swaggering, ruthless style, he easily defied 12st in the Irish Grand National, and 12st 7lb in the Hennessy (twice), Whitbread and other handicaps. He displayed outstanding pace, stamina, jumping ability and courage under crushing burdens, never falling and always giving his best. He is the only horse who, by his sheer brilliance, has forced a change in the rules, resulting in the present 'long handicap' system.

The assertion that some of Arkle's feats will never be equalled is not the delusion of an old fogey but a simple statement of fact. It was only in handicaps, conceding up to 3st to top-class rivals, that he revealed the full extent of his greatness, whereas more recent champion chasers have run only in level-weights and conditions events, and have therefore not been asked such searching questions. Best Mate is kept in cotton wool and is not risked unless conditions are in his favour; even in the Gold Cup he has to carry only 11st 10lb in these indulgent times.

In the decades since Arkle's last race we have looked for a worthy successor, but in vain. He was a freak, an unrepeatably lucky shake of the genetic cocktail, the nearest thing the sport has ever seen to the perfect machine.

1 Arkle **2** Brigadier Gerard **3** Flyingbolt

why I voted for
Desert Orchid
by Emily Weber

EVERYONE I've asked has been able to say straight away the name of their favourite racehorse. Not me. I've got so many.

Could anything be more moving than Crisp losing the Grand National in the last strides? So moving that I couldn't face the rest of the day and went to bed at teatime, feeling slightly sick. Or could anything ever mean as much again as whether Mill House could, this time, beat the hated Arkle? Who was I more thrilled by, that underrated bruiser Dawn Run or the old warhorse Persian War a couple of decades earlier?

It is an impossible question to answer. Or, perhaps, near-impossible. If it comes down to one single memory, then I never got more pleasure from a race than when Sea Pigeon won the Ebor, carrying top weight. We had to wait for the result of the photo and I'll never forget the roar that went up from the Yorkshire crowd when the announcement came through "First, Number One".

Strictly speaking, I suppose, he was my favourite horse, the one with the most character, the one I would have most liked to look after and fuss over at home. But it isn't as straightforward as that, for was he my favourite racehorse?

The answer is no, not quite. It is a fine distinction, but I just couldn't put him ahead of Desert Orchid, simply because of the sheer number of hours of pleasure he gave over the years.

When Desert Orchid came along, I thought I had experienced just about every thrill racing had to offer. Yet he gave so many that by the time he was three-quarters of the way through his career – and here Desert Orchid was wildly different to my other favourites – I barely cared whether he won or lost. The bank was full. Yes, I willed him on every time, shaking with excitement, but his failures no longer registered: it was literally irrelevant when he was beaten. He had done so much, given so much, that the results had become incidental. Now I had experienced racing's every thrill.

I saw Desert Orchid so many times that it is hard to single out one particularly special moment, but in some ways I was most touched by his defeat in his last Gold Cup. The glory days were over and as they turned for home he was miles behind, victory out of the question. Yet as he struggled up the hill, he was still giving it everything despite those tired legs, all those desperately hard races. He would never, ever say die. Happily he was retired not long afterwards and a succession of public parades in the years since has been the perfect retirement for a horse of his temperament.

And recently I heard the old superstar is still dishing out the thrills. A friend of mine, nearly 80 and riddled with arthritis, went to David Elsworth's birthday party. When she turned up, David asked her if she would like to ride Desert Orchid. There and then, they went to the tack room, David himself tacked the horse up and after a certain amount of heaving, Rose was in the saddle and riding round the yard.

Apparently he still leads the two-year-olds in their work. That's Desert Orchid: a warlord from beginning to end.

1 Desert Orchid **2** Sea Pigeon **3** Persian War

why I voted for
Bartlemy Boy
by Howard Wright

ARKLE, Nijinsky and Bartlemy Boy: two champions, one other, and all on a par as favourite horses. Bartlemy who?

Bartlemy Boy, that's who, and despite his aura of unfamiliarity, a horse distinguished enough to provoke a response when his claims were paraded in my regular column in the *Racing Post* shortly after the chosen 100 were listed, and his name had not appeared among the most popular.

A reader came forward to point out a small error. That's what happens when you try to get away with relying on memory, particularly at a distance of nearly 40 years. Someone somewhere is liable to know that little bit more.

No matter. At least that meant there had probably been another vote for Bartlemy Boy, and no amount of correction could erase the reason for my picking him in the first place.

For 14 months I edited a pocket-sized weekly racing magazine called – with little regard for ingenuity – *The Racing Week*. It was published by Timeform and had been launched by Phil Bull in 1964.

Despite having a deserved reputation for reflective, informed and profitable content, the magazine was under sentence of death. Circulation, through subscription and appointed newsagents only, had reached a plateau, and Bull was disinclined to forgo a percentage of the cover price to the wholesalers.

Among the features was a coded selection, which appeared in four daily newspapers and could be unscrambled only by reference to the current issue.

On Friday, February 10, 1967, the code led to the last race at Sandown, a novices'

hurdle in which the Josh Gifford-ridden Irish Moss was likely to start a hot favourite.

The magazine's imminent closure had a bearing on the selection. "Might as well go for a longshot," was the theory. But, in keeping with Timeform ethics, there was a sound reason behind the choice.

Another feature in *The Week* was 'Inside Information', in which a trainer talked openly about his horses – commonplace nowadays but unrivalled then.

Trainers of jumpers did not figure at first, but fresh enthusiasm from the new young editor was indulged, as long as he did the donkeywork on cold, winter morning trips to faraway places. Halifax to Chepstow in December was no fun in pre-motorway days, but Colin Davies and his family warmed the heart, and fuelled the racing senses, of this long-distance traveller.

Persian War was a season away from joining his string, but Davies told of a big, strong five-year-old, a horse who had run a promising third at Cheltenham that October, only to develop a splint soon after. He was fit again, would probably need his next run – unplaced at Newbury on New Year's Eve – but was, in Davies's words, "a really nice horse".

Bartlemy Boy started at 20-1 when he won at Sandown.

Four weeks later, *The Racing Week* was finished, but not before a memorable horse had provided the perfect riposte to the correspondent from Manchester who wrote: "Your coded horses are too pathetic for words. We the public are the mugs once again, paying 2s 6d (12$\frac{1}{2}$p) for such tripe!"

---

1 Bartlemy Boy **2** Arkle **3** Nijinsky

when a professional interest becomes personal

We talked to a selection of racing personalities to find out the horses who mean the most to them

 Andrew Balding
Chief Singer

The young are always impressionable, and I was ten years old and just starting to get really interested in the sport when this big, black, imposing horse with so much presence came along. He was called Chief Singer and won the Coventry Stakes by four lengths on his racecourse debut at Royal Ascot, yet that was to prove only the tip of the iceberg.

Clare Balding
Knock Knock

Knock Knock, on whom I won on my first time out at Kempton, is my all-time favourite. When he came to father's stable he was still a maiden and absolutely hated other horses – but he loved people and I loved him. My orders were to ride him like a non-trier – I had no choice as that's the only way I've ever been able to ride, but it worked like a dream. He was a 25-1 chance and I was so excited to win on my first ride in public.

 Jack Berry
O I Oyston

He wasn't the best we trained, but he was my favourite. A 2,600gns Doncaster yearling, he won 26 races. I always said there were two things I wouldn't sell: the missus and 'Olly'.

 Clive Brittain
Pebbles

Pebbles achieved almost everything I hoped she might – winning a 1,000 Guineas, a Champion Stakes against the top older horses and a Breeders' Cup, the first horse from England to beat the Americans on their home soil. She had a bit of character but it is the trainer's job to overcome that. I've been lucky enough to have had some great fillies over the years, but Pebbles was a racing machine.

 Tommy Carberry
L'Escargot

L'Escargot won two Cheltenham Gold Cups and a Grand National for me but he did very much more than that. He was placed in the National three years running, finishing third and then second to Red Rum before beating him on the third occasion. Two months before he won his first Gold Cup he won the season's top novice chase, the Wills Final at Haydock. The previous summer he went to America where he won a big chase at Belmont and as a five-year-old he won the Gloucestershire Hurdle by six lengths.

 Willie Carson
Arkle

Arkle has to be my choice because he was the finest chaser there has been or is ever likely to be – truly a phenomenon. He did everything, beat the best, often giving away huge amounts of weight, and seemed to run every other day. He was a genuinely great horse. Dayjur would be my choice of the horses I rode – easily the fastest I've ever ridden and possibly the fastest anybody has.

Victor Chandler
Dawn Run

Her win in the 1986 Gold Cup taught me the biggest lesson of my life – not to put my eggs in one basket. I laid Jonjo O'Neill's mount to lose more than I wanted to or ought to have done, and then some. I thought Wayward Lad had it won and was counting my money and preening myself when disaster struck. Afterwards, I bought Jonjo's boots and whip and, if ever I feel very opinionated about a horse, I look at them on the wall of my office as a warning.

Ray Cochrane
Desert Orchid

Desert Orchid was an inspiration to anyone who rides horses and I watched him from a very early age with the greatest admiration. He was not only a brilliant jumper but he had an extraordinary character. I can remember, long after the horse retired, Colin Brown cantering him past the stands at Sandown one day – only to be absolutely carted on the way back. The same thing happened once when Lester had a go – Dessie ran away with the most famous jockey in the world. I'd love to have given it a try.

Luca Cumani
Falbrav

Of course my favourite is Falbrav. He was simply a star, and was a brilliant racehorse for many reasons. His physical power was unique, he was determined, versatile and durable – all the things you look for in a champion. An awesome horse that always let you know he was boss, as he didn't like being pampered.

Kevin Darley
Attraction

I voted for Celtic Swing at the time of the poll. He was the horse who put me on the map and he never got the recognition he deserved. But while he was a true star and will always hold a special place in my heart, I've got to say Attraction now. I'm lucky in that I just ride her on the track where she is so straightforward and gives so much, but

she has her ins and outs at home, probably because of her conformation, I guess. She is perfect from a jockey's point of view, so easy to ride on the track, and we had quite a year in 2004. Whatever happens now, I'll never forget her.

Frankie Dettori
Fujiyama Crest

Dubai Millennium would be the best horse I've ever ridden but my favourite has to be Fujiyama Crest. He will always hold a special place in my heart after completing my 'magnificent seven' at Ascot, and he's now become a real family pet.

George Duffield
User Friendly

User Friendly provided me with my first Classic success in the 1992 Oaks and she will always be my favourite horse. She was very tough – her Oaks victory came on just her third start – and the great thing is she just kept improving, going on to land an Irish Oaks, Yorkshire Oaks and St Leger. Very few horses ever do anything like that and people forget just how good she was.

Richard Dunwoody
West Tip

It has to be West Tip, simply because I don't think my career would have taken off the way it did without my success on him in the 1986 Grand National. He finished fourth in a Gold Cup, so he wouldn't have been far behind the very best I rode, and he was very intelligent, very clever, and you could not have wished for a better horse round Aintree. If there were horses making mistakes around him, if he so much as saw a tail twitch in front of him, he'd be twisting in mid-air to get out of trouble. I owe him so much. I don't think I'd have got my job with David Nicholson if it hadn't been for him, and I doubt that I'd have got the ride on other great horses like Desert Orchid.

the professionals' choice

Mark Dwyer
Forgive'N Forget

We arrived in Britain from Ireland at the same time and he was my first high-profile success over jumps when he was a well-backed winner of the Coral Golden Hurdle at Cheltenham. I also won the Gold Cup on him and he ran at the Festival every year of his racing life; there's not many horses who have done that.

Pat Eddery
Dancing Brave

Dancing Brave was special. From my point of view the best thing about him was that he was so easy to ride. Okay, he liked to come from off the pace, which can sometimes cause problems, but that was only because he idled once he hit the front, as he did with me in the King George. What made him a lovely ride, though, was that he travelled extremely well and switched off. When you asked him he took off – that's why he's my favourite.

Mick Fitzgerald
Raymylette

When I was a kid, I always dreamed of riding a winner at the Cheltenham Festival so Raymylette, who won the Cathcart, just gets the edge over See More Business. The walk back to the unsaddling enclosure was simply amazing – I've ridden more than 1,000 winners but that one will always be special.

John Francome
Crisp

I was lucky enough to ride out on Crisp when he first came over from Australia and he was a marvellous horse with the most lovely nature. Early in his career here, I remember him winning the Two-Mile Champion Chase

under Paul Kelleway, a tremendous performance from a brilliant jumper. Most people's memory of him will be in defeat – losing out to Red Rum in that amazing 1973 Grand National – but it was certainly no disgrace to be beaten that day by a horse who later proved himself outstanding around Aintree.

Barry Geraghty
Moscow Flyer

He is the best horse I've ever ridden and everything you want in a National Hunt horse – he can battle, jump and is brave – and he also has scope. He's won the Arkle Trophy and the Queen Mother Champion Chase for me, but I am hopeful that he will become even better. He is a machine. He was also a very good hurdler and I won some good races on him including the December Festival Hurdle at Leopardstown and the Shell Champion Hurdle.

Josh Gifford
Aldaniti

How can I do Aldaniti justice? It was a truly wonderful fairytale, and he was such a generous horse, who wanted to please. He fractured a hind fetlock early in the Hennessy, yet was still so brave that he finished third. In the thick of Aldaniti's problems I told his owners, the Embiricoses, that they were pouring money down the drain but they refused to admit defeat – and it was the same with Bob Champion in his battle against cancer.

Alex Hammond
Desert Orchid

Desert Orchid is my favourite because he captured my imagination when I was still at school. I remember sitting in the school library, where I was supposed to be working, with my Walkman on, listening as Desert Orchid won a big race. I was so excited that I didn't do any work for the rest of the day. You could say it's been downhill ever since.

Nicky Henderson
See You Then

Arkle was the greatest horse of all time but my favourite without doubt has to be See You Then. He won three Champion Hurdles for us, and really put us on the map, as he was our second Festival hero after River Ceiriog. He was a peculiar horse as he had dodgy front legs and liked to kick and bite us. It was impossible to get him to the track very often because of his make-up, which is why he probably never got the recognition he deserved, but I have never seen a hurdler jump faster than him.

Barry Hills
Further Flight

He just gave it his all every time he raced and was a wonderful character. He wasn't that difficult to train and was totally reliable – he had to be to win the Jockey Club Cup five times from 1991 to 1995. Sadly he broke his leg when enjoying a lovely retirement at my son Michael's home.

Richard Hills
Tingle Creek

Tingle Creek was probably my all-time favourite, both back in his racing days and then during his retirement as a hack at Tom Jones's yard in Newmarket. His jumping was superb and, in a race, he was really bold. But after he retired, he was just a fantastic character – I even rode him out on a couple of occasions.

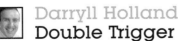
Darryll Holland
Double Trigger

He has to be my all-time favourite, not just

because of his ability, but because he was a public hero who overshadowed even the likes of Persian Punch at the time. He was a very proud and brave horse, who always seemed to know when he had won. There always seemed to be a huge buzz around the place when he was on the course, and the roof almost came off the stand when he beat his brother, Double Eclipse, at Goodwood.

Simon Holt
Red Rum

Red Rum was the horse who got me interested in racing – when I was a nine-year-old – and I remember his first Grand National win vividly. It was one of the great horseraces, but it was especially exciting for me as it was also the first time I'd ever had a bet. Red Rum was 9-1 and I won nearly a pound! By the time his third National victory came around, even my father was hooked – and he used to want to switch channels when racing came on. At the end of the race, he was on his knees in front of the TV, screaming.

David Johnson
Arkle

I think few would argue that Arkle has to be the best of all time and therefore he gets my No.1 vote. Any horse who wins over all distances, gives weight to the best around, runs season after season and totally dominates the sport has to be special. I think it is insulting to Arkle that any horse is compared to him either now or in the future.

Richard Johnson
Viking Flagship

I got to ride Viking Flagship only towards the end of his career but before I ever sat on him he was already a favourite of mine. He must be one of the toughest horses to have ever raced and he really didn't know when he was beaten. Although I wasn't on board the day he won the Melling Chase at Aintree in a three-way photo with Deep Sensation and

the **professionals' choice**

Martha's Son was very special. Adrian Maguire gave him a fantastic ride in what was one of the greatest races ever – and Viking Flagship proved what a great horse he was.

 Mark Johnston
Attraction

I voted for Yavana's Pace at the time of the poll – he gave everyone involved with him such enormous pleasure. He may not have been the best there has ever been, even though he was very high-class, but he was so game and genuine – and he tried to his absolute limit. But my favourite would have to be Attraction; it doesn't get any better than that. It was incredible to train a horse who won four Group 1s in a season, and in a way it was even more fun after she'd been beaten, as we didn't have to worry any more about maintaining her unbeaten record.

Gay Kelleway
Sprowston Boy

I became the first woman to ride a winner at Royal Ascot on him in the 1987 Queen Alexandra Stakes. As he was trained by father, it was a great day for the family – and what makes it really special is that no other woman has had a winner at the meeting since.

Tony McCoy
Lady Cricket

It wasn't easy to choose my favourite horse but Lady Cricket eventually got my vote. For pure gameness you just couldn't beat her, and she tried her heart out every time. She was a lovely mare, while the horse who was my No.2, Gloria Victis, was also very special – it is such a shame he didn't have the chance to fulfil his potential.

Joe Mercer
Brigadier Gerard

I must admit to a misunderstanding when I chose Ribot originally when my choice was published in the *Racing Post*. Obviously my own personal favourite has to be Brigadier Gerard, without any question of doubt. He was exceptional and we had such a great rapport – I was lucky enough to ride him for three seasons, and his record in Group races still stands.

John McCririck
Arkle

I couldn't select any horse in front of Arkle, because he was unquestionably the greatest chaser there is ever likely to be and it would be a crime to put anything above him. Zafonic runs him extremely close as a favourite of mine, however, as on the day he won the 2,000 Guineas I don't believe any horse I've seen could have beaten him.

 Paul Nicholls
See More Business

He was a great horse to me and without him I probably wouldn't be where I am today. Winning the Gold Cup was obviously the highlight, but his triumph at Wincanton in 2003 also sticks out. The reception he got brought tears to everyone's eyes. His CV is unbelievable – there will never be another like him.

 David Nicholson
Viking Flagship

My selection is all to do with his exceptional courage. Running 17 times on the Flat at three and developing bowed tendons at the end of his four- and five-year-old season didn't diminish his determination, and he was only a novice when winning twice at the Punchestown Festival. There was no braver horse on a racecourse, but if his stable was rearranged in any way, he would refuse to go in!

Conor O'Dwyer

Imperial Call

He was a serious, serious racehorse, the complete article. You could sit him in or make the running and he could win over all distances. He had every sign of being a proper racehorse from an early age but, of course, winning the Gold Cup on him was the moment that capped it all.

Jamie Osborne

Large Action

I always felt that I was half-married to Large Action – we were virtually inseparable for so many years. I won 13 times on him, and he was never the most natural jumper, but he'd give you everything and was a joy to ride.

Martin Pipe
Sabin du Loir

He was a brilliant racehorse – he beat Desert Orchid every time they met. Basically he was unlucky at Cheltenham because he needed a two-and-a-half-mile championship race, but he still won loads of top races, including the Sun Alliance Hurdle. The amazing thing about him is that we got him after he'd had three years off the track and he won his last race at the age of 14. He was a true gentleman, just like his owner Brian Kilpatrick.

Jenny Pitman
Corbiere

Corbiere took me to places I never thought I'd ever go and, as well as loving him to bits, I built up an enormous respect for him as a character. He was a cantankerous old sod at home – I'm not sure if he got it from me or whether it was the other way round – but he was so willing in everything he did

on the racecourse. He would have galloped until he dropped if he thought that's what you wanted from him. Corbiere was the horse who started the ball rolling for me, the one I have most to thank for all the pleasure I've had and the many smashing people I've met.

Richard Pitman

Crisp

I must stay loyal to Crisp. To have flown over those Aintree fences with him was the most fantastic experience and if any horse deserved to win a National, it was him. He did everything out of joy rather than duty – gallop, jump and race – and, while he was a very gentle horse at home, he was also immensely strong. I remember we used to go down to Mandown Bottom in Lambourn at the start of his work and, once he got there and was pointed up the hill, he was just unstoppable.

Richard Quinn
Ibn Bey

I have ridden plenty of very good horses, but pride of place has to go to Ibn Bey, who won four Group 1s, including the Irish St Leger. Blinkers transformed him and he went from being a mile-and-six horse to finishing second in the 1990 Breeders' Cup Classic. It was astonishing, because he was running on dirt for the first time and, aged six, it was the shortest trip he had run over since he was a two-year-old.

Peter Savill

Chaplins Club

What a character! As David Chapman's horsebox pulled into the yard, 'Charlie' would poke his head out to see if it was his turn. If it wasn't, he'd put his ears flat back and lean on the wall of his box and sulk. He loved racing and, between 1982 and 1992, won 24 races from over 160 starts. He twice equalled the record of nine handicap wins in a season, but his most phenomenal achievement was to run nine times in 19 days, winning seven.

the professionals' choice

Jamie Spencer
Desert Orchid

I would have been only five or six when Dawn Run first caught my imagination but it was Desert Orchid who became my favourite. I would follow him in every race from that time through to when he won the Gold Cup to the end of his career. He was my No.1.

Charlie Swan
Istabraq

He was a very easy horse to ride – I often said that riding him was like driving a Rolls Royce. You could put him anywhere in a race, it made no difference – and he had all that ability. He was so good he was almost freakish; he was a jockey's dream.

Andrew Thornton
Cool Dawn

He was spot-on when he won the Gold Cup. I went down to Robert Alner's yard ten days before the big race to school him, and I have never seen a horse look better. He was gleaming and, having ridden him out, I told Robert that I felt he was 10lb better than when winning his previous race at Ascot.

Ruby Walsh
Papillon

Any horse who wins a Grand National is special and Papillon provided me with the greatest day I had ever had in racing. We always thought he had ability and he was such a good jumper that you felt so safe when you rode him. He definitely put me on the map.

Ted Walsh
Commanche Court

The kindest, gentlest horse, he's given me the best days I've had in racing. He was bought to win the Triumph Hurdle, and he did, giving me my first Cheltenham Festival success as a trainer on an unforgettable day for the family. He went on to win the Irish Grand National and finish second in the Gold Cup – and he became the family pet. He's also the only 66-1 winner I've ever backed!

Peter Walwyn
Grundy

Grundy cost only 10,500gns as a yearling and we sold him for £1 million. When you see how many expensive purchases these days fail to reach their potential, that was some bargain. He was a bonny little horse with wonderful limbs, and he was such a fabulous mover that he would have galloped down Beachy Head. He won four Group 1s in a row and was so tough.

Norman Williamson
Alderbrook

People forget that he had only one run before winning the Champion, where he was a complete novice against stars like Large Action. He jumped super that day and was a class horse. His victory was my first at the Festival and also a first for Kim Bailey, which made it extra special.

Geoff Wragg
Teenoso

It was a great thrill when he won the Derby, as it was Lester Piggott's last victory in the race. But the thing that made Teenoso so special was that he was so easy to train. He was always very relaxed and never had problems – until the eve of the Arc, when he was lame for the first time in his career. He didn't race again.

the readers' choice winning letters

*The Racing Post asked readers to submit a short
argument in support of their choice, with prizes for the
best five after the hundreds of letters and emails had
been sifted. Here, we reproduce the winning five – and
letters editor Martin Smethurst explains exactly how he
made his choice.*

ALL RIGHT, all right. But it wasn't easy, you know, picking just five winners
from the vast number of excellent letters we received from *Racing Post* readers
nominating their favourite horses.

Those that appear in this volume, the writers of which won a copy of the Racing
Post *Flat Horses of 2003* annual for their efforts, were deserving in every respect.

The response to the search for the nation's favourite was phenomenal, and if the
letters proved one thing, it is this: once the politics of the sport have been set aside
– gently, of course, as we don't wish to bruise any egos – what remains is a glorious
celebration of the inviolable relationship between horse and human.

Whether they were writing having owned the animal in question, whether they
were inspired, as so many were, by a love-at-first-sight relationship struck in childhood, or simply enjoyed a happy accommodation between horse and wallet, a glass
was well and truly raised to all. That's the good, the bad and, quite possibly, the ugly,
at least in the case of Prof Mary McCabe's beloved Sir Desmond – "He was a strange
shape when I first saw him; head too small for his body".

And lest anyone is tempted to perform a double-take at the brevity of the letter
in celebration of Rondetto, consider the first sentence properly and ask yourself
whether anything you have read better captured the spirit of this entire exercise.

Mind you, if someone had suggested to me, as a schoolboy, that Rondetto should
be kept in the bedroom, I would have thought it ridiculous, even then. I mean, where
would I have put Red Rum? The bathroom would have been far too small . . .

Martin Smethurst

Hero never flinched in the face of adversity
Brigadier Gerard's groom explains why the champion's brilliance is unlikely ever to be equalled

BORN IN a stable on March 4, 1968, of humble parentage, his mother a lightly
raced maiden and blind in one eye, his father a rather lowly rated and inexpensive
sire, my favourite racehorse succeeded in putting the great firmly back into
British racing and breeding, at a time when it needed it most. Like the star of
wonder, his brilliance shone again and again during three magnificent seasons and
his achievements will surely never be equalled.

Answering the call to arms on ground he loved and on ground he hated, over all

the readers' choice winning letters

distances, racing from the front and from behind, in sickness and in health, never once did he desert the battlefield or flinch in the face of adversity. During this, an incredible era, my hero challenged their finest on the Heath at Newmarket then whupped 'em with all guns blazing in a never-to-be-forgotten Mayday Massacre.

He was rated the best he has trained by a great British trainer, the best he has ridden by a great British jockey, the highest-rated-ever British Flat racehorse by *Timeform* and was nominated the British Flat Horse of the Century in the *Racing Post*. At a time when hyperbole and superlatives are too freely used, he is the one British Flat racehorse who can genuinely and unequivocally claim the mantle of greatness. My favourite racehorse is, of course, Brigadier Gerard.

LAURIE WILLIAMSON, Brize Norton, Oxon

The most ill-tempered horse in training?
Kind Emperor, who has such a following at Yarmouth his trainer doesn't run him anywhere else

HE WON'T make the top 100, but my favourite horse has been described as quirky, enigmatic, unco-operative and a complete rogue. Having taken 30 attempts to register a victory, this horse has only ever won at one track, Great Yarmouth (albeit four times now), and has been branded an impossible ride by one jockey. He must rank as the most ill-tempered horse in training.

I nominate Kind Emperor, the gelding trained at Newmarket by Pat Gilligan. I have followed the (mis)fortunes of this equine maverick since his two-year-old days with Mark Polglase. Actually persuading the horse to race is a complex operation in itself. He is usually taken down to the start early and skulks around at the back before being hooded for stalls entry and led in last. Kind Emperor works alone, as he hates other horses and will permit only the trainer's wife to exercise him. His owner-breeder recounted the time he was shown his new quarters and responded by trashing his stable!

Given his unpredictability, the achievements of 2003 are all the more remarkable, as three further course victories testify. The horse has quite a following among the Yarmouth holiday crowd, so much so that his trainer doesn't bother to run him anywhere else. Kind Emperor – mean, moody and magnificent!

CHRIS BROOKS, Wilford, Nottingham

He is my first, second and third favourite
Arkle, the greatest steeplechaser who ever lived and a measure for any modern-day champion

IS IT really 37 years since Dad and Grandad took me, aged 11, to Kempton Park on that fateful day in 1966, to see the greatest steeplechaser who ever lived?

My childhood hero was the incomparable Arkle. Runners at Kempton, in those days, would walk across the middle of the racecourse prior to racing and my Dad and Grandad walked out there with me in the hope of seeing the great horse. And

the readers' choice winning letters

there he was, walking along with his lad and two security guards just feet away from me. I was so excited, I said: "Look, look! There's Arkle!" He stopped in his tracks and looked straight at me, those lovely big ears pricked. His lad laughed and said: "Well, you did call his name." I was enthralled.

When Arkle died I was 15 and was sitting eating my tea when his death was announced on the 6pm national news. Can you imagine the death of a racehorse being announced on the national news today? That was the immensity of his greatness and his popularity. To this day, almost 40 years since he ran in his last race, all modern-day chasers are measured against Arkle. He was truly the greatest and no horse, in my eyes, has ever, nor will ever, come close. Really he is my first, second and third favourite horse – I just loved him.

LESLEY PERKINS, West Hoathly, West Sussex

Excitement mounts and the seed is sown
Kif Kif is responsible for a love affair with racing that was still growing 46 years later

It's July 17, 1958. The pits have shut down and Dad's at home all day. As far as a near 50-year-old can remember, being then three, I remember the train to Catterick. A small girl sings *The Happy Wanderer* to her grandfather's harmonica accompaniment. The long walk from station to course is tiring for little legs and I hitch a ride on Dad's shoulders.

The picnic is set out on tartan rugs in the middle of the course and we drink Tizer and savour the special taste of egg sandwiches, always somehow different eaten *al fresco*. The talk among the men is all about Kif Kif in the last. At a time when Dad's bets were scattered like confetti, the powder would remain dry all afternoon. It soon becomes clear that 'going to see the horses' is different to the regular visits to the pit ponies enjoying their summer break at the pithead.

They're all brown, for one thing, and they have little coloured men on their backs. But the impression burns deep in the consciousness of one small boy.

I gaze in wonder at the shine on their coats and at the speed and power as the legs flash past the rails at eye level. "Come on Kif Kif" I parrot, as wild excitement mounts. I have no idea why. The seed is sown. A precocious love affair has begun. Forty-six years later and it's still growing stronger.

ERIC NAPIER, Banham, Norwich

He deserved to win the National
Rondetto, an all-time favourite

RONDETTO: I kept him as a pet in my bedroom and took him to school every day, but no-one knew! Should have won a Grand National – certainly deserved to do so. My favourite horse of all time.

LIZ CRESWICK, Horsham, West Sussex

selected bibliography

The Racing Post

The Sporting Life

Timeform Racehorses/Chasers & Hurdlers annuals

A Century of Champions, by John Randall and Tony Morris (Portway Press, 1999)

Oaksey on Racing – Thirty years of writing and riding, by John Oaksey (Kingswood Press, 1991)

Vincent O'Brien's Great Horses, by Ivor Herbert and Jacqueline O'Brien (Pelham Books, 1984)

Lester's Derbys, Lester Piggott with Sean Magee (Methuen, 2004)

Arkle – the classic story of a champion, by Ivor Herbert (Pelham Books, 1966, available as Aurum Press paperback)

Notable English and Irish Thoroughbreds, edited by Mary Mountier and Tony Morris (Alister Taylor & Genesis Publications, 1983)

Bloodstock Breeders' Review annuals 1912-1981

The Winter Kings, by Ivor Herbert and Patricia Smyly (Pelham Books, 1989)

Lester Piggott – My 12 Greatest Races (video, Castle Vision, 1991)